C000091137

The Celeste Beard Johnson Story
The Exclusive Biography

This book is the only book written from my perspective. It depicts the events in my life and contains relevant, previously undisclosed information. My story, as I told it to the authors, is exclusive in its entirety.

-Celeste

Nancy Hall

W.R. Mesiano

Trade Paperback

Copyright: 2019

Library of Congress: 1-7029639351

Requests for information should be addressed to:

A Vegas Publisher, LLC

www.vegaspublishers.com
vegaspublisher@gmail.com

First Edition: 2019
ISBN: 978-0-9968437-5-1

Cover Design by: Zoran Petrovic

Table of Contents

Only truth and transparency can guarantee freedom.

-Senator John McCain

During therapy, it is encouraged to keep a therapeutic journal. We are told to be honest and to write our deepest, most inner thoughts. This activity is helpful in allowing us to come to terms with what haunts us the most and to help overcome the obstacles that cause us harm. I would write some journal entries by hand in a notebook and sometimes use the computer. During the criminal trial, I was humiliated to have my highly personal and private thoughts made public. This unedited journal entry was presented to the court and read to the jury. It was stolen off my computer by my daughters and given to the assistant district attorney.

Sexual abuse from father. Stayed in trance during actual abuse. Should have been able to acknowledge the abuse. Maybe it would have stopped. Could have and should have been able to stop the abuse. Honor thy father and mother. Confusion regarding hatred toward father. I did something wrong. I deserved it. I am evil, bad, denial, weak, crazy, incompetent, undeserving, no will power, hopeless and life-threatening. Learn to not be able to feel. Learned to lie to be secretive. Once I asked my mom to take me to the doctor because my private area was really itching. The doctor scolded me and told me never to put anything up myself again. Then my mom threatened to tell my father. Bad, nasty girl. Religion told me I was a sinner, unclean, damned to hell. I feel unlovable, even to God. I feel really evil. If my own parents thought I was no good, then why shouldn't everyone else? Married Craig because I was running away from home. I tried not to notice that I was in a bad relationship because I thought I could change things. I could not face any obstacles. Coward. Thought my presence made him feel bad -- made him feel bad and abusive toward me. If I only did something right, everything would change. Raped by Craig twice. First time, gave birth to twins. Was too afraid to have an abortion. Second time, gave baby up for adoption. I must have done something to let him find my house. Did not secure home enough for him not to get in. Married Harald. Ruined marriage by having two tubal pregnancies, then ovarian cancer. God was punishing me for giving daughter up for adoption. Devastated by divorce. Started dating my 65-year-old attorney. Betrayed by him. My fault for getting involved. Started going out drinking to ease the pain. Married Jimmy. Ruined marriage because could not accept the fact that he cared about me and that he was a man of true integrity. Married Steve. Ruining marriage. I freeze, withdraw and manipulate any situation to avoid conflicts. I view myself as bad and Steve as perfect or at least better. I can see only pain and suffering and often view him as my attacker. Subconsciously tried to sabotage marriage. I feel I do not deserve to be loved by Steve. Craig died. Should have helped him more or else I helped him too much. May have sent him over the edge. Angry that he was able to commit suicide first. Can't accept his death. Still thinking he will come back for the girls. I am reliving the trauma. I see my father on top of me. I feel him touching me. I feel him making me touch him. I can't take it anymore. I can't make it stop. I feel helpless and overpowered. I feel the abuse happening all over again. I believe I don't deserve to live. I am consumed with the feelings of unworthiness and emptiness. Suicide seems to be the only way to gain some control of my life.

Prologue

When reading the events of someone's life, many people identify with certain segments and think "Wow! That happened to me." I have learned that most of our memories from early childhood are not going to be precise.

Well-known child abuse expert, Dr. Jim Hopper, states: "Most memories before the age of five and six will usually be just a 'snapshot' process."

Traumatic experiences will affect our relationships. Childhood sexual abuse causes some people to have frequent flashbacks. Mental, verbal or visual moments take people back to the past, bringing the hurt to the present. Flashbacks involving the abuse can disrupt all parts of adult life, including one's work. Triggers for flashbacks can be as simple as a spoken phrase, a body movement, a smell, or a look from someone, whether real or imagined.

Ultimate Judgment, written by Meg Clairmonte and Aurora Mackey, is a story of emotional corruption and betrayal involving a young girl, Meg Clairmonte, and her millionaire stepfather, who abused her into silent suffering for nearly three decades. Her attorney asked, "Why did Meg allow the abuse to continue? Why didn't she report it?" The evidence showed that she simply could not tell anyone because the abuse was horrible and shameful. Meg continually heard him whispering, "I told you no one would believe you, Margaret. Who'd you think they would believe? A rich white man like me or a little nigger girl like you?"

Studies show that few victims report abuse and are powerless to stop the violence until the abuser's control ends. The latest "Me Too" movement and causes, including Bill Cosby and Harvey Weinstein, confirm how rampant and widespread the abuse is.

I anticipate some readers will not believe parts of my life or will ask, "Why did she put up with such abuse?" Sometimes the mind has to 'play out' the abuse, like a ball of yarn rolled up wrong. You must unroll it, and then roll it up again to make it right.

Strong minds can work through this process with God's help and help from others. Facing abuse is a difficult task for family members to address because alcohol or drug dependency often accompany the behavior. With professional help, a beautiful human being can emerge.

My lifestyle was chaotic and violent. This book is written to reveal the real me. There are no excuses given. The sordid details of my bad choices have been laid bare for all to read. I am not seeking sympathy or pity. The writing is not a vendetta. It is my chance to speak up and share my experiences. It is a testimony which was denied at my trial, in my marriages, and with my daughters. When the media are writing their articles, maybe this time they will place me in the human race.

I am learning to stop fretting over what I have lost and what has been taken from me. Worrying prevents me from healing what remains of my shattered heart. I have learned to worry less. Abuse has surrounded my life in my homes, marriages, court, and now in prison. I have discovered that I cannot let abuse control who I am or what I choose to do because I am no longer a victim. I am an advocate.

It is important to disclose the life I shared with Steven. By revealing our lifestyle, I can paint a clear picture, for the first time, about the opulent world he created for us. Our obsession with material things came from Steven wanting the finest things life had to offer. He reaped the benefits of his lifetime of hard work and enjoyed living in a life of luxury. I was portrayed as a monger during my trial, but the truth is, my husband enjoyed luxury and viewed it as a marker for success. He wanted our homes to have a museum-like quality; he loved us to drive fancy cars, to wear designer clothes, to dine at fine restaurants, and to travel extensively. That is what made him happy and he relished in sharing his wealth and knowledge with us. Since my incarceration, I have learned to become a minimalist.

I have come to accept that I should have been more of a parent to my daughters; I should not have tried so hard to be their friend. I should have held firm boundaries during their most formative years. However misguided the raising of the twins may have been, it was born out of love for them. My daughters know exactly what they did and why they did it. Even if they never contact me, they will know how I feel and it will affect them. It is difficult to go on living under a lie. By telling my story, my message will get through. If I handled things differently, perhaps the girls would not have grown up to become greedy and vindictive young women.

1

The Formative Years

From a very young age, I aspired to be like Hollywood's Elizabeth Taylor. Her beauty graced the covers of various magazines published during my childhood. Her many husbands appeared to be a glamorous benefit of her lavish lifestyle. Despite acquiring the numerous husbands and the affluence of Liz's lifestyle, my life has deteriorated into a parody of tawdry "Hollywoodesque" drama.

I did not know my birth mother, Cathleen Joan Cook. She was 35 years old when I was conceived. I was given up for adoption as a newborn at Culver City Memorial Hospital in Orange County, California on February 13, 1963. When I was grown, I did make contact with her. When we met, I was crushed at how callous she was. She made it clear I was not wanted and that she would have had an abortion, had they been legal. She was angry about my birth and told me she was "just an incubator." Those words stung. Her career high up in the Republican National Committee was more important than

I was. The identity of my birth father was never revealed because she said she could not remember who he was. She never had any other children and made me swear to not let her mother or sister know about my existence.

I was the second of four children adopted into an everyday dysfunctional American family. I have an older brother as well as a younger sister and brother. The age gap separating the four of us is between 8 to 18 months. We were not wealthy, but did have more than just the necessities of life. I attended parochial schools until the eighth grade. Both my parents were of above-average intelligence and were active in our church. From childhood to junior high, I was forced to attend church, Wednesday night Bible studies, Sunday school, and Sunday evening services. Their radical religious activities led me to resolve firmly, that once I was free from parental domination, I would never again darken the doorstep of a church. I steadfastly followed this resolution for the next thirty years, except when circumstances made it socially unacceptable to be absent.

Only now, in prison, I have come to understand that God puts us in situations to make us stronger and to help others. I have returned to loving God. Even though I am currently living in miserable circumstances, beautiful things can still emerge. Only God can bring good out of my situation. He is showing me that no tragedy will bring evil to me if I take it to Him.

My disdain for organized religion left me in conflict because I was raised with a puritanical viewpoint towards sex, womanhood, and motherhood. I was sexually and morally confused from childhood through adolescence due to years of molestation by my father and brother. I was left feeling filthy and dirty and I blamed myself for the abuse. I believe this is the reason I cannot stand the feel of dirt; the association awakens the pain and suffering of my insides being torn apart while the molestation occurred. I believe this is where I developed the peculiarity of not wanting my skin touching and going to bed fully dressed beneath my pajamas, I never wore a nightgown for this very reason. I bare painful scars to this day.

The private schools I attended were at least an hour's drive from our home. On the outside, my life was orderly and structured. I was a member of the local swim team. I attended swim practice every day before and after school. My hair was always wet, and I usually went to school looking like a drowned rat. Every day, by the time I got home, I was exhausted with barely enough energy to eat and do my homework. I was pleased to be a grade A student. On Saturdays, I competed in swim meets, and excelled, placing third in the Nevada Junior Olympics for the breaststroke. When I was not attending swim meets, I participated in speech and debate tournaments around the state and won many awards. Even though I was a perfectionist and highly competitive, I never felt I fit in anywhere or was accepted by my peers. This is precisely how I feel in prison.

We were not allowed to associate with any neighborhood kids. We were told it was because they attended public schools. In hindsight, I suspect the truth was because of the fear of others finding out about what was going on behind closed doors. My friends from the private school I attended lived long distances away. The weekends, when I was not competing, were spent at Eileen's house. She was my best friend with whom I had gone to school since the age of seven. To this day, we remain close friends. One day she did confide that her mother suspected I was being sexually abused, but back in the 60's and 70's everyone turned a blind eye to the behavior. With my adoptive father being very close friends with the Chief of Police, any complaints would have fallen on deaf ears.

Around the age of twelve, I secretly made friends with some girls in the neighborhood who were on my swim team. I began relentlessly asking my mother to allow me to go to the local public school so that I could be with these particular girls. I had skipped the sixth grade and advanced to junior high. I was willing to risk all that was familiar to experience the freedoms I perceived these girls had. Their lives seemed so relaxed compared to my rigid schedule and, oh -- how I wanted to be like them! Finding a weakness in the family structure and using it to my advantage, my requests to change schools coincided with the time I overheard my parents contemplating divorce.

Female bodily functions were never discussed at home or in school, so I had no idea what questions to ask or what to expect as I matured. Things I have learned came from my fellow teammates along with a lot of misinformation. Many girls on the team were having their periods, but I had no idea why mine had not yet started. To participate in their group conversations, I told the girls every day, for over three years, that I, too, was on my period. When I learned that a woman had a period once a month, I could not help thinking back to my teammates, who must have thought I was weird and probably laughed behind my back. My monthly cycle did not begin until I was almost sixteen when vacationing in Hawaii with Eileen and her family.

Attending the public school, where I was not popular, and only a few students knew me, turned out to be traumatic. I was bullied and shunned by my new classmates. The reason for rejection was nothing short of silly: My eyebrows were too thick; my teeth were too white; my hair was too green from pool chlorine; my pants were too baggy; I was a virgin. It seemed everything about me was cause for ridicule and taunting. By then it was too late to return to the private school, as my mother no longer wanted to make the long drive back and forth. I had convinced my mother that I wanted to switch schools and was afraid to admit to her that I was wrong.

At age thirteen, my parents separated and later divorced. My brothers went to live with our dad, while we girls stayed with our mother. From then on, life became the girls versus the boys. The divorce was contentious, taking over three years to become final. To date, I have not seen my brothers in over forty years.

My mother became the sole provider after she and our dad split up. To help make ends meet she sold her blood plasma to a company that turned it into a treatment for RH-negative mothers. She religiously drove over 100 miles, round trip, twice a week to the clinic, located in a dangerous downtown area of Los Angeles.

It was my responsibility to keep the house clean, do the laundry, and cook the meals. Some nights when she was late getting home, I was so terrified of her dying, that I would call the hospitals and police stations to see if she had been hurt. My biggest fear was being left alone, and now in prison, I face that fear every single day. Only the desire of finding truth and justice keeps me going. My sincere hope is to one day reunite with my loved ones.

Celeste

My mind is either a sieve or a vacuum. Personal experiences I have refused to accept have left voids in my life. Sexual matters were out, but love was compulsively engulfed in my life. Stories in books and movies became a large part of my existence. Some girls I knew were having abortions; a thirteen-year-old girl had a baby, which she put up for adoption. These experiences gave me no insight into the emotions between a man and a woman. The next few years as a teen were nothing less than turbulent, with endless attempts to open and understand these voids and blocks.

In the tenth grade, I became a wrestling cheerleader and did anything for attention. I turned my legs orange with suntan liquid just before a meet; bleached my hair platinum blonde; over-tweezed my eyebrows; and wore excessive amounts of make-up. I enjoyed the attention from the boys when I wore the short skirt and tight sweater from my cheerleading uniform. On the outside, I looked to be in my early twenties, but on the inside, I was a naïve, immature, and gullible teen.

My sister's boyfriend introduced me to a young neighborhood man, Craig Bratcher, whom I eventually married. He was 18, and I was almost 16. He was a high school dropout, and I often saw him hanging out with some of the boys with whom I went to high school. It was around that time his father went to work in Florida; leaving Craig

21

unsupervised for a few months at their home. When Craig had nightly beer parties, he invited me to come over after his friends had left.

Being young and foolish, I did not realize that Craig was taking advantage of me. Because I had fallen in love with him, he could do no wrong in my young eyes. When Craig's father returned home, the parties stopped. We rented an apartment and moved in together. Craig became so jealous and would not allow me to go anywhere without him. Initially, the jealousy was flattering, but soon, along with his suspicion, came abuse, especially when he thought another man was looking at or talking to me. Craig began hitting, shoving, burning, and stabbing me any time he felt I might be paying attention to anyone but him. He hurled objects at me; whatever he had in his hand at the time, or happened to be within his reach. To this day, scars cover my body from cigarette and lighter burns, knife wounds, broken beer bottle pieces, forks, and even pens.

No one visited our apartment because Craig made sure that we had no furniture other than what was in the bedroom. He never allowed me to buy anything to sit on that might encourage friends to visit, so I consoled myself with decorating the walls. My bedroom furniture and sparse furnishings adorned the apartment. My mother gave me her Sear's credit card to buy dishes, towels, pots, and pans. She gave me a car to drive, because I wanted to find a job. Craig's mother visited the apartment once and ridiculed me, saying that I was too lazy to find a job so that we could afford furniture. She belittled me with words like, "You are the only person I ever met that decorated the walls of a home that was devoid of furniture." I was crushed but did not dare tell her what her son was doing to me.

Craig made me a virtual prisoner in our apartment. I was afraid to go anywhere without him and forbidden by him to work. Every morning he removed the coil wire from my car's engine, to ensure that I could not go anywhere during the day. He also kept a log of the car's odometer reading.

Any errands that needed to be done, such as grocery shopping, were only done with Craig, who drove my car. His obsession ran so deep that I was not allowed to use the laundry facilities at the complex; it was under his watchful eyes at the laundromat every Saturday that our clothes were cleaned. It did not matter how late at night he arrived home or how intoxicated he was. It was frightening to be his passenger when I knew it was dangerous for him to be behind the wheel. I never voiced my concerns because I feared his wrath more than I feared to die in a car accident.

Cleaning became my obsession so that Craig would know I remained "inside and busy." Desperately seeking any acknowledgement from him to validate self worth, the joy of having a spotless and sparkling house consumed me. I leafed through my cookbook collection to find the most complicated entrées to create for Craig's dinner. I discovered my hidden passion for baking and prepared delicious and picturesque pies, cakes, cookies, and other desserts. I never cooked any food from a can or box, firmly believing that taking a shortcut would mean that I was a thoughtless and careless person who did not deserve to be loved or respected.

A few months after we moved into our apartment, and unbeknownst to Craig, I walked across our small city to a doctor's office. I had been throwing up for days. When the doctor told me I was pregnant, I was shocked. I had always assumed the man determined when the woman would get pregnant. I had no understanding of how this could have happened, especially since nobody discussed pregnancy or how to prevent it with me. On the long walk home and in my childishness, I convinced myself that Craig would be thrilled with the news. Continually feeling so isolated and alone, I assured myself that a baby would be just like taking care of a new puppy or kitten. I could hardly wait to tell Craig the excellent news.

When I told him I was pregnant, he threw me against the closet doors so hard that they broke in half. He called me a "stupid bitch," then tried to convince me to have an abortion. In high school, I accompanied a 15-year-old friend

24

to Planned Parenthood for an abortion; after that heartbreaking ordeal, I was sure I did not want an abortion. He hounded me for weeks, but I did not relent. He often punched me in the stomach hoping I would miscarry. My thought was, it's not that I have a moral dilemma or that I still want a child, but I am just plain scared. If I ignore the problem, it will either go away or eventually solve itself.

I was 5'8" and weighed less than 110 pounds. I endured physical and emotional abuse and had countless stays at the hospital. Despite the violence, I married Craig on December 6, 1980. I did not want my baby to be labeled illegitimate.

Late in my pregnancy, I was hospitalized, again, because I could not keep down food or water. It was then that I found out I was pregnant with female twins. I was terrified. My doctor had me convinced, early on in my pregnancy, that I was having a large baby boy. All my preparations were for a boy baby, not two girls. The doctor kept me isolated in a private room because he suspected that I was being abused. He would not allow me access to the telephone; the few visitors I had were closely monitored because I refused to tell him who was hurting me.

In my seventh month of pregnancy, I was no longer in danger of having a miscarriage. The private hospital would not allow me to continue to stay since I did not have health insurance. My doctor ordered me on complete bed rest, and I reluctantly went home with Craig. My mother had no idea what Craig was doing to me, and I was both scared and unwilling to tell her. Craig had convinced me that he had total control over me. He repeatedly said he would hurt my mother if I spoke up. I was only seventeen, and I believed him. Craig sternly assured me that even though I might be able to fool the doctor that I was frail, I could not deceive him.

The house was a mess, and I was ordered to have it cleaned before he returned from work. Within a few hours, I was in labor. By some miracle, Craig had left the coil wire on my car, because in his haste to get back to work, he forgot to remove it. I drove by Craig's job to tell him I was in labor, but he accused me of lying, accused me of looking for attention, and ordered me to go home. Instead, I stopped at a pay phone and called my mom. I was frightened about disobeying Craig but was terrified about giving birth alone. My mom was too far away for me to risk waiting for her to pick me up. I drove the 15 miles to my doctor's office. His office was across the street from the hospital. There was barely enough time to get me into radiology to find out that one of the twins was breached. The doctor delivered my twin daughters by cesarean section. I was almost 18 years old when I gave birth to my identical twins, Jennifer and Kristina, on February 6, 1981.

Celeste

The girls barely weighed over three pounds each. The hospital did not have a Neo-Natal Intensive Care Unit; I was unable to see my daughters before they were whisked away by helicopter to the county hospital in Ventura, California. Due to the need to provide immediate medical care, the girls were not thoroughly cleaned before departure. My sister saw the twins, as they were being prepared for their flight. She came into my room and hatefully said,"You make ugly babies."

My doctor kept me in the hospital for an additional five days after the birth; I was very worried about my babies. What was happening to them? Were they all right? Were they deformed? Craig would not tell me anything.

Upon my release, I went straight to the hospital where the twins were being cared for; Craig did not visit them at all. I was horrified to see the mass of tubes coming out of their little bodies. I broke into tears.

My mother had convinced Craig to allow me to drive to the hospital every day to see my babies. The hospital did not let me hold or touch them for several weeks, because of their weak condition. It is my belief that is the reason why, in the future, they never bonded with me. All I could do was sit in a chair hour after hour, day after day, watching them. It was a difficult time; there was no place I wanted to be, except with my babies.

Celeste

I found consolation with a stray dog I named, Shiloh. He showed up at our house one day and Craig allowed me to keep him. He was a German shepherd mix and thought he was a lap dog. Shiloh followed me everywhere I went, both inside and outside the house. I loved this dog more than I thought possible, and in return, he loved me unconditionally. I truly believed that God sent him to help me while my daughters were fighting for their lives in their incubators. Over time, Craig began to abuse the dog.

The local La Leche League gave me a breast pump to feed the twins. As much as I tried, I was unable to produce more than two ounces of breast milk at a time to feed my precious babies. This lack of milk upset me as I accused the nurses of giving my milk to the other babies in the unit. The hospital gave them more canned than breast milk. I always cried, believing my babies would die. Craig was harsh with me, demanding to know why I would not stop crying. He would break things that meant so much to me, and tore up my photographs and yearbooks. I was fearful of being left alone with him because his violent behavior began to increase. He said that if I stopped crying, he would stop destroying things. I tried, but could not stop crying. I finally realized that he had no feelings for our daughters or me. His drinking and carousing with prostitutes began to escalate. He tried to inflict emotional pain by flaunting his infidelities; instead, I was relieved that I did not have to have sex with him. Intimacy with Craig filled me with complete and utter disgust.

I prepared for the twins to come home. I purchased another car seat and crib, changed the color scheme from blue to pink, returned all the 'boy' items, and doubled up on all the necessities.

When our daughters were three months old, I was able to bring them home. They weighed less than five pounds each. My marriage became more strained because I could not bear for Craig to touch me. I still believed it was his fault that I became pregnant. Birth control was still foreign to me and was never discussed. I could not ask my mom or friends about birth control because I was afraid to risk anyone finding out that my "happy marriage" was nothing more than a sham.

Before we left the hospital, my pediatrician told me the twins, being premature, would sleep continuously and would need to be woken to be fed. Otherwise, they would die. He instructed me to feed them every three hours. It took, what seemed like an hour per baby, to get two ounces of milk into them. Keeping them awake long enough to drink their bottle was tough.

Exhaustion soon set in because I had no one to help me care for the babies and I occasionally overslept. Once, I slept for fourteen straight hours, and when awakened, was terrified the girls were going to die. They were all right, but that episode frightened me. The girls developed an allergic reaction to disposable diapers, so I had to use cotton diapers. This added to my workload. I made their baby food and diligently watched their diet so that they would grow and thrive. I believed, with all my heart, that anything they endured, such as diaper rashes, colds, usual bumps, and bruises, was a direct result of my ability to be a good mother. I would cradle my babies and promise they would not endure the sadness and hurt that I experienced. I wanted everything to be perfect for them.

Once, Craig let Shiloh out front to relieve himself while I was asleep, and instead of watching him, he shut the door and came back inside. When I woke up, I asked where he was. When Craig told me what he had done, and that he had been outside for a few hours, I instinctively knew something terrible had happened to him. I found him dead along the roadside. He was hit by a car. Craig buried him in the yard. It took me over a year to come to grips with my grief. Shiloh had become my only friend.

In the early spring of 1981, I discovered that Craig was a full-blown alcoholic and drug addict. He was arrested many times for countless attacks on me. One of the stipulations of his release from jail required him to be admitted to an in-patient treatment program for alcoholism and drug addiction. He tried numerous times to stay clean and sober, but never made it longer than a couple of months. I was horrified when one of his rehabilitation counselors told me that Craig was also an IV drug-user and snorted cocaine.

Craig was in and out of rehab and he became increasingly abusive. In the early summer of 1981, he and his counselor assured me, that after his release from rehabilitation, a move to the state of Washington would solve all of our problems. The counselor reasoned that we would have a fresh start because Craig would no longer be tempted by all the bad influences currently around him. We would live in a house next door to his mother. The counselor convinced me this would be a blessing to me because Craig would be forced to change his behavior because he wanted his mother to be proud of him.

He was released from rehabilitation in the late summer of 1981. With sheer reluctance, I agreed to move to Washington. This less than ideal living arrangement included a short stint of staying with his mother until she moved into her father's house next door. His grandfather convinced Craig to let me get a job. We needed the extra money to take care of the girls. I began working shucking corn at a cannery, where Craig and his mother also worked. The cannery operated twenty-four hours a day, so I worked the midnight shift while Craig worked the morning shift. We arranged this schedule because the twins were now sleeping through the night.

31

Things were getting better at home, and as far as I could tell, Craig had stopped drinking and drugging.

This lull in my stormy life was short-lived. Craig's mother told him I was seen talking to a young man in the cannery break room. He brutally beat me and accused me of having an affair. He was entirely out of control so I called his mother asking for help. She let me know that she was in the middle of a Bible study and hung up the phone. Craig broke my arm that night, and by the time the police arrived, he had destroyed the contents inside our house. Arrested and sent to jail, his mother refused to intercede. She told me that it was my fault because I should "not be flirting" with other men; I was only talking to a fellow worker at break time. A friend of hers told her she saw us talking and it scared me because I realized I was under constant surveillance by Craig's mother and her friends.

After the E. R. staff put a cast on my broken arm, I went home and packed my meager belongings into a U-Haul truck. I put the twins in their car seats and drove home to California. It was 1981, and I was eighteen with no cell phone or GPS device to help me in an emergency.

Driving only in the right lane, the trip took almost 24 hours to travel from Washington to California, I was petrified of having an accident. I could not stop to rest. I had no idea how to back up the 24-foot rental truck. The best I could do was to drive the truck around in circles, making it difficult to stop for gas. By the time I arrived in California, I was exhausted. I stayed with a family friend for a short time and began feeling safe again.

During the 1980's, police did not take domestic violence seriously and rarely intervened. A low priority was assigned to domestic-disturbance calls that came into the police departments. By the time the police arrived at the scene, Craig would be gone. The police could not arrest him without a warrant unless he was at the scene. Once a warrant was applied for, it would take days for the DA's office to issue it. The few instances where he did receive judicial penalizing, it was always minor and not a deterrent to him because he had no fear of his punishment.

Eventually, Craig located me, begging and pleading for us to come home. He threatened suicide unless I took him back. To convince me, he was arrested for attempting to jump off the roof of a downtown hotel in Ventura, California. Fool-heartedly, I took him back. I was fearful that my daughters would hate me if I turned my back on their father, and he killed himself. I still believed that I deserved the abuse.

One night, after Craig had been drinking and using drugs, I was forcefully woken by him; I never knew when or why he would erupt into a rage. He was shoving cat poop, straight from the litter box, down my throat. I will never forget how the cat litter gravel felt, clinging to the feces, as I choked.

He and his family continued to blame me for his drinking and drug abuse. I never had a normal mate experience with which to compare a relationship and believed that all our marital discord rested solely on my shoulders. This belief filled me with immense shame and made me think that I could never be the wife and mother that Craig and his family wanted me to be. Because of the cat poop experience and the death of my dog, Shiloh, I remained terrified of having a pet for over a decade.

In the process of shoving the cat poop down my throat, Craig crushed my nose, breaking it in several places; he also broke my front-teeth roots. Even though the roots are permanently broken, I have been blessed to have the teeth intact without any dental intervention. It took two extensive surgeries to repair the damage to my nose, and for months, the whites of my eyes were completely red and my face black and blue, causing me to look like I had been thrown through a car windshield. Craig was again arrested and sent to jail, only this time he was allowed to work during the day. The county referred to it as their Work Furlough program. He reported to the jail every afternoon and stayed there until it was time for him to go to work the following day. Several times he stopped by my house and assaulted me, either on his way to work or when returning to the jail. Luckily, he was required to stay in jail on the weekends. It was the only time I had any restful sleep, knowing he could not abuse me.

I was never unfaithful to Craig, even though, all during my time with him, I continued to endure physical and mental abuse. He broke my arm, wrist, leg, nose and several of my ribs; burned me countless times with cigarettes or hot metal objects; and stabbed me multiple times all over my body. Still visible is a crescent moon shaped scar on my forehead from when I was hit with a beer bottle after refusing to have sex; it is a constant reminder of the violent man he was. Most of his physical abuse occurred when I was sound asleep after he had been out drinking and using drugs. I became a night owl for self-preservation, afraid to fall asleep, never knowing how I might be awakened. To this day, I suffer flashbacks when the guards make their rounds and hit the metal walls to disturb the inmates. Under the guise of wellness checks, they abuse their authority and laugh at us for their amusement. I was diagnosed with PTSD and become startled when woken in this manner.

By 1983, my life was filled with depression and hopelessness. I entertained thoughts of suicide. It did not seem that things would ever change. Nothing stopped Craig. He had shot my neighbor in the leg while trying to shoot me, and in the process, Kristina was cut on her head by flying glass shards from the living room window. It was the first time one of the girls was injured by their father.

A few years had passed since I talked with my mom or sister. I hid my whereabouts from them because I was humiliated and ashamed. I was fearful for their safety; Craig often threatened to kill them if I divorced him. I believed I deserved his control over me because I did not know how to make him happy.

In the fall of 1983, after summoning all my courage, I left Craig and enrolled in college, where I earned straight A's, earning a place on the Dean's list. At the same time, I began seeing a therapist, while working part-time at McDonald's and Straw Hat Pizza to pay my expenses.

I could not afford a divorce attorney so I went to the courthouse to obtain the necessary paperwork to file for a divorce myself. The clerks were very helpful and patient as they answered all of my questions. The local library allowed me to use the typewriter to prepare the documents. Within two weeks, I had successfully filed for a divorce. The decree was finalized in September of 1983.

Craig was allowed visitation with the girls, even though he never paid the court ordered child support; I was too afraid to report him. The court ordered me to deliver the twins to Craig's house for weekend visits because he was not allowed to drive a vehicle with the girls inside. It mattered little to the court that he had dozens of arrests for assaulting me. No one was willing to consider my needs as a victim or give any thought to my safety.

Craig's family made sure he always had excellent legal representation for all his criminal and domestic problems, but I had no one. Looking back, I realize that legal assistance would have secured the essential safety net I desperately needed. I would have received help to improve my economic position through child support. The fears Craig planted in my mind about losing custody of the girls would have been nonexistent. I would have been informed about the available government benefits.

One occasion when I arrived at Craig's house to pick up the twins, he came to the door and offered to bring their suitcase to the car for me. I was following the girls down the driveway when Craig ran up behind me and karate-kicked me in the back. I hit the side of the car so hard that I was knocked unconscious. I woke to find him kicking me all over my body. He kicked my arm so hard that he broke the scaphoid bone in my wrist. This injury required a full arm cast for almost nine months. I quit going to college because I was afraid they would find out about what had happened to me. I never could get past the deep seeded belief that I deserved whatever Craig did to me. Being so terrified of Craig, I stayed in a battered women's shelter. I feared for our lives and was afraid to stay in my apartment. At first, they did not have room for the twins. I was forced to put the twins in protective custody until I secured housing. I hated myself.

Many years later, my adult daughters would whine to everyone that they were in foster care because I did not want them. Little did they know, I was protecting them from their father while trying to keep myself from being killed at his hand.

The shelter helped me find a safe place to live with the twins and helped me write a proper resume to use in my job search. I managed to get a job as a receptionist. As a hard worker, I was soon promoted to project supervisor of an industrial complex, supervising and scheduling sub-contractors for the finish-out on industrial properties.

In 1985, I was 22 years old; Jennifer and Kristina were four years old and enrolled in preschool. Craig's visits with the twins were being supervised. Not wanting Craig to know where we lived, I drove the girls to his father's house for the weekend visits. I knew that his father would not idly stand by while his son physically assaulted me. He was more concerned the neighbors would think ill of him than for my safety. For the first time, I started to have a good feeling about myself. When Craig saw me, he called me a whore even though I was professionally dressed. It eludes me to this day why I took his insults and accusations to heart.

Celeste

The girls and I lived happily, contented, and alone in a small apartment in another city and away from Craig. Until one day, I came home from work to discover that every piece of clothing I owned had been cut, ripped, or shredded. The word "whore" was sprayed with black paint over all of the walls of every room except for the girls' bedroom. My underclothes, make-up, hair dryer, and curling iron were nowhere to be found. Craig left a message on my answering machine to let me know it was his handiwork and that I could retrieve my belongings from the local landfill. The recording confession led to his arrest.

By January of 1986, I was dating Gary, my 65-year-old boss, who owned the complex where I worked. He became my protector and treated me like a princess. I delighted in escorting the twins to their daycare in his limousine. He asked me to marry him, and we planned a February wedding. I would be his sixth wife. He bought me a breathtaking four-carat diamond ring. I felt safe for the first time in my life. As the wedding drew near, he came into my office one day and said he had a confession to make.

I felt as if everything was too good to be true, and assumed he wanted to break things off. Instead of breaking up with me, he disclosed that he had herpes. I never asked why he did not make love to me; I thought he was a gentleman waiting for our wedding night. The full impact of what he had just told me had not registered, so I began laughing hysterically, filled with relief that he did not wish to break up with me. Gary was offended because he thought I was laughing at him for having herpes. He was so upset, he left town for the weekend, agreeing to talk with me again when he returned.

Later that night it hit me like a ton of bricks... herpes. He might as well have said he had leprosy. I was not entirely sure what herpes was except that it was contagious and incurable. How naïve of me. I could not get the imagined picture of open sores oozing out of my head and became frightened that I could contract it. I left the ring Gary had given me on his office desk with a "Dear John" letter since I was too much of a coward to face him. I mailed back the office keys, and we never spoke again.

I had convinced myself that I could not survive without a man in my life. I believed that only a man could provide love and security to my daughters and me. The twins were elated that I left Gary, desperately wanting Craig and me to get back together. The girls begged me to go back to him, because every time Craig saw or spoke to them on the telephone, he pressured them. They would cry and tell me they were mad at me for refusing to reunite. I worried that my daughters would grow up hating me because I believed it was my fault that Craig drank too much and used drugs. Craig's

40

family reinforced this idea every time they saw the twins; they told them what an awful person I was. The girls were young, so they had no problem relaying all of my faults to me. It became second nature; I wanted to run and hide and try to put my troubles behind me.

After the destruction of my clothes and the apartment, Craig had moved to Phoenix, Arizona to live with his brother. In February of 1986, I stupidly called Craig and told him I wanted to get back together, as he was someone familiar. Again, I rented a U-Haul truck and left for Arizona, sure that I could manage the 10-hour drive.

A few days after arriving in Phoenix, Craig's brother moved out, and we moved my belongings in. When I unpacked my answering machine, Craig went berserk, accusing me of having it to keep in touch with Gary. Even though he was demanding sex, I still was not ready to have intercourse with Craig. The only intimacy I could manage was to allow him to rub his penis on my back until he ejaculated. I was repulsed at the thought of kissing him.

That night Craig became incensed, believing that my denying sex with him was because I was still in love with Gary. Considering all I had been through, penetration was impossible for me. He beat and raped me and in the process, he stabbed me in the hip with a five-inch blade. To this day, I still remember feeling the warm blood rushing down my leg.

Celeste

He kept trying to force me into admitting that I had relations with Gary, refusing to accept "only him." I thought he was going to kill me and quietly prayed to God to let me die. After he was through with me, he left and went to his brother's house. I packed up the girls in the middle of the night, and the police took me to the emergency room to have my leg stitched. The doctor rushed me into emergency surgery to repair the femoral artery Craig cut during his attack. He was arrested again and the twins blamed me for hurting their dad. It was a blessing that one of the nurses took care of the girls until I was released the following day.

To get even with me, Craig had his brother come to the apartment the next afternoon, with the landlord and the police, to evict me because my name was not on the lease. The police put me in contact with a battered women's shelter in Tempe, Arizona, where my daughters and I lived for a few months. The shelter helped me get a job as an accounts payable clerk, which enabled me to get an apartment. Soon I became violently ill, and took the girls with me to the emergency room. I was told that I would have to be admitted. I was pregnant and severely dehydrated, putting the baby's life at risk. The hospital contacted Craig and told him he needed to come and pick up the girls. When he arrived and found out about the pregnancy, he became furious. He called me a whore, took the basin containing my vomit in it, and

42

threw it in my face. He began yelling, "I'm not the father!" When the nurse came into the room, she found him choking me. He ran out of the hospital, leaving the twins with me as I cried, hysterically. The doctor said I had no choice but to place the girls in protective custody while I remained in the hospital. I would jeopardize the life of the baby if I did not stay. Craig's mother was in town, visiting from Washington, and she refused to take care of her granddaughters. The girls were barely five years old, and once again, were taken away by strangers, while they cried and begged me to let them stay. Years later, the girls held me accountable for having to go into foster care. They would not listen to reason; their grandmother refused to care for them while I was hospitalized, leaving me no other choice than to depend on the care of strangers.

After being released from the hospital, I lost my job. The court released my daughters from protective custody, and they came home to live with me. Again, I was pregnant, and no one would hire me, so I felt I had no choice but to go back to Craig. The twins were happy. We moved into a house in Glendale, Arizona, where every day I could walk my daughters to and from kindergarten. Craig would not allow me to drive anywhere; I was grateful the school was within walking distance, given my condition. My time was consumed with being their Daisy Scout Troop leader and room mother at their school. I made their clothes, trying to be the mother they deserved. During that time, I ignored that I was pregnant. I relived the rape on a daily basis. Craig had penetrated me with such force; I was paralyzed with fear that Jennifer and Kristina would find me dead by the hand of their father. I did not think I would live to see my 24th birthday. The girls and I slept in the living room in sleeping bags, pretending we were camping out. I planned this sleeping arrangement because I was afraid Craig would try to have sex with me. I slept between Jennifer and Kristina to keep Craig from touching me.

When his brother moved into our guest bedroom, I had to deal with the physical and mental abuse from both of them. Being pregnant did not stop either one of them from hitting me every time I expressed my disapproval of their smoking marijuana or snorting cocaine in front of the girls. By the time I was seven and a half months pregnant, I realized it would be impossible to raise an infant under these circumstances and decided to give up the baby for adoption. When I told Craig my decision, he did not try to talk me out of it; he never believed that he was the biological father of the baby. This choice caused many nights of fitful sleep. I knew firsthand how it felt to know that my biological mother had not wanted me. I anguished over this decision and believed I was making the right choice to give this baby a better life than to grow up in a dysfunctional house filled with abuse. I wanted my baby surrounded by love. It was a painful, but proper resolution.

At first, I contacted adoption agencies from the Yellow Pages, but they were distant and uncaring. The agencies gave me no say in who would adopt my child. While the girls were in school, I walked to the library to look up the adoption ads in the newspapers from across the country. I called several of the couples and met with dozens of prospective parents before narrowing the choice down to two families. One couple lived in upper New York State, and the other was a single 42-year-old woman from California. Craig and I, along with the twins, met with the woman from California and over the next month we became friends. We gave this woman a false impression that we were a happily married couple with the inability to provide for the baby. This woman was single and affluent without the help of a man, that is why I chose her.

The baby was delivered by Cesarean on November 18, 1986. My doctor, who openly despised Craig because I had confided in him about the abuse, verbally shamed him into being in the operating room during my surgery. He told me later, that when he cut my stomach open, Craig immediately passed out. Along with the birth, I convinced the doctor to perform a tubal ligation, not wanting to take a chance of getting pregnant again. Being a Catholic hospital with strict birth control policies, the doctor performed the surgery under the guise of saving my life. I had never used any birth control methods that were available to women, such as IUDs, birth control pills, condoms or a diaphragm.

At that time, an Arizona law required that an adoptive baby could not be released from the hospital to the adoptive parents for 72 hours after the birth. To get around this law, I had to have Craig check the baby out of the hospital and give her to the new mother at the curb. Before Craig gave her the baby, the new mother, Janet, came into my room to make sure I did not want to hold the baby before she left. I could not stop crying, so devastated that I contemplated canceling the adoption and told Janet, "To hold the baby will only change my mind about the adoption." Janet sent me baby pictures for the next couple of months. The beautiful baby girl looked exactly like her twin sisters. I no longer kept in touch, because it was just too painful for me. People would inquire about the baby as I walked the twins to school. My answer was a barely audible, "She's just fine." To admit that I gave her up was too shameful.

The ordeal traumatized me to the point that I never signed the adoption papers. I believed that if I did not sign the adoption papers, then none of this had ever happened. I hated myself for giving up that precious baby and convinced myself that I was a coward.

I came to realize that I had to get away from Craig or kill myself, those were my only two choices if I ever wanted a peaceful existence. The heartache of giving my daughter up for adoption was far more unbearable than any physical or emotional abuse I have ever endured. I can only hope my daughter will be able to forgive me someday when the truth is exposed.

Giving up my baby gave me the strength and determination needed to leave Craig for good and never look back. All the broken bones could never measure up to the pain of giving up my daughter.

I left Craig at the end of 1986, and he began stalking me. This time I resolved to die before I would accept him back into my life. He chased me in his car several times trying to run the girls and me off the road. Once, he ended up chasing me to the local police station, where he crashed into another car carrying a mother and her children. When he went to court, the Judge made it clear that if he violated his restraining order, he would go to prison and not to the county jail. This threat scared Craig enough for him to move back to Washington.

My babysitter introduced me to her husband's friend, Harald. We hit it off right away and decided to live together in February 1987. Considering my violent past, I was able to overcome some intimacy issues with Harald. The girls lived with us, and we finally had a real family. Harald was in the Air Force, and I got a job as an accounting clerk for a local ice-manufacturing plant. He was dependable and doted on us like a faithful husband and father. We were married on August 26, 1988. Harald desperately wanted to have children of his own and had divorced his first wife because they could not conceive.

Once, while carrying bags of groceries from the car, I tripped over a parking curb and broke my ankle. Harald took me to the hospital, and I left with a cast; not 20 minutes later we were back at the hospital with Jennifer. She fell off the slide during school and left the hospital with a cast on her arm. We were a sight for sore eyes.

Another time, a painful back problem forced me to see a chiropractor, who told me that when I had my right leg in a cast for six months, it probably knocked out my back. Daily, Harald took me to see him for two weeks, but my back pain steadily got worse, and I began missing a lot of work. The misery continued and I started vomiting, so much, that I had to carry a Tupperware bowl with me at all times. Being sick did not seem to concern the chiropractor even as the pain escalated. I started getting chills and Harald put me in the bathtub with scalding hot water. I was so cold that my teeth would not stop chattering.

Celeste

Harald bundled me up and took me to the hospital. Even though the temperature outside was 115 degrees, I wore my winter coat. My temperature was close to 105 degrees when they admitted me to the hospital. We were young and did not know that all the blankets, warm clothes, and coats were making me sicker. The nurses covered me with ice. I never felt so cold in my life. The doctor said my kidneys were so infected, that if I had waited another day, the infection would have entered my bloodstream. I was hospitalized for over a week. Harald took leave from work to spend all his time with me at the hospital.

It felt stable being married to Harald and I was blissfully happy. About a year later, I became pregnant, even though I had the tubal ligation. He was so excited that he stopped at the first pay phone he saw and called all of his friends with the good news. For me, it was a dream come true. We had discussed with my OB/GYN doctor about the microsurgery to reverse my tubal ligation.

About two weeks after finding out I was pregnant, the twins were turning nine. We wanted to give them a huge birthday celebration. We hired an ice carver to shape a 300-pound block of ice that was dyed pink, to resemble a Popsicle, and we had the girls' names carved on both sides. After a long afternoon of playing outdoor games, I began to have pain and started bleeding. I kept quiet until the party

49

ended, then had Harald take me to the hospital. I had an ectopic pregnancy; gestation had occurred outside of my uterus, and I needed surgery.

My doctor was not on call that day and I would not let the hospital send me to surgery without first seeing him. As he was the only doctor I trusted, he knew what this baby meant to Harald and me. The doctor on duty contacted the hospital Chaplain to convince me to have the surgery right away. Their warning was ignored because I only felt confident with my doctor. Later that evening, my doctor arrived in his tuxedo and said that I needed the emergency surgery. He had witnessed my devastation and understood my angst when I gave up my baby girl for adoption. Harald remained at my side the entire time I was in the hospital. My doctor assured me that microsurgery was still a viable solution.

I was only at home two days before I became severely ill again and was readmitted to the hospital with meningitis. Luckily, my job was held for me during these extended illnesses. The four of us remained a close family unit throughout those difficult times. We desired a child and set the date to have the microsurgery in hopes of a successful conception.

In 1989, Harald and I were waiting for me to have the tubal ligation reversed. My doctor was confident the procedure would be a success. I still had not used birth control. My physician never suggested it, and I never gave it any thought. The date had been set for my fast approaching surgery when I collapsed at work because of another ectopic pregnancy. I was rushed to the hospital where emergency surgery was performed. The Fallopian tube had ruptured, causing internal bleeding. At the time the surgery was done, the doctor found a large tumor on my left ovary, leaving him no choice but to perform a total hysterectomy.

When Harald and I found out that we would never have a child together, our lives forever changed. My steadfast belief was that God was punishing me for giving up my baby girl for adoption. Harald was furious with me that I did not have the ambulance transport me to the emergency room at the hospital on the Air Force base where he was stationed. It never occurred to me. The ambulance driver said I was being taken to the closest hospital, Thunderbird Samaritan Hospital. I could not think straight and went along with whatever they thought was best. I wanted my own trusted doctor to perform the surgery, but he was not available.

I believe that Harald felt I had betrayed him. He could not get past the fact that I signed a blanket authorization permitting the surgeon to perform any procedure deemed necessary to save my life. Harald concluded that our fate was sealed at the moment I chose to go to a civilian hospital.

Celeste

As communications between us ceased, we started going our separate ways, even though we were still living under the same roof. I sought comfort from a female friend at work while Harald received emotional support from his male friends. A few months later, Harald received orders to go to Japan. The Air Force authorized the twins to go with him to Japan, but not me because of my ongoing medical treatments. His orders were then abruptly changed to go to Iceland, a place where I assumed dependants could not go.

After he left, I felt desperate and alone, that there were more than just miles between us. It was a challenge to reach Harald by telephone, and my letters were not being answered. I called the commander of the Air Force base in Glendale, Arizona because Harald stopped having his paycheck deposited into our joint account; something I discovered when twenty-two bounced check notices came in the mail. His commanding officer told me that Harald was the one who requested the transfer to Iceland and to go alone. My world ended.

I returned to moonlighting at a department store for a second job to pay off the bounced checks. I was behaving recklessly when I filed for a divorce and simultaneously enlisted in the Air Force; I had enough college credits and could become an officer. Considering Harald was an enlisted man, I thought I could pressure him to come back to me if I outranked him. However, there was a snag in the enlisting process. I could not enlist unless I gave custody of the twins to their natural father. The recruiter assured me that once boot camp was completed and I was stationed at my assigned base, I could regain custody of my daughters.

Craig had since met his soon-to-be second wife and assured me he was drug and alcohol free. I assumed that he was clean and sober because of his second wife, further convincing me that his family was correct in claiming that it was my fault he had not been able to stay sober around me. I surmised Craig's second wife was religious because of her matronly and frumpy appearance. I felt she would be a good influence on the girls while they temporarily lived with Craig. He was thrilled when I signed the girls over to him. We agreed that the girls would only live with him for a short time in Washington until I received my orders.

This life-changing decision was not contemplated for my twenty-six years of age; it was merely my reaction to missing Harald. In the interim, I started dating my divorce attorney, Stuart, who was close to 70 years old. He was appalled at the thought of me enlisting in any branch of the armed services. Stuart was able to convince the Air Force not to demand that I honored my commitment and asked me to marry him.

He lived at the Arizona Biltmore Estates and we met

every night for cocktails at the Ritz. In addition to drinking and eating dinner, we went to my apartment, stayed overnight at the Ritz, or went a few times to his condo. At his place, I mentioned to Stuart that I noticed the feminine décor and he told me his daughter had done the decorating. I never spent the entire night at his place; Stuart said he was worried about what the neighbors would think if I stayed overnight and they saw me leaving at daylight. He persuaded me that he was chivalrous, wanting only to protect my reputation.

Stuart was handling my divorce along with preparing for our upcoming wedding in September of 1991. When scheduled for minor surgery, Stuart accompanied me to my doctor's appointment to receive post-surgical instructions. The doctor kept asking him, "Are you sure you're going to stay with her after the surgery?" I became irritated because I thought this was an ignorant question, I knew they were close friends, and it seemed he should have known I would be safe. Stuart was intimidating; his mere presence commanded respect, and I was completely enamored by him.

I woke up in unfamiliar surroundings after the surgery. Having to go to the bathroom, I could not get out of bed without help. I was heavily sedated and could not move my body, so I began shouting for help. I was filled with panic and was disoriented about the unfamiliar surroundings. I could not understand why I was alone and unable to get out of bed. I could not recall leaving the doctor's office. The last thing I remembered was the doctor leaning over me and telling me to count backward from ten.

The door opened, and a strange man came in to tell me he had been given a number to call, if I needed assistance during the night. He said that I had been abandoned at the Ritz. The attendant took me to the restroom and left. I was too sedated to comprehend this news. I stayed at the hotel for a few days. When I was able to get up and around on my own, the attendant took me back to my apartment. I was pitiful still not understanding why I was abandoned at the Ritz.

A couple of weeks later I ran into Stuart's daughter at his office. Trying to make small talk, I mentioned that she had done a beautiful job decorating her father's place. She looked bewildered, saying; "Oh, it was Nancy that did it." His daughter was very masculine looking and I assumed Nancy must be her lover. She told me Nancy was a flight attendant and that she and her father had lived together, sharing a romantic life, for the last five years; she owned the residence, as well as the $90,000 Porsche that Stuart drove occasionally.

Suddenly everything made sense with the secretive behavior that Stuart consistently displayed along with the unusual meeting places and odd hours. We were spending almost every weekend in Palm Springs, where I saw him making whispered telephone calls. I foolishly thought they were privileged attorney/client conversations. I was offended that he had approved my surgery to be scheduled on a weekend that Nancy was in town. He chose her over my well-being and dumped me off at a hotel, treating me like a discarded piece of luggage. How could he ask me to marry him while he was sharing a bedroom with another woman and lying about it?

After that, I was on a mission. I still met Stuart for cocktails at the Ritz, but feigned a headache every night so he would take me back to my apartment. Once home, I fluffed up my hair, put on more make-up, a miniskirt, and boots, then headed out to the local country and western nightclubs in search of another man.

Knowing I would need to find a new attorney to attend to my personal affairs, I began dating another married lawyer. His spouse was a Dean at Arizona State University. When I tried to end the relationship, he became threatening and abusive. The affair came to an abrupt end when I told him I would let his wife know about the kink in his penis.

One night, as I was standing at the bar, trying to persuade the bartender to return my car keys, a handsome Hispanic man walked up to me and said, "I'm going to marry you and move you to Texas." I said, "Okay" and within two weeks Jimmy and I were gone. We moved to Dallas, where I signed up with a temporary agency and began working at

American Express auditing their capital expenditure accounts.

By August of 1991, Jimmy and I were off to Las Vegas to get married at the quaint "We've Only Just Begun Wedding Chapel" on the Las Vegas Strip. We chose Las Vegas because of the glittery, glamorous casinos and hotels. I did not know until years later that my divorce from Harald had never been finalized. Jimmy's family attended, and Neiman-Marcus planned a small, but elegant reception.

Jimmy had become fond of my Shih-Tzu, Charlie, so we took her to Vegas with us. The only place at the time that would allow dogs was Motel 6. If we walked on the carpet in our room without wearing slippers, the bottoms of our feet turned coal-black from years of filth. Everyone else stayed at the Mirage, but we did not care. I was Jimmy's first wife and he was my third husband. The girls were still in Washington with Craig, and we were in the midst of a full-blown custody battle in a Washington court. I had lost the fight for jurisdiction in Texas. Both courts decided the state in which the girls were now living should have jurisdiction. Kathy, Craig's wife, worked in the county courts and lent a helping hand against me in the finalizing of the custody battle.

Jimmy received a job transfer to Tucson, so we moved back to Arizona. We began having problems, because he wanted me to work in an office and I wanted to try my hand at waitressing, thinking I could earn more money while working fewer hours. A wife of one of Jimmy's coworker's assured me I could double the wages earned in an office job. My first job was at a Mexican restaurant, where my work was fun, and I liked the attention of the customers. I noticed the owner was shorting me on my pay. We only made $1.13 an hour because Arizona is a "right-to-work" state. I was upset with the owner because she was stealing, not only from me but also from all the employees who worked so hard for her. She was despicable and told us to recycle the uneaten tortilla chips, not caring when I found chewed-up gum amongst them. She told me to throw away the gum and serve the chips for another order. Afterward, I vowed not to eat anything else there as I did not know what she was telling the cook to do.

Because I was upset with the owner, I started drinking tequila, sneaking the most expensive brand into the customers' drinks, then drinking a shot myself. We were supposed to pour from the least expensive bottles, yet charge for the premium tequila. When no one was watching, I served only the best food and drink for the customers. It was my way of getting back at the boss for shorting our pay and for cheating the customers. Some nights I was so drunk that I became confused as to where my station was and what tables placed which orders. However, I made excellent money.

I started coming home late at night intoxicated, causing problems in my marriage. While my daughters were

Celeste

in Washington with Craig and Kathy, I vowed to keep the peace with Jimmy. I agreed to work daytime hours at another establishment. I still was not willing to give up waiting tables, because I was able to make more money by working fewer hours than if I had a desk job. I found a job serving breakfast, where all the various law enforcement agencies ate in Tucson. I received considerable attention from the male customers, and I received generous tips. Once again, Jimmy was transferred, this time to Austin, Texas. We were still fighting in family court, but Craig finally allowed Kristina to live with me, while Jennifer stayed in Washington. The girls were now twelve years old.

Not long after my arrival in Austin, I was admitted to the hospital, diagnosed with Legionnaires' disease, the more severe form of the infection that causes pneumonia. The U.S. Center for Disease Control investigated, identified, and then isolated the Legionellosis bacterium. They found the bacterium to be breeding in the cooling tower of the hotel's air conditioning system where I spent the night in Arizona. I remained hospitalized for over a week.

I was only home from the hospital a few weeks when I was readmitted to another hospital for five days. I suffered from a severe intestinal infection unrelated to the Legionellosis. One month later I was rushed to the hospital for emergency surgery because of a ruptured appendix.

59

Celeste

Jimmy took excellent care of Kristina during all three of my hospital stays, making sure she ate right, went to sleep at a decent hour, and got off to school on time. When visiting me in the hospital, she always told me to hurry up and get well because she said Jimmy was "too mean." I knew Kristina resented Jimmy's structured lifestyle, but there was nothing I could do to intercede. I begged her to do what he asked and promised her that we would have fun once I recovered. I considered Kristina my best friend and loved her more than I loved anyone and was anxious to be well and be together again.

2

Meeting Steven

I began working at the Austin County Club as a waitress. While working at the club, I received an excellent education about the true nature of many affluent people. Some of the members talked down to the wait staff and expected us to babysit their children, clean up after them, and take them to the bathroom. If the children had an accident, we were supposed to clean it up. The adults were even worse. If members had too much to drink, got sick or soiled themselves, we were expected to assist in the cleanup, fetch clean clothes, and dispose of the soiled ones -- all done, of course, with a sweet smile.

A few of the elderly male members treated the female staff as if we were nightclub strippers. I was offered $100 to $500 to let them see or touch my breasts. Rarely did the members show kindness or respect to the staff. In retaliation, I observed cooks and servers spit in, step on, or burn food for those members' who complained about the meal or the service. I had witnessed this practice in every restaurant that I have worked in and I begged Steven to not complain about his food or service for this reason. Steven bragged to everyone who would listen to him, not only was this country club the oldest in the state, it still did not have any black members. Steven loved to verbalize, "You can paint them red, white, and blue, but they still come out a nigger." I cringed every time I heard him speak like that. Without remorse, I sold the membership in 2000 after my husband died; I refused to pay dues to a club that was prejudiced. I still kept my memberships at both Barton Creek and Las Colinas. Steven was not a member of these clubs because they were diverse in their affiliations.

Jennifer was still living in Washington state with her father, his second wife Kathy, and her two small children from a previous marriage. Craig and I were in the midst of a vicious custody battle because we each wanted our daughters in our sole care. In addition to the turmoil of my going back and forth to court in Washington, Kristina was in a constant struggle with Jimmy. She detested that he was setting limits, enforcing rules, and giving her daily chores. This situation became more than a dispute, and our home life was a constant verbal battlefield. Jimmy said we should make parenting decisions together, but I felt caught in the middle. Kristina was my child, and she felt that his demands bordered on abuse. I believed that, as her mother, I was supposed to clean her room, make her bed, put away the dishes, and take out the trash. Since I had to do these things growing up, I was adamant that my children would enjoy growing up for as long as possible without having any responsibilities. Jimmy disagreed. When he told Kristina to do something, she just got on her bicycle and took off down the street.

The outside of her bedroom door was plastered with handmade posters like "I hate you, Jimmy." The guest bathroom was near her bedroom, so anyone who came to our house could see the disrespect. I allowed her to continue with this behavior, trying to be her protector and friend. Jimmy never abused her. To this day, I do not understand why he still loves and cares about all three of us, after the way we treated him. To demonstrate to Jimmy that he was not in charge of Kristina, and partly to appease her, I allowed her to miss 22 days of school in the 5th grade. We stayed up late and watched *Designing Women* together, getting to sleep well past midnight. She was too tired to get up, so I did not make her go to school. I would have allowed her more sleep-in days, had I not received a letter threatening her to be retained in grade 5.

As the arguments were escalating, I was afraid to leave Kristina at home with Jimmy. I did not fear that Jimmy would harm Kristina but did worry, that due to her headstrong nature, she might make decisions that were detrimental to her well-being. The sight of Kristina taking off down the street on her bicycle terrified me. I took her to school early in the morning, so that I could volunteer at the school's store. I returned in the afternoons to volunteer as a teacher's aide, sometimes even substitute teaching a class. I stayed until Kristina's school day ended. I took her home, made dinner, and was usually back at the club by 4:30 or 5:00 p.m. in time for the dinner crowd. I was always home by 10:30 p.m.

Jimmy had a friend he had known since kindergarten, whose wife was a social worker and they had three boys. Kristina and their oldest child were very close friends, so they took Kristina into their home for a few months to give her some peace and stability. Kristina loved this couple as if they were her second set of parents. Years later, after she concocted my involvement with Steven's shooting, she cut off all ties with them along with almost everyone else who had known us before the shooting. She could not keep up telling and remembering her many lies, knowing that they knew better. Regardless, they still miss her.

Steven and his first wife, Elise, were regulars at my workstation at the club. Partially paralyzed, she arrived in a wheelchair, having suffered a stroke from an inoperable brain tumor. Steven kept her plied with Scotch, even though he had to hand-feed it to her, the best he could do for her alcoholism. Before her stroke, Steven and Elise fought publicly, cursing at each other, never caring who witnessed their arguments. He said ugly things to her regarding their three children; they thought the black nanny was their mother because Elise was always out golfing or drunk. She countered that she enjoyed the peace and tranquility of having a separate bedroom. Steven condemned Elise for not taking an interest in the decorating of their home or the cooking of their meals. She responded that he was overbearing and obnoxious. He flatly stated that she dressed like a pauper and she yelled back at him that he looked like a pimp. She said unforgivable things about him because he was caught in the hot tub with his adult daughter, who was wearing only panties and bra instead of a swimsuit. In my opinion, their daughter Becky was also an alcoholic. Elise died from cancer in October 1993. Two of their children, Becky and Steven III, died in

2011 from a heart attack and cancer, respectively.

My boss asked me to go to Steven's house and help him with the laundry and meals because he was alone. When he came into the club after the funeral, I hugged him, a simple act of heartfelt sympathy. Ten days later, he asked me out on a date.

Even though I was still married to Jimmy, I had no trouble accepting the invitation since Jimmy and I had already decided that our marriage was over. We agreed not to make it public for fear that Craig would find out and use it against me in the custody battle.

Steven met me at Mama Mia's Restaurant and divulged that night over cocktails that he was overwhelmed by my hug. He said that most people were terrified of his abrupt and aggressive manner; I was the only employee at the club not intimidated by his obnoxious demeanor. He said that he appreciated me because I was feisty and unafraid of him, confessing that all his life Elise was the only other person to stand up to him. He said I was beautiful. He said he loved my smile. He said he loved my laugh and that he loved that I made him laugh.

Steven had a boisterous personality and enjoyed the power that came with his affluence and position in life. I was more than a trophy wife to him because of my age and looks. I was someone to whom he could completely open-up. Although we both had tendencies to let our tempers flare up, we both forgave quickly and did not hold grudges. He and Elise fought in public, cursing at each other, but I was different in this area, being mortified if he cussed at me in front of someone else.

I broke my husband of his cursing habit on a trip to Spain in 1995. He was belligerent because his friend and attorney, Philip, wanted to eat at a different restaurant. Steven said earlier that his only condition was that he wanted to eat at a place that served pasta. The restaurant chosen did have pasta but was not Italian. Steven pitched a fit and began cursing and screaming that he never got to pick the restaurant because Philip always did. I was on the telephone with Philip, and he could hear Steven yelling; I was embarrassed by his childish behavior.

I impulsively packed my suitcase and stayed in another five star hotel down the street. I booked a one-way, first-class, $8,000 airline ticket back to the United States, leaving early the following morning. It took me one more day to arrive back in Austin because of a delay in Miami by customs that caused me to miss my scheduled flight. The abrupt and costly change in my itinerary must have caused the officials to think I was carrying drugs in my luggage, as I was thoroughly questioned and searched.

After arriving back in Austin, I began shopping, as usual, comforting myself with jewelry and clothes. Steven did not want to leave because the entire trip was prepaid, so he finished out the itinerary. He ended up being delayed an extra five days because the pilots in Spain went on strike the day he was scheduled to depart. Arriving in the United States, he called from customs, in Miami, and asked, "Darling, will you pick me up from the airport when I arrive in Austin?" I picked him up, and we ate dinner at the club before arriving home. Nothing else was ever mentioned about that situation. He paid the bill for the extra hotel room, the flight home, and the shopping spree, but never again behaved like that in public. He appreciated my willingness to stand up to his behavior. He told me many times that he had never loved anyone, including Elise, in the ways that he loved me. He called us soul mates.

At Christmas of 1993, I had agreed to live with Steven and he agreed to do everything in his power to get Kristina back into my custody and care. He sweetened the deal by offering to adopt her. She had gone to visit her dad and sister for Christmas and was not coming home, as scheduled, because I lost the first phase of the ongoing custody battle. Kristina was devastated.

Steven had a provision, I must not work. He told me to give notice to the club. He did not want his woman to have a job -- period. He agreed to pay off all of my debts, even credit card balances that were considered joint and community property with Jimmy. He understood that Jimmy's name was listed as the responsible party on most of the cards, yet I was the one who made the majority of the charges. For Christmas, he gave me a three-carat solitary diamond necklace, a cocktail ring with forty-two diamonds, and a 1994 SUV. I found it difficult to buy for him because he already owned everything. I had a jeweler design a 14-K gold pill tube with his initials engraved, allowing him to carry his codeine pills discreetly. He had always wrapped his medicine in his handkerchief and kept them in his pants pocket, resulting in some being crushed. The pill tube was an elegant solution to this problem. I also gave him a 14-K gold penny-sized heart with our initials engraved on each side. Whenever he put his hand in his pocket to bring out a coin or key, the heart was there to remind him of the love we shared.

We spent Christmas Day, 1993, looking for property on which to build our lake house. We found the perfect place in Spicewood, and Steven gave Dana, our real estate agent and later a close friend, a check for the lot. We found an architect and purchased the adjacent lot, so we could save most of the trees by repositioning the house.

My divorce from Jimmy was finalized in April of 1994. In the midst of the house construction, Steven negotiated the sale of the Fox TV station to a CBS affiliate in New York. The negotiating was quite a coup, considering that Fox had recently acquired the NFL rights for Monday Night Football. This acquisition meant a considerable bounty for Steven and his partner. Being left with a lot of control over the lake house construction, I was amazed by my skills in the areas of design and decorating. In the meantime, Kristina came back to live with us because she formally accused her father of physical abuse. I discovered this fabrication years later; it was manipulation, so she could get her way.

As agreed, Steven instructed our attorney in Marble Falls to draft and start adoption proceedings. We set the date of February 18, 1995, for our wedding. The closing of the TV station sale was scheduled for February 1, 1995. I signed a prenuptial agreement that would give me one million dollars, should we divorce.

We were wed at the Austin Country Club with about forty close friends and family in attendance. He was

70; I was 32. It was well known by Steven, and others, that I married him for his money; it was no secret. He said he loved me and would provide for my daughters and me. He told me he wanted a companion, someone to share and enjoy his wealth, and someone who would enjoy being his traveling partner. He was lonely and wanted a woman to dote on, and he desired that person to be me. He told me there was no point to have all that money if there was nobody to share it with; little did I know, at the time, was that his generosity with his wealth would lead to a spending compulsion. We honeymooned in New Orleans, and subsequently, spent our future anniversaries there. Steven told me that I could choose to travel anywhere in the world for our honeymoon. I gave the offer considerable thought, remembering our first date at Mama Mia's when I had asked Steven where he would most like to visit in the world. He chose New Orleans, because of the food and the ambiance of the French Quarter.

The lake house was completed in the spring of 1995, and we were elated with the finished product. Tulips are my favorite flowers, especially the pink ones. Steven ordered two pink tulip trees, while we were in New Orleans, and surprised me by having them planted near the back patio at the lake house. The gardener tried to dissuade

Celeste

Steven, saying they would never survive the Texas climate, but he was wrong. The trees thrived and were a constant reminder of our wedding anniversary every time we sat outside visiting with each other.

Steven wanted Kristina to attend a private boarding school that was located within 10 minutes of our home. I knew there was a possibility that Kristina would not be able to pass the entrance exam. Kristina and I worried about the test and did not want her to fail so I made arrangements to hire a proctor. I would take the exam in Kristina's place without the school finding out. Her scores were impressive for a soon-to-be seventh grader. However, I was unaware that a personal interview with Kristina was required before the school's acceptance.

They said that Kristina's interview indicated that her aptitude was lower than what her written exams represented. They accused me of improprieties and returned our $26,000 tuition check. I convinced Steven that it was impossible to abide by their rigid visitation schedule, so I had her pulled from the school. I was ashamed of my indiscretion and embarrassed that Kristina could not meet their qualifications. I did not want her to be scolded by Steven with this information. He had a sharp tongue and could be very hurtful with his words after a few cocktails.

The cheating was another one of my poor choices; it remained unmentioned by the girls in my trial.

Kristina was apprehensive about starting middle school in a new public school district and, in the beginning, had a difficult time adjusting. The parents of the majority of the students were affluent, and the school was listed as exemplary by the state. To ease the transition, I coddled her. I never made her ride the bus and during the first quarter, brought her lunch daily from a fast-food restaurant and stayed with her until the lunch period ended. I started bringing in pizzas and enough fast-food to feed the other students at her table. She became an instant hit and was able to make several friends. In the afternoons, I always brought my puppy, Nikki, as I greeted Kristina at her classroom door. The children's natural attraction to the small Cocker Spaniel helped Kristina open-up to the other children, ending with having lavish parties at our house for her and her new friends. I allowed them to toilet paper houses in the neighborhood, securing my place as a "cool" mom. Kristina blossomed and joined the yearbook team as a photographer. Kristina had the privilege to take a school trip to England to see the newly renovated Shakesphere's Globe Theatre.

I sent Craig the papers to sign, allowing Steven to

adopt Kristina. As Steven kept giving me the run around regarding the adoption, strife began creeping into our lives. Everywhere in the house, I felt Steven's late wife Elise's presence. We had only been married a few weeks, when he changed his mind about adopting Kristina, giving me no explanation. This abrupt change of heart made me feel paranoid, leaving me to assume that he had tricked me. Because of this upset in our plan, a couple of months after we were married, I left Steven and requested a divorce. I was admitted to a hospital for depression because my life was spiraling out of control. Kristina remained in the house with Steven. After a few weeks, we were able to reconcile, and the divorce issue was dropped. We attended marriage counseling and Steven related that our Austin attorney, David Kuperman, advised him not to adopt Kristina since she was an identical twin. He felt it would be emotionally harmful for them to have two different fathers.

Had I have known this, I would have been able to understand this reasoning and not insisted he file for divorce. He was afraid of hurting my feelings and kept quiet. During this same marriage counseling session, Steven suggested we sell the house and live in the lake house while building a new house with our new memories. We decided to sell everything and start over. He deeded the lake house to me and the new house would be equally owned by both of us. After listing his home for sale, we celebrated our reunion by taking a trip to Mexico City.

Steven's house sold for $795,000 while we were on vacation. The buyers wanted some of the furnishings and most of the artwork. I was elated because I had initially assumed that Steven told me a fabricated story and that Elise had decorated the house since that is the traditional role of the wife. He assured me years later that she only cared about playing golf and drinking and went through a case of Scotch a week. He confided in me that he did all the decorating, cooking, and shopping.

This fact was natural for me to believe because he had donated my entire wardrobe to a battered women's shelter when I first moved in with him. He picked out my replacements right down to the lingerie. I enjoyed the attention at first, but after a couple of years, I no longer allowed him to dictate what clothes I wore. He abhorred jeans and refused to let me buy any. It was a struggle that took years to overcome, but he eventually relented and kept his opinions to himself when I wore a pair of jeans. My compromise was to never to wear a pair of jeans to the country club.

During the day I liked to be casual and comfortable,

wearing no make-up and cared little how my hair was styled. I had never been high maintenance in this area. For functions or evenings out, I dressed extravagantly. My husband loved showing off his elegant wife. He said Elise was an embarrassment because all she ever wanted to wear was nylon jogging suits. Steven took great pride and pleasure in buying my expensive clothes and jewelry. He was adamant that I never wore the same outfit twice when we went out. He viewed my appearance as a direct reflection of him.

Steven was both flamboyant and gregarious. Merely saying he loved me was never enough for him and insisted on showing me his love through material possessions. He was quite generous to me. I regret now that he let me do whatever I wanted and how he forgave me for everything and anything. I wish he would have put his foot down with me as he did with the twins and everyone else in his life. He was my constant champion, and no matter what poor choices I made in life, in his eyes, I could do no wrong.

On one occasion, I was asked to chaperone Kristina's high school yearbook class on an overnight convention in Dallas. I agreed but did not want to fly with the group, not wanting to smoke in front of them outside the airports. Instead, I drove the five hours and gave my ticket to a less fortunate friend of Kristina's, so that she could also attend. We stayed at the Hyatt, a beautiful hotel with rooms surrounding dining areas.

Curfew for students was 11:00 p.m. One of the female instructors and I decided to drive to a club in Deep Ellum and have cocktails and listen to some jazz. It never occurred to me that the teenagers would break the curfew. When we returned close to 3:00 a.m., the security guard stopped us in the elevator and told us that the students had thrown their clothes over the balconies and all the garments had landed on the chandeliers and tables below. Squirt guns were used on TV sets, and sex took place in stairwells.

When I arrived at my room, my roommate, a mother of one of the students, whom I had never met, was waiting for me. She chastised me for my negligence and dereliction of duties. I was informed by the school that I would never be allowed to chaperone another school function because I had disgraced the good name of the snooty school. It humiliated me, and I cried on Steven's shoulder. He assured me that I was "Mother-of-the-Year" in his book and surprised me the next day with another fur coat. He assured me that I made him proud, and that was all that mattered. He called them "gibbonies" for holding it against me that I had not known the students would break curfew.

During the summer of 1995, Kristina, Steven, and I started living at the lake house. We were building our dream house in Austin close to the country club and down the street from our impending upscale shopping centers. When school started in the fall, I took Kristina on the 30-minute drive to and from her new school in Marble Falls. She had to change schools because we lived in a different school district. When she joined the basketball and volleyball teams, Steven and I never missed a game. She had one particular friend who lived in Granite Shoals, and the girls alternated spending weekends at each other's homes. We bought two Waverunners and took them out on the lake every weekend. Steven did not have the patience required to back the trailer in and out of the lake or storage units, so he coached me, and I became an expert.

We always took my dog, Nikki, with us wholly attired in her all-pink visor, sunglasses, and life vest. Her leash was specially made to resemble a water ski rope. Other boaters videotaped her on the Waverunners, as she stood up, front paws on the steering wheel and her ears blowing in the wind. She was quite a sight to behold, especially when we reached speeds more than 50 mph.

We ended up with two stray cats as house pets because Jennifer and Kristina insisted on keeping them. I had a compulsion to check the litter box innumerable times during the day to make sure it was empty of any waste. Steven was so proud of me for doing this because he had an intense dislike for cats. He regularly commented on how well I looked after all of the animals. I was too ashamed to tell him how tormented I was regarding the litter box and the horrific memories of Craig shoving cat feces down my throat.

My husband enjoyed taking the Waverunners to the local marina where we had a long, relaxing lunches together, just the two of us and Nikki. Anywhere I went, Nikki also traveled. I loved this dog as if she was my child. Steven called her "little asshole," because she would never obey him. The more frustrated and loud his demands became, the farther she would back away while barking non-stop at him. I felt bad because he was never able to entice her with a treat or table scrap. Steven told me that the love and devotion Nikki and I shared with each other brightened his days because he was the purchaser of the dog and therefore responsible for my happiness. It was around this time my husband asked me to affectionately call him "Big Daddy."

Celeste

On July 30, 1998, I signed the Marital Trust
Agreement Steven had drafted with our attorney. I
understood two things: It was irrevocable and a tax shelter.
My name would be used in the trust and I would pay the
taxes on the income received. For my agreement, Steven
gave me two houses and $500,000. He told me by paying
this amount; it was far cheaper than paying any estate
taxes.

Any funds that were removed from the Marital
Trust had to have the consent of the trustee. Steven was the
only trustee until his death, all of my expenditures required
his approval. No matter how much money I spent, my
husband always approved the payments. I knew that after
Steven's death, I would have to go to the Bank of America
for spending approval, knowing they would not be
generous to me, or even kind, so the longer Steven lived,
the better off I would be. The twins would inherit nothing
until I died or was disqualified with a murder conviction.

3

The Twin's Father, Craig

By the spring of 1996, the Toro Canyon home was over half-way completed. In mid-June 1996 I received a telephone call from Jennifer in the middle of the night. Hearing her voice, I was ecstatic. Weekly, I had sent her a letter along with a small gift. She never wrote me or came to the telephone when I faithfully called every Sunday night, regardless of what continent I happened to be visiting. She had not communicated with me in almost two years, blaming me for the abuse Kristina accused her father of doing. Regardless, I wrote to her regularly and reassured her how much I loved her.

Jennifer told me she was calling because her father was in dire straits and she needed me to help them. Craig's mother lived 10 minutes away, but Jennifer did not feel comfortable calling her. She told me that Craig's wife had asked them to move out of the family home and that they were now living in an empty apartment. She made me promise I would not force her to live in Texas because she wanted to stay with her dad. I asked Steven for his advice on allowing Jennifer to remain in Washington with her dad. He assured me that whatever I decided to do, he would back me. That same day, Kristina and I went shopping, and our purchases were shipped to Washington so they would have everything they would need to set up a new household, including new bedroom furniture for Jennifer.

I spared no expense and was thrilled to be in a position to help my daughter. She had turned to me, knowing I would not let her down. I spoke with her several times a day on the phone. A couple of days after the first shipments of household goods arrived, Craig came on the phone to thank me. He sounded extremely depressed, and I was genuinely worried about him. Both he and Jennifer never hinted that he was, again, struggling with alcoholism and drug addiction. I surmised that time would heal the sting of his recent separation from his wife. I knew Craig suffered from mental illness and addictions. I believed those traits, coupled with my depression, would likely appear in the twins as they mature. Regardless of what I thought the future would hold, I allowed Jennifer to stay with him because I thought they needed each other.

Celeste

Craig and I began a nightly ritual of talking on the phone for hours at a time, exchanging stories about the girls and our spouses. These calls did not interfere with my time with Steven, considering the time difference, he was already asleep. The calls were long distance; he was well aware of the length of our conversations and never complained about the telephone bills. He was just relieved that the anger had dissipated between Craig and me.

A few months before Jennifer's distress call to me, Kristina confessed that she lied about her father's physical abuse. She showed no remorse. Kristina said she lied because she knew I would believe her, considering the abuse I had endured at the hands of her father. She told me that she just wanted to live with me and did not care if it hurt her dad. After Kristina said this, I again turned to my husband for advice. He told me not to disrupt Jennifer's life by coming forward with the truth. I was torn, not wanting to lose Kristina, but at the same time, understanding that Jennifer had every right to push me away because she knew that Kristina had lied. Jennifer believed I put Kristina up to the abuse fabrication.

I noticed how distraught and depressed Craig sounded over the telephone. I questioned his alcohol and drug usage and he flatly denied both. I still believed that he would eventually overcome this hurdle. When Craig told me that Jennifer was scheduled to visit her paternal grandfather in California, I made arrangements for Kristina to meet her at the airport so they could spend time with their grandfather together; they had not seen each other in over two years. When Craig suggested Jennifer visit me after her two-week stay with her grandfather, I was elated. To bolster his spirits, and against Steven's advice, I sent a letter telling Craig that Kristina had told me the truth about the abuse. I asked for his forgiveness because Steven and I had let him have it with both barrels over the alleged abuse.

When the girls' visit was to end with their grandfather, I had our travel agent make arrangements for me to take them to Disney World, thinking this would give the three of us a fun reunion. I sent Craig a letter about wanting him to go to Disney World with the girls and that Steven had agreed to pay for the trip. Years later, while stealing documents off my computer to give to the DA to use at my trial, the teenagers never gave a copy of this saved letter to the prosecution indicating I wanted the three of them to mend fences. I explained to Craig that I would be with the girls until he arrived, then return to Texas. The plans were that when the weekend was over, he and Jennifer would fly back to Washington and Kristina would come home to Spicewood. This plan would give Craig private time with the girls, and he would not be uncomfortable because of my presence.

In the letter, I also included a $5,000 cashier's check for a retainer for his divorce attorney and $500 in gift certificates to Albertson's grocery store. He said he was looking forward to spending time with both girls and was overwhelmed by my generosity and forgiving spirit. He was pleased that I was available to him, despite physically and emotionally abusing me in the past. I explained to him that Steven had taught me how to forgive and not to live in the past. I told Craig that Steven had never held a grudge against me no matter what I did and that he taught me how to love unconditionally. I was able to reach out and offer financial and emotional support to Craig because he would always be the biological father of the twins. Steven explained to me that to help Jennifer, we had to help Craig. My husband was a wise man, and I admired that about him.

Craig agreed with all the travel plans, and we each sent one of the twins to California. After two days I still was unable to reach Craig and grew concerned. Steven and I thought Craig might be out late drinking to drown his sorrows; this seemed highly plausible, but I did not want to alarm Jennifer. By day three, Jennifer called in a panic over not being able to reach her father. I promised her that I would locate him. My first reaction was to fly to Washington and find Craig. Steven convinced me to call Craig's work, only to find out he had not been seen in two days. Steven had me call Craig's mother, and she told me, "Mind your own goddamn business." I called his workplace again and spoke with one of his friends and asked him to go and see if Craig was at his apartment. He went, but no one answered the door, and he then became concerned, when he noticed Craig's vehicle in the parking lot.

I grew apprehensive, afraid that Craig must have blacked out from alcohol; afraid Craig was the way I had seen Steven many times after excessive drinking. I was mainly concerned because no one was living with Craig that could get him medical aid if he needed it. I relayed my concerns to Steven, but he still insisted that I remain in Texas until we knew Craig's whereabouts. Steven called the apartment manager and made arrangements for the friend to enter Craig's apartment with a family member present. In the meantime, Steven and I were preparing to fly to Washington when I spoke to Craig's friend. With reluctance, he was able to convince Craig's mother to accompany him to the apartment. His mom assumed that he was having drug and alcohol problems, and went only to save face in their small community. Craig and his mom both worked at the same cannery, and now she was embarrassed because we were calling everyone we could think of.

Upon entering the apartment, they discovered that Craig had committed suicide; it was apparent he had been dead for a few days. The coroner determined that he had been dead for three days. Craig had placed a sawed-off shotgun to his head, which meant he had committed suicide hours after Jennifer's plane left Sea-Tac Airport. The last call he made was to his wife, but only she knows what was said.

When Jennifer was notified at about 1:00 a.m., she called me, hysterical. I immediately booked a flight to leave in the morning. Steven did not accompany me because I did not want to wait to make arrangements for the pets and reschedule appointments. I wanted to be with my daughters as soon as was humanly possible.

I flew to California, picked up the girls from their grandfather's house and brought them back to Texas. Their grandfather wanted them to stay, but I said no, feeling it was imperative that I be the one to comfort and console them. Having not seen Jennifer in nearly two years, I hardly recognized her. She was dressed in gothic style with her hair dyed a burgundy color. I held and comforted them to the best of my ability all the way back to Texas. There was no doubt about where Jennifer would be living. Steven and I never questioned each other, because we both understood her place was with us. Kristina was extremely distressed, wanting me to allow her sister to live with one of Jennifer's friends in Washington. They were 15 years old; I never gave this idea any consideration.

Kristina treated Jennifer as an unwanted intruder, as she did not want her sister in our lives. Kristina's attitude broke my heart because Jennifer had been emotionally distraught. Kristina was rude and obnoxious to Jennifer, even in Steven's presence. Her behavior angered Steven, and to compensate; he began favoring Jennifer over Kristina at every opportunity. Steven and Kristina's relationship soon became irreparable. They had verbal battles that continued to escalate up until his death. After all he had done for them, the girls should have been more respectful to Steven. They admitted to many people that they hated him and some witnesses testified in court to their hatred of Steven. I believe these battles contributed to Kristina's decision to blame me for his death -- her way of "getting even."

I took Craig's suicide extremely hard, blaming myself for not flying to Washington to check things out for myself when I sensed something was wrong. Jennifer had entrusted me to take care of her "beloved dad," and I had let her down in a grave and fatal way. I was inconsolable. My daughter's lives had been forever changed, so I had to be strong and be the girls' advocate.

Since Craig's brothers had also physically abused me, I was frightened to go to Washington with the girls. Steven felt his presence would be an intrusion, so I asked my best friend Dawn to accompany us. My mixed emotions caused me to feel it was important for the girls to attend their father's funeral; I was scared to death to go to the community where Craig and his brothers had terrorized me so I asked Dawn to go with us.

The four of us left the following day, not even knowing when or where the funeral was to be held. We stayed in Seattle because it was two and a half hours away from Craig's mother's house. Craig's dad and brothers picked up the girls at our hotel, under the condition that Dawn accompanied them to the services. When Craig's brothers saw me at the hotel in Seattle, they faced me and threatened bodily harm if I were to attend the funeral. I was far too afraid to consider attending the funeral and had already promised Steven that I would go nowhere near those people without a hired bodyguard. I was grateful Dawn wanted to accompany them and provide them with emotional and moral support. I bought them each a Bible, a lace handkerchief, and a gold cross pendant so that they would feel my presence and have something to bring back to Texas to comfort them since I had assumed Craig would be buried in Washington.

We stayed five days waiting and wondering why the funeral had not been scheduled. With empty days to fill, while the girls were with relatives, my husband suggested I spend my time with the coroner and also at the courthouse trying to piece together the events that led Craig to end his life. The autopsy report was gruesome; my daughters never forgave me for not allowing them to read a copy of it. I was afraid the visual imagery described in those reports would forever haunt and torment them. They never understood that I disallowed the reading because I loved them enough not to want their last memories of their father to be wretched and miserable.

I did some research at the courthouse and discovered that Kathryn Bratcher had filed numerous restraining orders against Craig. He accused her of over-indulgence of marijuana, while she charged that he was addicted to crystal methamphetamine along with alcohol. Kathryn Bratcher's statement on her petition for Order of Protection against Craig read as follows:

"May 26 and 27, 1996, respondent broke into family home where he has not resided since April 1st. He gained entry by crashing through the kitchen door and did further damage to the home and property by punching his fist through an interior door, throwing things, leaving holes in the walls, etc. On April 28, respondent forcibly and in a very threatening manner caused the children and I (and a friend with her 9-yr old son) to leave the home with no notice or right to do so. After we left, he ransacked my office, destroying a PC monitor, important paperwork and several other personal items (pictures, candlesticks, etc.) of mine. Respondent also urinated on my son's bed and personal belongings. April 1st, stalked family home peering through windows and threatened his nine-year-old stepson with violence. Respondent is an alcoholic and methamphetamine user. His ability to reason is severely impaired by his addictions, and the acts of violence continue to escalate. Respondent has demonstrated that he cannot stay clean and sober more than eight days unless being in an in-patient treatment program, should be ordered to undergo an acute treatment program. May 31, 1996, at Everett, Washington, Kathryn J. Bratcher."

When Craig realized she was not going to take him back, he planned his demise. He knew he would have to get Jennifer away from him to be successful. Craig held it together long enough to convince us he would make the trip to Florida. I will always be grateful to him for not allowing Jennifer to find his body and also now understood that he and Jennifer turned to me because they both knew I was a good person, not the evil witch as his family portrayed me. It finally became apparent to me that his alcohol and drug addictions were defects in his character and not in any way precipitated by me. I blame his deep rooted emotional issues, his violent behavior, and addictions on his dysfunctional family. This realization was like a boulder being lifted off my shoulders.

Jennifer was unaware, and I never did find out what happened to the $5,000 cashier's check and $500 gift cards to Albertson's I sent Craig. I suspect his greedy, selfish mother cashed the check and spent the gift cards for groceries.

Steven's direction helped me solve the mystery and uncover the truth. Thank goodness I had my husband by my side. He gave me the inner strength that I would need to battle Craig's wife, Kathy, and his family on behalf of the twins.

The girls expressed deep anxiety, they advised their paternal grandparents that they did not want their father cremated. The girls told their grandparents that Steven would give them a blank check to pay for all the expenses so that Craig would not be cremated. There was no casket or urn at the funeral. The girls hounded me daily to find out the location of their father's body. After about 45 days, the funeral director finally told me if I would pay for the funeral expenses, he would send Craig's remains to Texas for the girls. He explained that the ashes had been sitting on a shelf in a "plastic utility box" since the funeral and could not be displayed at the service because the ashes were not even in an urn.

I was appalled at this discovery because Craig's mother had received $10,000 from his life insurance policy from his employer; his funeral expenses were barely $3,000. To treat one's child in this manner was beyond my understanding.

The girls wanted their father buried in Arizona since he was born in Phoenix. Steven and I paid the funeral home and had Craig's ashes sent to Texas and interred in a black granite urn. I made arrangements for the twins to pay their respects in a viewing room at the Cook-Walden Funeral Home. They stayed for about an hour, and I took photos of the urn for them. We told stories of happy times we had each spent with Craig.

The funeral home shipped Craig's ashes to Paradise Valley, Arizona. I had purchased two plots under a tree by a pond with swans, not wanting anyone buried right next to him. The cremation plots were already extremely close to each other. I ordered an ornate black granite headstone, and when it was in place about six weeks later, I took the girls to see where their father was buried. I had a beautiful silk floral arrangement made in a granite vase and paid for its care to be preserved in perpetuity.

Over the duration of about eight months, I took the girls with me to California once a month, when I visited my mom. On each trip we stopped in Phoenix for several hours, giving me enough time to rent a car and drive them to the cemetery to pay their respects. It was essential to me that they work through the suicide, so I arranged individual counseling, which was helpful and lasted a few years.

Before Jennifer and Kristina started ninth grade, Jennifer asked to visit her friend in Washington. Steven refused, saying, "Those people (the friends) up there are trash." That remark hurt Jennifer's feelings, even though I must admit he was correct. We came up with an alternative plan; we would tell Steven that Jennifer was going to Camp Longhorn in Texas, while Kristina was attending Camp Buckner in Burnet. Steven was delighted that Jennifer took an interest in camp. Less than three days after Jennifer was supposed to be asleep at camp, I received a call in the middle of the night from the Stanwood Police Department in Washington. Thankfully, Steven was passed out. Jennifer had been arrested for driving under the influence of marijuana at the age of 15. I secretly hired an attorney to get Jennifer out of jail that morning and eventually, he successfully had the charges dropped; Steven never knew anything about this. Helping get Jennifer released from custody without a record of this happening was never brought up by my daughters in the long list of my extraneous offenses during my trial. How convenient for them that they forgot to mention this.

I was fighting Craig's wife for Jennifer's personal belongings and asked for a picture of Craig. All Jennifer had from Washington were the clothes she had packed in her suitcase for her trip to California. Of course, Steven and I did not hesitate to buy her a new wardrobe. It was just so sad to us that no one in Washington cared enough about Jennifer's feelings to send her the belongings she so desperately longed to have. My daughters had no personal mementos by which to remember their father. Craig had long ago destroyed all photographs we had accumulated during our marriage.

I purchased several full-page advertisements in newspapers serving the surrounding communities, where Craig had resided. The heading *"Wanted"* was in four-inch bold lettering, followed by a plea requesting anyone who had a photo of Craig to send it to the girls in Texas, at my expense. This plan further fueled their grandmother's animosity towards me, as she was only concerned about how this made her appear in the community. She still refused to send them any photos. The local sheriff's department, on Camano Island, sent us an 8" x 10" booking photo of Craig taken of him after one of his many arrests. This sincere gesture was very much appreciated, but not what I wanted the girls to have as a lasting memory of their father. KOMO –TV, out of Seattle, picked up the story and interviewed the girls in Austin via satellite at our local station. The wrath of Craig's mother was further incensed, and she swore never to give them a photo.

4

We Are Family

In November 1998, just two and a half months before the girls 18th birthday, Steven adopted the twins; he made it clear that he agreed to adopt them because he loved me. To get my way, I threatened Steven with divorce if he did not adopt them. By this time, neither one of them wanted anything to do with Steven. Our house had become a verbal battlefield between the trio. My husband found it extremely difficult to be civil, especially with Kristina, unless we were out in public. I convinced the girls to allow Steven to adopt them by assuring them they would receive great wealth when the day came time to distribute the estate. At my trial, both daughters said I wished Steven dead. For their gain and greed, I guess they thought back on this conversation and twisted the truth to make me look evil in the jurors eyes.

Steven was not in good health. His medical records included alcoholic, heart disease, severe sleep apnea, hypertension, elevated blood sugar, chronic asthma, fluid retention, gout, erectile dysfunction, obesity, bipolar, and back problems from a fracture. I knew that he would probably die before me because he was 39 years my senior. I was not in denial about that and wanted to be sure that the twins were protected financially. There had been so much stress and strain in our house between the three of them. Very few people knew about the girls' hostility towards Steven. They complained endlessly to my close friends and their maternal grandmother about their relationship. They would only refer to him as "Steve" and flatly refused to call him "dad." Kristina held so much contempt towards him she would become indignant or angry if he used any bathroom in our home other than his own. She would not use the room after him unless the maid cleaned and disinfected it after his use.

All of this negative behavior made me an emotional basket case. The three people I loved most in the world were always at odds with each other. I was torn, knowing the twins would be going off to college soon and starting their own life, and that Steven's health was deteriorating. As I sided more and more with Steven, Kristina continued pulling away from me; she treated me as if I had betrayed her. I was fighting a losing battle, trying to make everyone happy. The undue pressure led me to hold a gun to my head. I did not know how to use the gun, or know if it was loaded. I just wanted the fighting to end.

Steven had always insisted the four of us sit together for hours as a family for the dinner meal during the week, and remain seated until he was finished drinking. Steven did not drink alcohol with his meal, either at a restaurant or home. With this annoying peculiarity, he expected us to wait for him to finish his cocktails before we could eat. We did not enjoy his cooking; I think this was mainly due to the food being dried out from waiting for him to be ready to eat, rather than his lack of culinary talent. Often he drank in excess before dinner and would not remember eating with us. The following mornings he would ask if we had dinner the night before and asked what we ate. Considering he prepared all the meals, I saw this as a warning sign that his alcohol consumption was out of control and he was experiencing blackouts. He would forget entire conversations and ask what we talked about; he would ask if he was belligerent because he could get mean after his second drink. There were times he could not remember if the girls were home for dinner. If I drank too much alcohol, I would need to lay down. Steven could remain functioning and it was difficult to know if he was in a blackout mode or not.

We had a warming drawer installed beneath our broiler oven. Steven cooked the meal by 4:00 or 5:00 p.m. and put it in the warming drawer, until he was ready to eat. It was not unusual for our dinner to stay in the drawer for more than five hours. Steven was usually inebriated and he never noticed the food going under the table to the dogs. He was verbally abusive and torturous to all three of us. If he passed out at the dinner table, I had no choice but to leave him there overnight, as he was too heavy for me to help to bed. In the morning he had a daily ritual of asking me if he had been a "bad boy" the previous evening. No matter what had transpired, I always told him "never." We just gave each other a kiss and a hug and started our morning routines.

I am a very organized person, and he adored that about me. We met for lunch at one of our favorite places almost every day. I usually had our leather family day planner with me, and we read it over while eating lunch together. He spent his afternoons working on the Davenport Village shopping center plans and ended his day at the grocery store. I think Steven's love for grocery shopping was because he enjoyed the personal attention the employees showered upon him. He insisted on going to the grocery store every day for fresh ingredients, despite that it was not in a convenient location to our home. I never shopped for groceries, so when the girls said I would buy dented cans of food in an attempt to poison Steven, it was clearly a false accusation. I cannot imagine any high-end grocery store selling dented canned goods.

The twins shared a bedroom when Jennifer first moved in with us because Steven wanted them to bond. The more they argued with each other, the more he insisted. The new house was designed and built U-shaped with two separate wings. As far as I know, Steven said he never roamed to the girl's side. We designed the house so that they could live on their side and not have to interact with him until dinnertime, solely Steven's idea. He never knew that I had allowed Jennifer to move into and take over the guest bedroom. I decorated it in an eye-catching Oriental motif with the color scheme being black, red, and gold; Jennifer loved it.

Had Steven ever ventured to that side of the house and discovered clothes in the walk-in closet and dressers, he would have never raised a question. He lived with three women who owned an excessive amount of clothes. He knew he was partly to blame for this extravagance because he purchased the bulk of my clothes. He came up with the brilliant idea of building a storage room in our garage when our architect was working on the plans for our home. The third storage area in our massive garage was the size of a small bedroom, air-conditioned and built to resemble a walk-in closet to handle the overflow of seasonal and formal clothes, shoes, purses, and accessories.

The twins had their separate entrance to the backyard and the garage. They had complete privacy and could come and go without ever being seen or heard. Our home had two different street entrances, which allowed the girls to leave the house in a vehicle unnoticed by Steven. During the trial, Tracey Tarlton testified that she entered the door that was off the pool area. Mr. DeGuerin asked, "Is that a sliding door or a door that was on hinges?" Tarlton answered it was on "hinges," but Tarlton was wrong because this was a sliding door. The stained glass doors in our main entry were the only glass doors on hinges. All other glass doors were sliders, there were fourteen in total. The doors looked like French doors, but the only hinged doors were the red oak doors going into the bedrooms, the garage, or closets.

5

The Affair

My best friend, Dawn, had been attending beauty school so that she could open a manicure business. She graduated in November 1998, and we celebrated with a girl's night out. We had dinner and then began drinking at several bars on 6th Street in downtown Austin. As the night progressed, we realized that neither one of us was in any shape to drive home. To sober up, we walked to Katz's Deli for a late night snack. On the way to use I the restroom I called Jimmy collect and asked him to give us a ride home. When I returned to the table and told Dawn what I had done, she suggested that I call the twins and have them pick us up instead. The twins gave Dawn a ride back to Spicewood, and I left with Jimmy. My going home with Jimmy started our affair. The twins picked me up at Jimmy's in the early morning hours. We drove back downtown, located my vehicle, and arrived home shortly before Steven woke up.

I went out with Jimmy during weeknights. I think Steven never put a stop to the affair because I never allowed it to interfere with the time I spent with him. I was always home in time for our morning rituals and breakfast. I am ashamed of my behavior and regret betraying my husband. Even though he forgave me, I still live with guilt and cannot help but feel like my incarceration is my karmic retribution for my infidelity. I do hope, however, that over seventeen years, and counting, in prison will be enough time served for being unfaithful to my husband.

David Kuperman, our attorney, testified at my trial that in 1999 Steven told him about my affair. David asked Steven if he wanted a divorce. My husband told him no. This is when he decided to put the European trip together so we could give our marriage a fresh start.

6

Terrific Traveling Times

Traveling became a way of life for us. Steven showed me how to become a seasoned traveler, and he loved planning trips for us. It was such fun traveling around the world with Steven. Those were happy times. Steven said we should spend our money freely when traveling; he wanted to embrace the world's many, diverse offerings, regardless of the cost. We traveled extensively, no sooner arriving home from one vacation before jetting off to another location. These extravagances were not mentioned at my trial; the fun, wholesome times were not regarded because those great times showcased the loving side of our relationship that the prosecutors did not want the jurors to see.

I made at least three major trips a year as a couple, with my daughters, with friends, or by myself. If I traveled alone, Steven would have had all the arrangements made in advance and have the itinerary written down for me to follow. He would book flights, make hotel reservations including salon appointments, have limousines scheduled, and dinner reservations at the top restaurants were arranged. His travel plans were always perfect. He would have bouquets of pink tulips and roses ordered for each hotel room, and he would surprise me with lavish, pink satin ribbon wrapped gifts sitting on my pillow, awaiting my return to the suite. Steven learned to spend his money wisely and was an educated consumer. That is what made his gifts so exciting to unwrap; you never knew what was inside. I would call him, laugh with him, tell him about my day, and thank him. I loved his thoughtfulness and attention to detail. It made traveling alone less anxious.

One of the first trips that Steven and I took together was to Atlanta, Georgia, in 1994, to watch the Dallas Cowboys win their 4th Super Bowl victory (30 to 13), against New York's Buffalo Bills. We sat on the 50-yard line and had a blast watching Troy Aikman and Emmitt Smith lead their team to become the fifth in history to win back-to-back titles. Steven could not believe that he was able to witness Steve Christie's 54-yard kick – the longest in Super Bowl history; that was all he talked about for days. Steven ended up giving all of the Super Bowl XXVIII memorabilia and souvenirs we had amassed to my ex-husband, Jimmy. He said that since Jimmy was a devoted fan, he would appreciate the collectibles more than we would.

While in Atlanta, we attended numerous Super Bowl parties, because Fox Network recently acquired the rights to broadcast the NFL games, and Steven sat on its Board of Governors. One evening we enjoyed the dinner company of Bryant Gumble, former co-host of NBC's *Today Show*; Terry Bradshaw, former quarterback of the Pittsburgh Steelers, football analyst and Sunday co-host of *Fox NFL Sunday*; and Howie Long, former Oakland Raider's defensive end and studio analyst for Fox. Terry Bradshaw affectionately refers to Long as "Buckethead."

We stayed at the luxurious Ritz-Carlton. Steven hired a limousine to take me shopping, while he attended meetings during the day. Two days of shopping by myself was enough for me, so Steven had our concierge hire a guide to escort me to see the MLK Historic Site, the Botanical Gardens, and many of the beautiful plantation homes. Atlanta was in the midst of transforming the metro area into a modern city, in preparation for the upcoming 1996 Summer Olympics. I found the flurry of activity interesting around the town and enjoyed sightseeing.

After arriving home, we headed to California in

search of architectural elements, treasures, and inspirations to aid us in designing and furnishing our lake house. We hired an architect and a decorator, as we both wanted the "unique and unusual" to make our lake house a show place. We stayed at the Beverly Hills Hotel and invited my sister Caresse, my niece Amanda, and my nephew Michael to join us for the weekend.

With our teenage company, my husband insisted on taking everyone to Steven Spielberg's unique restaurant, Dive. The restaurant resembled a gigantic yellow submarine. They offered valet parking and had a wood-burning oven to cook its excellent submarine sandwiches. Once every half-hour sirens blared, red lights flashed, and commands of "Dive!" reverberated around the room, as giant video screens filled with bubbles. The whole scene was a little loud for Steven's liking, but he was a good sport and made sure the teenagers had fun.

We ventured into an antique district in downtown Los Angeles. We came across two wood panels, each ornately carved with a topless sea nymph. The panels were antiques from Spain, and we loved them. Steven came up with the brilliant idea of having the panels pieced together to use as a door. We were both thrilled because this was our first of many purchases for the building of our lake house. Steven explained to me that the front door of a home should be treated as if it were art, to be viewed by visitors, patiently waiting for the door to be answered. Steven's most treasured pieces of art were all or partially nude women.

Steven had to travel to Chicago on business, he insisted I join him. When traveling, I preferred two suitcases. Steven told me, "Using more than one suitcase tells the world you are a tourist, not a traveler." I heeded his wise advice. We stayed at the Ritz-Carlton, high above prestigious North Michigan Avenue. Our luxurious suite offered stunning views of majestic Lake Michigan. While Steven was in meetings, I went shopping with a limousine escort. I asked the driver to take me by the Willis Tower, formerly known as the Sears Tower. This fantastic building rises to a height of 1,450 feet and is one of the most recognizable landmarks on the Chicago skyline, as well as in the world. In 1994, the tower had held the record for the world's tallest building for 25 years, until the Petronas Towers in Kuala Lumpur, Malaysia was built in 1998.

Our first evening there, we had dinner at The Chicago Chop House. The restaurant is located in an immaculately restored, century-old Victorian brownstone in the popular River North neighborhood. Its ambiance is like visiting Chicago's colorful past. Steven ordered their awe-inspiring 64-ounce Porterhouse steak for himself and the 16-ounce New York strip for me. Amazingly, he devoured all four pounds of meat, ordered charred to perfection, while I barely ate half of mine. We both agreed on how delicious the prime-aged flavor was with our steaks.

We were home for a couple of weeks when my husband decided we should fly to Santa Fe, New Mexico, to get ideas for the type of wall art we wanted to hang at the lake house. The architect had nearly finished the house plans, but I was still feeling overwhelmed and unsure of my ability to choose a color scheme. Steven gave me carte blanche` with decorating the lake house, but I was feeling incompetent and worried about disappointing him. At the same time, I did not want to leave all the decisions with the decorator.

We stayed at the plush La Fonda on the Plaza, because it is located just steps from museums, galleries, shops, and restaurants, where the work of the local artisans is always shown. We chose this hotel, so that Steven would not require a wheelchair, and was able to walk short distances with the aid of a cane. Santa Fe has long been recognized as the center of arts and culture, and the restaurants are known for their creative and delicious southwestern cuisine. We found Santa Fe to be a very romantic place.

I fell in love with a painting titled, "Rainbow Wolves," by Robert Holland. This painting is enormous, with two wolves in bright acrylic reds, teals, oranges, purples, yellows; a venerable rainbow, as the title depicts. I was enamored with the dazzling colors; their striking yellow eyes appeared to follow me, no matter where I was standing in the room.

Steven never haggled over the painting's $5,000 price tag. He beamed, as he wrote the check because I had made my first decision without any prodding from him. I was now confident that the central theme of the decorating to be animals, all bright and colorful, using the colors of the wolf painting. My husband agreed with my choice, and we went to eat to celebrate. During lunch, I recall thinking: Steven and I always enjoy each other so much… it's wonderful!

After lunch, we strolled happily, hand-in-hand, into Malcolm Moran's Studio. Steven was drawn to Malcolm's work, because, he explained to me, the artist's gallery and home were used in Clint Eastwood's movie, *Play Misty for Me*, one of Steven's all-time favorites. What intrigued me with Malcolm's art was his ability to unite bronze with jade, using children as his subject matter. Not leaving empty-handed, we purchased two sculptures, "Girl with Frog" and "Kite Boy." Leaving Santa Fe for home, we were loaded down with packages. Steven was agitated, as he did not like being burdened with purchases, even though I assured him I did not mind. After this trip, I opened a Federal Express account so that we could ship everything home ahead of us, no matter where we found ourselves in the world. My husband said I was "brilliant" for coming up with this idea.

At spring break in 1994, we took Kristina and her friend Kristopher with us to Nashville. Kristopher is my third husband, Jimmy Martinez, best friend's son. Steven, only wanting the best for us, had encouraged a continuing friendship with Jimmy and his friends to keep some normalcy in Kristina's life. When Jimmy bought his house, Steven and I gave him a stainless steel, side-by-side refrigerator as a house-warming gift. Steven called the store and ordered the same refrigerator that we had purchased for our lake house, and had it delivered to Jimmy's new home as a surprise; luckily it fit in his kitchen. My husband taught me that life and love are all about giving. He believed, as do I, that what you give will come back multiplied. Showing me that it is impossible to love and not give, he also consistently demonstrated to me that love must be debt-free or it is not real love. Because of this belief, Steven allowed me to give lavish parties and buy expensive gifts for all my friends and family; he loved the attention showered on him due to his generosity. I could never figure out why Steven gave his daughter, Becky, the used furniture that he had when married to Elise and refused her the new furniture that she wanted. Becky asked for a new car, and Steven refused again. He told her to buy her own car. I am sure this added to Becky's hatred towards me. During her deposition in the civil trial, Becky said, "My dad could be a demanding man, and he wanted things done a certain way, "It was the Steven Beard way, or the highway."

Steven could be unreasonable. He told his son, Steven III, he would not be a cosigner when he needed help getting a credit card. He told his son he needed to learn to manage money on his own. His son forged Steven's name, regardless of his father's wishes. When Steven found out about this deception, he punished his son by deducting $100,000 from his inheritance in the will.

One year we gave Jimmy, and all three of Steven's adult children, Steven III, Paul, and Becky, satellite dishes as Christmas gifts. Whatever Steven purchased for his three adult children, he always included Jimmy. When I first moved in with Steven, he showed his love by giving material things, not with physical intimacy.

On the plane to Santa Fe, we had seen a brochure for an amusement park in Nashville; we thought the teenagers would enjoy it. Unbeknownst to us, the brochure was outdated, and the amusement park was no longer in operation. This closure was a huge disappointment for the kids, which we found out after our arrival in Nashville. We stayed at the Opryland Hotel, attended the Grand Ol' Opry, and toured the City Music Hall of Fame, all without Steven. Thank goodness the teenagers loved country music, which at least kept their interest for a short time. Not being a country music fan, Steven declined to join us, he was happy to relax in the hotel room with his Wolfschmidt vodka.

The first time we went to the Cracker Barrel Country Restaurant, we were hooked on their down-home Southern-cooked food. The entrées were loaded with fat and unhealthy ingredients, which always makes the food taste better. We ate breakfast and lunch there every day. This was a side of Steven I had never before seen, as he never wanted to dine in this type of restaurant. He said he had done it to please the teenagers, but I knew he genuinely liked the food. The kids thought that Nashville was the "most boring place on earth." We begged to differ.

Steven and I toured Alaska for almost three weeks while Marilou stayed with Kristina. In Anchorage, we stayed at the Hotel Captain Cook, and from there visited endless places. We flew to Fairbanks, where we took a jet boat excursion to Barrow, which is surrounded by the arctic tundra. We enjoyed a ride on a historic paddlewheel boat on the Chena River. At Denali National Park, I was awed by the sight of grizzly bears, moose, and caribou. We privately toured a glacier by float plane, we also flew over Prince William Sound. The Alaska Railroad tour in a private car was breath-taking, as was the boat cruise through Resurrection Bay where we saw orcas, seals, and sea lions. Steven had a blast, watching my excitement every time I saw one of the animals. He said, "Watching me on this trip gave him the idea to have the enormous stone mantle above the lake house fireplace carved as a scene of deer foraging in the woods."

I took the tramway, by myself, to the top of Mt. Roberts in Juneau, because Steven was having breathing problems caused by the elevation. At the time we blamed the problem on his asthma. I made a note to call the

115

medical supply store, when we returned to Austin, to see if they had any portable breathing equipment that we could take with us when next we traveled. I am a bona fide list-maker for everything, and my husband admired this habit.

The following day I went rafting through the Chilleat Bald Eagle Preserve by myself because Steven drank in excess the night before and was not up to the rocking of the raft. In Ketchikan, it was exciting to observe totem poles being carved. As the trip was coming to an end, we enjoyed a cruise headed to Vancouver, offering endless, spectacular views of the Inside Passage. I enjoyed the trip immensely, but at the same time silently prayed that Steven would get better so that we could share the sightseeing. I wanted to spend more time with Steven because we had many laughs from his sarcastic humor.

Steven always enjoyed driving his Cadillac up and down the beach. He had special-ordered the car from the Cadillac Coach Division, which makes limousines. Having it cut in half and extended, he had this custom feature added to the design of the car to offer passengers additional leg room in the back seat. The extra-long car barely fit in our garage, and our garage was more significant than most others. Steven loved that long car.

I asked him if I could try my hand at fishing the

next time we went to Port Aransas. He bought all manner of fishing needs: poles, tackle boxes filled to the top, deck shoes, hats, and gloves, then loaded all into his car trunk, waiting for the weekend to arrive so that we could go fishing together. All the way to Port Aransas, Steven gave me advice and tips on how to fish and promised he would hire a boat and a captain, once we checked into the hotel.

I excitedly looked forward to my husband participating in the fishing with me, something we could do together, while he could remain seated. I often felt lonely on our vacations, always having to make excursions or side trips alone. We did not go fishing for a couple of days. Never sure why, I did not question the delay, not wanting to make him feel bad. Once out on the water, I was anticipating the fishing experience, even wanting to learn to bait my hook. Steven had other ideas, as he instructed our guide to bait both our hooks. He cast his line and told the guide to cast my line for me, then hand it to me and I could slowly reel it in. I do not know why Steven thought I was incapable of doing anything other than reel in the line. When I caught a fish, I had to give the pole back to the guide to reel in the fish for me. It was such a let down and not the fishing experience I expected.

I caught the biggest fish, but was disappointed,

because I wanted the fishing experience to be more of a hands-on one. Steven never baited his hook, and the fish we caught was given to the captain. I disappointed Steven, never wanting to return to Port Aransas, and we never did. This small reaction caused me tremendous guilt because he always did what I wanted to do. Instead of acting like a spoiled child, I should have just compromised and gone along with whatever he wanted to do.

Steven saw a television documentary about the St. Louis Union Train Station and wanted to see how they transformed a 114-year-old National Historic Landmark from a train station to the most significant adaptive reuse project in the United States. He coaxed me into accompanying him, by telling me that the unique retail shops offered fine fashions and one-of-a-kind gifts. This landmark, of unmatched beauty and elegance, is now one of America's great marketplaces. Steven was indulgent and bought me a new wardrobe. This trip inspired him to build his upscale-retail shopping center, eventually to become known as Davenport Village.

Steven wanted to drive to Missouri, so on the way there, he could show me the ranch he once owned in Muenster, Texas where he raised Beefmaster cattle.

I insisted that we visit the Gateway Arch, an edifice

built between 1963 to 1965 as a monument to the westward expansion of the United States. Its width is 630 feet at its base, and its equal height of 630 feet makes it the tallest monument in the United States. The hollow arch contains a unique tram system that takes visitors to an observation deck at the top.

With a bit of prodding, I convinced Steven to get into the egg-shaped "elevator," that only accommodates five people at a time, and takes about four minutes to reach the top and three minutes to travel back down. Because of Steven's size, we only carried four passengers in our tram, so this space was a challenge. Near the top of the arch, we exited to find thirty-two windows, 7" by 27", which gave us a spectacular view of the Mississippi River.

Steven and I traveled to Austria, the Czech Republic, and Hungary with a large group of people from Austin. We went sightseeing in Vienna's historic district, toured the Hofburg Palace, known as the Imperial Palace, and took a romantic carriage ride for two. We attended the Vienna Orchestra, featuring music by Mozart and Strauss, which was held in a historic palace, Ringstrasse, the Opera House.

We traveled the Danube River to Budapest, Hungary, a city that is split in half by the river. One half is called the "Buda" side, the other the "Pest" side. On the "Buda" side, we enjoyed views of the city from Gellert Hill and admired the stained glass windows in Matthias Church. On the "Pest" side of the city, we toured Hereo's Square and viewed some of the most beautiful Hungarian architectural works. We were both awed by the opulent State Opera House with its gilded, vaulted ceiling, murals, and a three-ton chandelier. We saw the Parliament Building, a neo-Gothic masterpiece.

The Danube River boasts being the longest river in Europe. We floated past fairy-tale castles and medieval villages, taking me back in memory to the storybooks I read while growing up. Hungary is also where I discovered my love for the beautiful hand-painted Herend porcelain figurines. Each piece is an individual work of art and is painted with exquisite detail. The distinctive figurines usually depict various animals. Steven bought me so many pieces for our hallway bookshelves at the lake house that I lost count. I love all animals and was so pleased with his selections.

We traveled by train to Prague in the Czech Republic, where I took a walking tour, by myself, to the old town and the ornate Charles Bridge. I visited Hradcany Castle, built in the 9th century. It is one of the largest ancient castles in the world and is the country's traditional seat of power, incorporating palaces, museums, monasteries, and halls for knighthood ceremonies. I admired the Czech Republic's Gothic, Renaissance, and Baroque architecture.

Steven and I wandered into a Czechoslovakian glass shop, not then realizing that visiting this shop would be the foundation for establishing my scent bottle collection. The shop showcased an incredible variety of beautiful perfume containers, either blown in cranberry glass or clear crystal, both antique and modern. My favorite was the cranberry glass, made by adding gold chloride to the molten glass. The glass fixtures above our vanities at the Southlake home were all hand-blown cranberry glass. These fixtures were transformed into a dark-pink color, as the glass was blown into individual glass shades. Steven often remarked that my sizable scent bottle collection looked stunning on my granite vanity in the master bath and around my sunken whirlpool bathtub.

During Kristina's Christmas break at school, we decided to visit our friends, Ana and Philip, at their new vacation home in Carmel, before traveling on to San Francisco. We stayed at the Pine Inn on Pebble Beach, ate dinner at Clint Eastwood's Hogsbreath Restaurant, and enjoyed walking through the quaint shops and miniature homes along Ocean Avenue.

We stayed at the luxury Compton Place Hotel in San Francisco, located between Chinatown and Union Square. We explored the city by limousine and crossed the Golden Gate Bridge. At Kristina's insistence, we drove by the house that had recently fallen into an aquifer sinkhole because she had seen it on the news. Steven did not want to see it, but gave in at my pleading, on Kristina's behalf. We shopped in Chinatown, on the Embarcadero, and in the specialty shops at Fisherman's Wharf. My absolute favorite was buying pounds and pounds of Ghiradelli chocolate at Ghiradelli Square. I could eat nothing but chocolate for days, if given the opportunity.

Steven and I took our honeymoon on February 18, 1995. When we arrived in New Orleans, he was much like a kid at Disneyland. His love of New Orleans showed all over his happy face. We stayed at the posh Loews New Orleans Hotel, located one block from Bourbon Street. We enjoyed a romantic dinner at Commander's Palace in the middle of the garden district and were greeted by the owner and his friend, Ella Brennon. Our honeymoon night we had intercourse, and it was the only time during our marriage that we shared this intimacy. Medical issues made it difficult for my husband to make love.

To please my husband, I did make a romantic deal with him: every Sunday, before the cocktail hour would render him flaccid, I would offer him oral pleasure. This was the only way he could achieve sexual gratification, due to his erectile dysfunction. He playfully dubbed this the "Sunday suck." It was brought up at the trial, by the prosecution, to make it appear I was prostituting myself with my husband for money. This suggestion could not have been further from the truth; it had been another tactic of the prosecution; conforming my character by twisting the truth to fit an alternate hypothesis. Having no bearing on the charges I was facing, the sexual relations within the confines of our marriage had no business being discussed in the trial.

We spent each subsequent anniversary at this award-winning landmark, toured plantations by limousine, and shopped in the warehouse and arts district, where I found a painting to hang in one of the bathrooms in the lake house. It featured a long line of dogs waiting to use an outhouse in various states of angst, depicting their dire need to relieve themselves; it reminded us of a secret joke between my husband and me. When Steven was outside at either of our houses, he urinated on the grass, instead of going inside to one of the restrooms, because it was too far to walk. The dogs always walked over to where he had urinated, sniffed the spot, gave him a disgusted stare, and then they urinated on the same spot. Steven cracked up every time he saw the painting because it reminded him of my dogs.

In the French Quarter, we happened upon an Adult Sex Shop. I am no prude, but was embarrassed when Steven pulled me inside and proceeded to handle the dildos and vibrators while making silly faces and loudly asking the sales clerk lewd questions while telling him that we were on our honeymoon. I was mortified. Steven's attention turned to a stack of Rainbow/Gay Pride Flag stickers. He explained to me that these were well known gay symbols to show support for the gay/lesbian community. Steven purchased a couple dozen of the stickers. He kept them in the glove compartment and stuck them on car bumpers of the country club people he did not like. I doubt that anyone ever suspected Steven of playing that boyish trick. I imagine his doing this silly prank was the reason Steven put up with my toilet-papering and signing of houses with the teenagers during sleepovers.

For Kristina's 1995 spring-break vacation we wanted to make up for the 1994 "boring Nashville trip," but remain within the continental United States, since she had only a week long break from school. After getting ideas from Kristina, we decided to travel to Washington, D.C. I had never met Steven's son, Paul, who lived in Virginia, and I asked if we could also visit him. At first, he refused, but then gave in with a list of stipulations. He insisted that we have a brief visit because he could only take his daughter-in-law, Kim, in small doses, claiming that she was both dense and dull. He always referred to her as "muttonhead," which I soon realized after meeting her, was not a term of endearment.

To appease me, Steven agreed that we lodge in Williamsburg and that the visit must transpire over lunch or dinner at a restaurant of his choosing. Usually, we both had equal input regarding our vacations, but this trip was an exception. Steven allowed me to select places I wanted us to tour while in Washington, D.C. He let me know that the Virginia portion of the trip would be scheduled by him because he did not trust me to stay within the parameters to what we had agreed while visiting with his son and daughter-in-law.

I was awed at the Williamsburg Inn; it was quaint with charm and picturesque accommodations. The Inn successfully combines 21st-century comforts and conveniences with the classic American style of times past. Steven insisted that Kristina and I "dress up" for the relaxing afternoon tea. He surprised us with two beautiful outfits that he had Saks ship to the Inn. That was my husband, always so thoughtful and with excellent taste. He was generous to a fault and loved gift giving. He included stylish shoes and a matching handbag with any clothes he purchased for me, and sometimes, completed the outfit with pieces of fine jewelry. Always smitten with his selections, Steven was so charming when giving gifts.

Steven had planned for us to meet Paul and Kim at Nick's Restaurant, in Gloucester Point. When he called to let them know we were on the way, they insisted we come to their home first, as Paul wanted to show us their antiques. Steven complained and fussed during the entire drive, but luckily, the distance from Williamsburg to Gloucester Point was less than 25 miles.

We stayed at their home for less than an hour when Steven loudly cleared his throat, stood up, adjusted his waistband, and abruptly announced that we were leaving. He backpedaled on the lunch invitation, using the excuse that we were behind schedule. I felt sorry for Paul; Steven made it clear they shared nothing in common. I was embarrassed by my husband's rudeness and felt terrible for having insisted on the meeting in the first place. All the way to Jamestown, he ranted about how he painfully suffered being forced to interact with what he referred to as "vittle-eating, raccoon-wearing hillbillies."

Steven was so infuriated by the visit that he insisted I drive so he could drink his Wolfschmidt (now called Wolfy) vodka. He was never one for small talk, and like me, said the first thing that popped into his head, regardless of who happened to be around to hear it. I am sure this is why his son, Paul, and daughter-in-law, Kim, had never visited, even when Steven was in the hospital with only a 10% chance of surviving. They did not attend his funeral. I found this treatment repulsive. Although, they were eagerly in attendance in the courtroom during the civil trial to fight for Steven's money.

After the 160-mile drive to Washington, D.C., we arrived at the Capital Hilton Hotel. Steven had long been passed out, and the quiet ride had also lulled Kristina to sleep. I smoked to stay awake during the trip, with my window cracked. It was unusual for me to smoke in the car if Steven was with me. Since he had asthma, I did not want him to inhale my smoke. He never complained about my smoking, because he was used to his late wife, Elise, smoking everywhere, even in their house. I never smoked in our homes, just something I chose not to do. I cared about Steven's health, but needed to stay awake for this rare time.

I did not have my prescription glasses with me; I always kept a pair in both of my vehicles to wear while driving at night. Both my ski goggles and dive mask were also fitted with prescription lenses. I did have my prescription sunglasses with me, but they were too dark to use that late at night. Steven often surprised me with Gucci, Fendi, Dolce and Gabbana, and Chanel because he loved me wearing the large round frames that resembled the ones Jacquelyn Onassis wore in the magazine photos. He bought so many because he feared one day they would no longer sell them. Driving in the dark, smoking one cigarette after another, and without glasses, my nerves were on edge. Steven refused to wear a seat belt because it was uncomfortable for him. I worried myself sick that I would either miss an exit or crash the rental car. During the trial, the ADA made several disparaging remarks, intentionally loud enough for the jurors to overhear, "I only was wearing glasses to look 'innocent,' once the trial ended, I probably would not be seen in glasses again." During my trial, I wore the glasses because I am nearsighted and wanted to be able to look at each person directly in the eye as they testified on the witness stand. Without glasses, I could only see a silhouette of the witness' faces.

Steven initially wanted to hire a driver and limousine to take us from Virginia to D.C. I begged, pleaded, and finally cajoled him into renting a car, by telling him that it would make me happy to have him sober before he visited Paul and Kim. I told him that he would not be tempted to drink if driving since he had already had a DUI. I should have just let him do what he wanted to do in the first place. Paul and Kim blame me for their father's rude behavior.

The following day we visited the White House. Steven had prearranged for a private tour given by a Congressional aide. He wore a suit and tie, and I wore a beautiful St. John's knit jacket and skirt, with which Steven had surprised me to wear on the tour. Kristina wore a pleated skirt and sweater also recently purchased by Steven for this occasion. Steven schooled us that wearing casual clothes to the White House would be disrespectful, so we honored his wishes. Steven, in his wheelchair, was able to accompany Kristina and me on the tour. We had our limo driver waiting for us, and once the tour ended, he drove us around D.C. to view the landmark sites and monuments that symbolize America's rich historical heritage.

Celeste

When the Vietnam War ended in 1975, I was in the 8th grade and proudly wore a metal ID bracelet honoring one of our POW's (Prisoners of War). I did not personally know of anyone who had fought in this war. My information came from what we learned in school and what was in the newspaper and broadcast on the evening news. While walking the pathway of the nearly 500-foot wall with Kristina, I tried to impress upon her that the nearly 60,000 names etched into the black granite represented servicemen who were either confirmed as KIA (Killed in Action) or remained classified as MIA (Missing in Action), when the walls were constructed. I do not think that she fully understood the significance of the Vietnam War.

We visited the Holocaust Memorial Museum the following day, a bit boring for Kristina. When we were planning the trip, I let Steven know this was the museum I most wanted to visit. I read that President Bill Clinton's Commission established a committee for the Museum on Consciousness to "work to halt acts of genocide or related crimes against humanity." The tour moves through three floors, starting at the top: The first floor, "Nazi Assault" – 1933 to 1939; the middle floor, the "Final Solution" – to 1945; and the final floor - "Last Chapter." At the beginning of our tour, Kristina and I were each given a Jewish passport, a replica of those owned by an actual Holocaust victim. At the end of the tour, the guides informed us that neither of our passport owners survived. What I remember vividly is looking down on an enormous, metal vat filled with thousands of old and heavily worn leather shoes.

The "Final Solution" was not only systematic murder, but systematic plunder. Before victims were gassed, the SS confiscated all of their belongings. This mass pillage at just two of the six concentration camps generated over 300,000 pairs of shoes. These shoes, distributed among German settlers in Poland, now seeing them in this humongous vat made me cry.

The museum is a living memorial to the Holocaust that inspires its visitors to confront hatred, promote human dignity, and prevent genocide. I left the Holocaust Museum with a more in-depth and renewed compassionate understanding of the cruel and inhumane atrocities inflicted upon millions of people just because they were Jewish.

Early in our marriage, for a brief time, I insisted Steven file for divorce, but decided against it. We cemented our renewed bond with listing Steven's house for sale along with a trip to Mexico City. While in Mexico, I bought a dozen masks to decorate the walls of our lake house, and those purchases pleased my husband immensely. He confided to me that my purchases made him relax and feel at ease because it meant I was not leaving him. The first mask I bought was beautifully carved of stone, marble, and turquoise. This mask was prominently displayed on a glass shelf in the living room because it had a special meaning for the two of us; it was the only mask in our collection not displayed on a wall. I found exquisite masks made out of jade, onyx, wood, paper-mache`, gourds, and sterling silver.

Steven chose the Hotel El Presidente', because of its world-class accommodations and breath-taking views of the city's most elegant cultural business and shopping districts. We ventured downtown to eat at an upscale restaurant the La Mansion. I foolishly tried to keep up with Steven drink-for-drink of vodka on the rocks. Before placing our food order, my head began to spin. Steven wanted to have a couple more drinks before ordering, and there was no way I could wait for him to finish without passing out at the table. Steven had the maitre d' call a cab for me, and when it arrived, I just fell into it. I was not a seasoned drinker like my husband.

After reaching the hotel lobby, it was still a long walk to our room. I tried and tried, but could not get the door unlocked. I left the card key in the slot in the door and staggered back to the front desk. A bellhop escorted me back to my room and told me that the card key had been inserted upside down. Oops! I barely had time to enter the room, before I threw up and passed out until the next morning. I learned my lesson and never tried to keep up with drinks with Steven. He thought that was hilarious!

Upon our return home, we heard that there were many tourists in taxi cabs in Mexico City who were robbed and murdered during the time of our vacation. We had no idea that the U.S. State Department had warned that Mexico City crime had reached critical levels. Tourists in cabs were being targeted and murdered. Steven was upset with himself for not taking the time to investigate where we were vacationing. I told him that I was equally responsible; after all, if I had not insisted on a divorce, we would not be taking a "reconciliation trip." Steven would not stop apologizing to me about that situation when we returned to Austin. He surprised me with another fur coat and a diamond necklace, saying that the gifts were to prove that he loved me.

The following day, he hired a limousine to take us to the Mayan Settlement, Teotihuacan, 25 miles northeast of Mexico City. The city's broad central avenue, called "Avenue of the Dead," is flanked by impressive ceremonial architecture, including the immense Pyramid of the Sun. I climbed all 248 steps to the top of the massive pyramid while Steven sat in the shade, patiently waiting for me. He said his enjoyment came from watching me discover new and beautiful sites. He said he loved vacationing with me because he could see the world and its entire splendor through my eyes.

While in Playa del Carmen, I found a large oil painting of Calla lilies to hang in our master bedroom. The enormous painting depicted the flowers over-flowing in a beautiful copper basin. I fell in love with the artwork the minute I laid eyes on it. Steven tried to dissuade me from this purchase by telling me that the Calla lilies reminded him of vaginas, thinking I would cringe and not want it in our home. I just rolled my eyes and bought it anyway. Eventually, he recanted, letting me know that it looked stunning in our bedroom.

Still looking for various pieces to decorate the lake house, we made several trips to New Mexico and California in the hopes of finding the extraordinary and unusual to complement the décor. Now we were able to ship our purchases home ahead of us by FedEx.

In the fall we traveled with Ana and Philip Presse, and some others from Austin, in a large group to tour

Celeste

Spain. Barcelona and Majorca were my favorite places.
Steven found a beautiful leather jacket for Kristina in
Madrid. She did not like it, so she gave it to Marilou.
Steven did not mind, because he loved and doted on
Marilou, like the little sister he never had. He also
purchased a strand of pearls for Kristina and two strands of
cultured pearls for me. I was transfixed by the priceless art
treasures at the Procto Palatial Museum.

Steven did join us for a flashy flamenco show, but
bowed out when I asked him to go with us to the Valley of
the Fallen tour. He felt his failing health would keep us
from enjoying the excursion. The monument precinct
encloses almost 3,500 acres of Mediterranean woodland
and the granite boulders on hills are over 3,000 feet above
sea level where stands the basilica, the Benedictine Abbey,
the Hospedria, the Valley of the Fallen, and the Juanelos.
The most prominent feature of the monument is the
towering 500-foot cross erected over a granite outcrop 500
feet over the basilica esplanade and is visible from over 20
miles away.

Spain is where I became enamored with antique
crosses, especially those depicting the crucifixion. Steven
bought me several that dated from the 17th and 18th
centuries, and most were carved from olive wood. To me,

135

the cross is the most important symbol of Christianity. I handled the crosses with reverence because they symbolize Jesus dying on the cross to save humanity from sin.

When I married Spencer Johnson, five months after Steven's death, we moved to our house in Southlake, Texas a year later. Over the years, I had amassed a stunning collection of over 75 crosses, all displayed in the large alcove above the front door. I strongly felt that they protected us. I whole-heartedly believed that because I hung the crosses at our lake house, and not in the Toro Canyon house, that this was the reason Steven was shot and my daughters became estranged.

I have come to realize that I wrongfully placed my faith in these antique artifacts, and in the process, had unintentionally transposed them into idols. I firmly believed that, through Jesus, the crosses would protect my family and me. Because of this belief, when I left the Southlake house through the garage door, upon returning, I walked around the house with my dogs and entered through the front door, purposely walking under the crosses. By performing this ritual, I believed that no harm would ever come to us. I trusted that by having all of the crosses above the entrance to our house, we would remain safe and happy. Being arrested for Capital Murder placed those crosses into proper perspective for me.

Initially, my husband wanted to travel to a sunny destination for the Christmas of 1995 because we had been in chilly San Francisco the past year. Even so, for two reasons, I convinced him into going to New York instead. I felt that everyone should experience how fabulous Christmastime is in New York City and wanted Kristina to have this opportunity. My second reason was purely a selfish one. We lived in the southwest, I had few opportunities to wear my fur coats. The first fur coat Steven purchased for me was because he lost a friendly bet between us. Then he began buying them often, usually giving them to me on the day following one of his drunken tirades. I had amassed twenty-six coats by the time Steven died.

Steven felt that my reasoning about Christmas in New York were valid and asked if I would be interested in traveling by train to Boston for the second week of our trip. Kristina was excited because she wanted to go inside the Cheers Bar, since it was part of her favorite television show. Unlike the song at the opening of the show, nobody knew our names!

We made reservations at the plush Plaza Hotel. Unbeknownst to us, our vacation coincided with President

Clinton's family vacation. Steven grew irritated because thousands of people filled the already-crowded, sidewalks and streets. Police cordoned off the main and side streets around the hotel. I teased Steven that he was just mad because he was Republican and Clinton was a Democrat.

In a short time, all three of us were feeling aggravated and put out by the Secret Service continually rerouting us throughout the hotel or making us wait to enter or leave our rooms. Every now and again we caught a glimpse of the Clintons; Steven neither appreciated nor condoned how star-struck Kristina and I were at seeing them. My husband became so infuriated by all of the hoopla surrounding the Clintons that at one point he refused to leave the hotel room.

We made sure that Kristina took a boat trip to Ellis Island, where Kristina and I climbed all 354 steps that spiraled to the top of the Statue of Liberty. The windows were tiny, considering how many steps we had to climb to get to them; we were both a little disappointed. We also went to the top of the 102-story landmark and art deco skyscraper, the Empire State Building. On another day we ate at the Tavern on the Green. By limousine, we showed Kristina Wall Street, Times Square, and Rockefeller Center. We ate lunch at Carnegie Deli, which Steven raved about for days. We had our driver take us through Midtown Manhattan and over the Brooklyn Bridge. Kristina and I walked through Central Park by ourselves during the day, because I was too scared to walk there at night.

After a week in NYC, we took a train from the famous Grand Central Station to Boston. I was taken with the bright city lights of Boston. Steven narrated that Boston was America's road to independence and encouraged the two of us to walk the Freedom Trail. It is a 2.5 mile-trail that leads to sixteen nationally significant historic sites, each an authentic American treasure. The site consists of museums, churches, meeting houses, burial grounds, parks, a ship, and historical markers that tell the story of the American Revolution and beyond. I took Kristina on a tour of Harvard University and the Old State House. We went to the Cheers Bar for lunch, but again Steven did not want to accompany us. Kristina bought T-shirts for Jennifer and all of her friends.

The three of us did tour the city by limousine. My husband was still feeling put out about New York because our hotel room was over $2,500 a night; too much to spend for all the inconveniences we had suffered. He told me I could not pick the Christmas trip next year because this one was such a disaster. I did not argue with his decision.

Steven and I took at least once-monthly, two to three day excursions to South Padre Island. On our first visit to the island, Steven introduced me to Ila Loetscher, who is affectionately referred to as the famed "Turtle Lady." She put together a not-for-profit organization to aid and assist in the protection of the Kempis Ridley Sea Turtle in an attempt to restore the Ridley population to a level that would ensure its survival.

Ila had once brought a turtle, donned in a dress and panties, on the *Tonight Show* with Johnny Carson. She dressed the turtles to catch the attention and interest of the public. Ila died in 2000 at the age of 95, a real inspiration to many. We made a sizable donation to her every time we were on the island.

Sometimes we would invite various friends to join us on the island. Once, our attorney friend Philip & his wife Ana joined us, and another time Chuck Fuqua, Steven's banker, visited. We flew into Harlingen, Texas and rented a car to drive about an hour to South Padre Island. This time we were not flying first-class. Southwest Airlines offered non-stop service to Harlingen, but with only coach seating. Steven was a sizable man and always required an extension from the airlines for his seatbelt. Southwest Airlines did not offer assigned seating; it was first come, first served. It did not take long for him to realize that they always first boarded the disabled, children, and anyone needing special assistance. At the gate to check in, Southwest issued a numbered boarding pass and then boarded in groups of 20 to 30 in sequential order. My tardiness always assured us of being in the last group called, which infuriated Steven. Flying via other airlines, we traveled first-class, so my lateness did not matter, as first-class boarded first.

Since I consistently broke a bone or strained a limb, we had all kinds of splints, braces, and walking casts at our home. Steven wanted to board first because he liked to sit in the first row of the plane. Due to his 300 + pound size, the other travelers passed us by, so rarely did we have to share our row with a third person. Since I had the problem being punctual, Steven insisted I feign an injury and don a brace or splint, so that we would be in the category of "needing special assistance," allowing us to board first. I faked injuries rather than listen to him complain when he did not get to sit in the first seat.

We both had handicapped placards for our vehicles. I never really needed one and am now ashamed of having used the special pass strictly for my convenience. Steven refused to get a handicapped license plate because the state only gave one or the other, not both. We traveled extensively and my placard hung from the rear-view mirror while our car remained parked in the handicapped area of the airport parking lot. We took Steven's placard with us and used it, no matter what state or country we had rented a car, and no one ever questioned its use.

We always stayed at the Bridgeport Condominiums on South Padre Island and rented a three bedroom condo, regardless if it was just the two of us traveling. Steven loved to sunbathe. I went to the pool with him to carry his iced drink and snack. I laid his towel on the chaise lounge and then oiled him up with suntan oil. He loved to stay by the pool for hours. I do not enjoy baking in the sun. I have always said that the sun is not a woman's friend because of its harmful rays and the damage it does to the skin. I religiously wore sunscreen regardless of the time of year or amount of time I spent outside.

Steven raved about Scampi's restaurant on the island, where he liked to arrive early enough to enjoy the island sunset while having cocktails. Amberjacks was another favorite because it offered panoramic views of the Laguna Madre. The beach is known as one of the nation's best windsurfing sites with its shallow waters and consistent breeze; I often wanted the twins to try it. Steven was a bona fide gourmand, who not only enjoyed eating but often ate too much; his waistline was ever expanding. He could not get enough of the fresh seafood the Gulf offered.

We took the girls with us to South Padre Island when Ana and Philip were visiting. I had worn a cast because of a broken arm from a fall. One evening, when my husband had long been passed out, Philip took the four of us to an outdoor-type carnival that we had seen earlier in the day. Jennifer talked me into riding with her on the Reverse Bungee. The ride consists of two telescopic bridge-like towers mounted on a platform that feeds two elastic ropes down to a two-person passenger car constructed from an open sphere of tubular steel.

We were strapped into the sphere and then catapulted vertically with a g-force of 3-5, reaching an altitude of almost 250 feet. The passenger sphere freely rotated between the two ropes, creating a feeling that was chaotic and disorienting. After several bounces, the ropes were relaxed, and we were lowered back into the launch position. We paid to have the ride videotaped so that Steven could see what we did. When I showed him the video, he was furious. He ranted on and on about me being "out of my mind" to do something like that. His overreacting rage made me cry.

The day after we returned to Austin, Steven gave me the largest diamond tennis bracelet I had ever seen. Placing it on my wrist, he told me always to remember his everlasting love. He apologized for yelling at me, saying that when he watched the video, it scared him. He made me promise never again to do something like that; I did not.

Because of Craig's death, I moved the Orlando trip to coincide with the Labor Day weekend. Steven did not join us on our trip to Disney World and told me that he was looking forward to being alone. I understood his feelings. After all, he was the only male in an all-female household, including two female cats and two female dogs that I treated like spoiled children. Whenever the girls traveled with me and without Steven, I boarded all the animals, as he was incapable of caring for them in the manner to which they were accustomed. I knew all their habits and quirks and gladly catered to them. Nikki aggravated Steven and Megan infuriated him because of her unpredictable skittishness. I always worried if I left Megan in his sole care, he would have her put to sleep because, to him, Megan was a constant threat. I did not trust the girls to take care of my "babies," either. So I boarded the animals, better safe than sorry. I knew they were treated well when boarded at our vet's office. The charge was $35 per pet, per day, but was well worth the cost for my peace of mind, and Steven never complained about this expense.

I was only home a couple of weeks when I was invited to go on a shopping trip to New York City with Ana and two other ladies. This trip was primarily for apparel, but we also wanted to squeeze in some of the Broadway musicals. Steven was unhappy that we were staying at the Helmsley Hotel; he warned that we would be "staying at a dump" and, as usual, he was correct. The hotel was in the midst of remodeling, so there was no room service or even ice or vending machines. He told me, unequivocally, that Leona Helmsley was a "piece of shit." He said anyone like her, who does not pay their taxes, deserves to be thrown in prison.

One day Ana and I went to an office supply store and purchased poster board and colored markers. We made a sign that read, "We left our husbands in Texas, but brought their money with us." We woke up early the following morning and secured prime positions at 30 Rockefeller Plaza; the "*Today*" show's stunning, glass-walled, ground-floor production facility was at the corner of 49th Street and Rockefeller Plaza, where annually, thousands of visitors peer through the windows to become a part of Matt Lauer's and Katie Couric's broadcast. Steven was thrilled when he watched the show and happened to see the two of us with our beaming smiles, and he loved the sign.

Ana and I went to see the 1996 revival of the musical, *Chicago*, at the Zipper Theatre. Bebe Neuwirth starred as a showgirl and killer Velma Kelly. She deservedly gained her greatest stage recognition for her part in this musical. Marilu Henner, who played in the role of Roxie Hart alongside Bebe, also gave a stellar performance. We thoroughly enjoyed the show.

We attended a matinee showing of *Rent*; a Broadway musical rock opera that told the story of a group of impoverished young artists and musicians struggling to survive in New York's lower east side, under the shadow of AIDS. I was grateful that my husband had arranged front-row seats for us, but the presentation was extremely loud for my taste. It was a moving production, which I was thankful to have attended.

Ana and I spent another evening seeing the Broadway musical *Titanic*, by far our favorite. I was surprised that the show adequately depicted the scope and humanity of events occurring during the ship's historic voyage. We thought the performance was both daring and visionary, not to mention a technological wonder.

The other two women did not participate with us after the first evening; Ana and I had a great time together. She had remarked about Princess Diana, with which one of the other two women disagreed, so after that, we were treated as pariahs. We did not care because we got along well together. Ana was my bridesmaid when I married Steven.

Craig's death was still recent when I asked Steven to cancel our scheduled trip to South America. He agreed and suggested that I take the girls to California for weekend visits with their grandparents every 4-6 weeks, insisting that we needed our family time together. I was a little taken back by his comment, because when I suggested that he spend time with his children, he said, "Hell, no." I stopped bringing up their names because that mention always seemed to elevate his blood pressure.

Christmas vacation was fast approaching. The previous Christmas we had spent a great deal of time being ordered around by the Clinton's Secret Service staff. Steven made arrangements for the four of us to island-hop in the Caribbean. Instead of using our travel agent, he let me pick half of the islands. I teased him mid-trip, letting him know that he should not make travel plans while having cocktails because he grumbled at all the different airports. It did not help matters when he reminded me that I had told him that Martinique, Dominica, and Guadeloupe were all Spanish islands. Steven had explicitly told me he did not want to vacation on any French islands. The names sounded Spanish to me.

The first island we visited was Martinique, located in the southern Caribbean. With the island's western Italian Creole traditions, I thought it was worldlier and classically French. While on the island Steven could not wait to school me on the fact that the island is still an integral part of France. The island continues to grow sugar cane and bananas and has a lush countryside.

Not long after our arrival, Kristina was plagued with a touch of food poisoning. It was not severe enough to warrant a house call from the local doctor. Steven volunteered to go to the pharmacy to get some over-the-counter medication for her. He returned with a package of small pills in a distinctly "French" package. I hesitated to give a pill to Kristina, because, to me, they looked suspicious, resembling our "American" laxatives. I started to question Steven, but changed my mind, because he could not stop reminding me that I lacked the mental capacity to discern the difference between a French and Spanish island. When he insisted that I give her two pills, so that they would work quickly, I complied.

Kristina took a turn for the worse. I was worried because she was white as a sheet and could not leave the restroom. I sent for the hotel doctor. When he arrived, I explained how Kristina was not getting better after the medication was given to her. Thank goodness the man spoke English! Looking at the box, he said, "Madam, these are laxatives." I glared at Steven.

Steven relayed what transpired between him and the pharmacist, who spoke only French. Steven pantomimed, by squeezing his eyes shut and clenching both fists in the air, while slightly squatting. At the same time, he made a loud farting noise. It was apparent to me while watching him that even a complete idiot would think he needed to use the restroom because of constipation -- the exact opposite of Kristina's problem. Watching him repeat the pantomime, the look on the hotel doctor's face was priceless. I was sure that he could not believe how stupid we both were. Of course, Steven tried to convince me the pharmacist purposely deceived him because he was an American. I made sure he knew I was not falling for that lame excuse. The doctor visited Kristina several times a day over the following three days. My thought was that he felt sorry for her because we were her parents.

Next, we went to Dominica. Steven did not utter one negative word about the island not being Spanish. It was too soon after Kristina's poisoning, as I repeatedly referred to her illness; he did not want to chance my bringing it up again. He spent his time sunbathing and took several trips up and down the beach to eye the topless women. Strangely, he stayed away from the hotel pool where the majority of topless women were very elderly. The girls and I were able to relax and experience Trafalgar Falls, a beautiful waterfall.   We rented a car for Steven to drive, but the island roads were very narrow, and he hit a few vehicles on the driver's side by driving too close. I relieved him as the driver. I felt that the poisoning incident with Kristina was beginning to work in my favor, as Steven did not argue about not driving. I insisted on driving for the remainder of our vacation.

The last French island we visited was Guadeloupe, one of a large group of islands, named an archipelago located in the Leeward Islands in the Lesser Antilles, the first overseas region of France. I saved face with my husband by pointing out to him that Christopher Columbus named the island after the image of the Virgin Mary that was venerated at a Spanish monastery. Steven told me that

Celeste

by 1815, the French had permanently controlled the island, making sure to reiterate it was still a French island.

We stayed at a luxury resort and spent our time snorkeling, while Steven sunbathed and sipped cocktails. He enjoyed going to brunch at the hotel because some of the women were topless. I found their nakedness offensive, especially that of the older women. I surmised that these women were not locals, but nationals from France. The pungent aroma of body odor was stifling in enclosed areas. True or not, I was told that many Europeans do not use deodorant. The other grooming standard I could not understand was the women's unshaven armpits. The girls made several whispered comments of shock when they noticed this strange habit.

One day, at the local grocery store, Steven and I watched the patrons in front of us chatting non-stop with the clerk, who was very friendly, as she packed their purchases into plastic shopping bags. When our turn came, we paid the clerk and waited for her to pack our few items. She glared at us, then abruptly pulled a bag out of a holder and rudely thrust it at us. Steven became incensed and started cursing, but I saved the day by packing our purchases, and we left post haste.

When in the car and seat-belted, I slowly turned the

151

key in the ignition, waiting for Steven to break the silence. At the same moment, we turned to each other and burst out laughing. He said, "Darling, I love you," to which I replied, "I love you, too."

That night we all retired around 10:00 pm. Around midnight, the girls and I were awakened by loud and boisterous partying at the pool beneath us. Since we had only been asleep for a couple of hours, we were irritated. I picked up the telephone and dialed the front desk to complain. I felt foolish, when he replied, "But madam, it's New Year's Eve." I quickly replaced the receiver and relayed his explanation to the twins.

We ran over to the balcony and looked at the party-goers dancing, drinking, and celebrating the arrival of 1997. Since Steven was passed out cold, he had heard nothing. The girls wanted to join the party, but I told them I was too embarrassed after my telephone call. We had our own little party and headed to the mini bar. We shared the small bottles of champagne and wine. I brought some of the candy and nut snacks to the balcony. Jennifer tossed one of the snacks to Kristina; it flew over the balcony, landing in the pool. We looked over the balcony and realized that no one even noticed.

One thing led to another. We began emptying out

the entire contents of the minibar while screaming Happy New Year! We tossed more items over the balcony into the pool: beer, sodas, nuts, chips, anything in the minibar. Even though we were doing something so childish, stupid, and ridiculous, we still had a ball and laughed until our bellies hurt; Steven slept through it all.

When Steven checked out of the hotel, he called me downstairs because of a concern about the over $400 minibar charge. I told him it was legitimate and to chalk it up to my being under the influence of alcohol. He responded with "But you rarely drink." I assured him he did not want details and to trust me that all was okay. I guess that he was looking forward to our next stop on St. Thomas, so he never mentioned the bill again. I cannot remember if I ever did tell him what we did that night, but eventually, I probably did because I usually told him everything I did, good or bad.

Steven chose St. Thomas because it is a small island, only 31 miles square. He said he had always wanted to vacation in the U. S. Virgin Islands. He planned to be sunbathing while the three of us went off on our own. Steven was only interested in meeting up with us for dinner. We stayed at the luxurious Ritz-Carlton Resort, nestled within a 30-acre waterfront estate of white-sand beaches and perfumed tropical gardens only a car trip away from the bustle of the shopping district. He was looking forward to the two of us indulging in several private couple's massages. Steven especially enjoyed the poolside bar amid the lush setting. Even though we were staying right on the beach, he never ventured past the pool. He enjoyed the Ritz-Carlton's full-service spa and four restaurants, stating that he felt as if he had "stepped into blissful solitude."

We were only at the Ritz-Carlton a few days when we were being rerouted throughout our hotel, as Steven called it, placed under "house arrest." He was furious that, once again, our vacation was being disrupted by the Clintons. It was more aggravating on this trip because Steven could not stay by the pool all day. The President had a poolside party; Steven was seething, nothing would appease him. We three girls decided to go with the flow. At one point the Secret Service allowed me to photograph Jennifer and Kristina with the President and First Lady after I explained to them the Clinton's were following us around the globe on our Christmas vacations.

We did not let Steven's lousy attitude hinder our fun that day. He fumed and stayed in the suite drinking his Wolfschmidt vodka. He always had his vodka shipped ahead of us to the various resorts and hotels where we had reservations. I know that FedEx did not know what was being shipped, because when I filled out the shipping invoice, Steven instructed me to describe the contents as "business documents." This instruction is why the teenagers' testimony that I was putting Everclear in his Wolfschmidt bottles was absurd. Being a heavy drinker with a distinctive taste, he would have spit it out and complained. All shipments were new, unopened bottles, and I did not dare risk one leaking, since we were less than truthful to customs about the contents. Because of the deceit regarding the contents, and knowing if discovered that criminal penalties could apply, I made Steven sign the invoices, as if that made the cheating better.

The girls and I explored the underwater world on a high-tech Atlantis Submarine. We had fun snorkeling around Buck Island, cruised to St. John's on a catamaran, and snorkeled at Trunk Bay Beach. We had fun renting Waverunners and went crazily speeding all over the ocean on them. We took day trips to Tortola and Virgin Gorda, which are the British Virgin Islands. While on Tortola, we snorkeled at Smugglers Cove. Our favorite spot was the baths on Virgin Gorda. We were able to snorkel in the extraordinary network of sunlit grottoes, and sea pools on the southern shore that are formed by giant granite rocks in a national park. My most cherished photo taken was the twins in one of these caves. They looked so happy because they were.

Every evening during dinner we would regale Steven with stories of our day's adventure. He listened patiently and with a smile knowing that we could not have been so fortunate if he had not provided us with the opportunity. On vacations with the girls, we did not have to wait for Steven to finish drinking before we ordered and ate our meals. He ordered when he was ready, even when we had usually finished our desserts by the time he stopped drinking. I never put my head on my pillow before thanking Steven for giving my daughters the world.

We remained home the entire month of January 1997, and in February we returned to New Orleans to celebrate our second anniversary. We spent the weekend at the Loews New Orleans Hotel, which my husband particularly liked because that is where we spent our honeymoon. The hotel is located just one block from Bourbon Street and the French Quarter. We did some shopping in the warehouse and arts district, but our primary focus revolved around our three meals a day. I did not mind, because I wanted to do what Steven wanted to do

since he always let us do what we wanted when
vacationing.

For the girls' spring-break vacation, we decided to
take a tour to Rapid City, South Dakota, Grand Tetons,
Wyoming, and Yellowstone, ending in Salt Lake City,
Utah. The girls would miss a few days of school, but
Steven said this trip was "educational" and that the school
would give them an excused absence. He called the
superintendent and, of course, they were excused.

Steven scheduled us to fly to South Dakota two
days ahead of the tour to give us time to recuperate from jet
lag and prepare for the long bus tour. The girls immediately
realized that they were the only teenagers and the three of
us were the youngest amongst the entire tour group. They
were annoyed because they were always asked to fetch or
retrieve things for other people on the tour. Steven and I
just laughed.

When our group arrived to view the Mt. Rushmore
National Memorial, we could barely see it through the fog;
this was a huge disappointment. Steven had just finished
assuring us that instead of heading home from Salt Lake
City, we would fly back here to view the massive sculpture
of four of the great American presidents carved into the
rock face of Mt. Rushmore. This incredible work of art was

sculpted between 1927 and 1941. Turning to leave, suddenly and miraculously, the fog lifted. What a sight to behold! The sculptures of Roosevelt and Lincoln are each 60 feet high. We took some beautiful photos, and Steven was elated that we did not have to fly back. We did not see the Crazy Horse Monument because it was still a work in progress; some day, I would love to see it. We drove through the Big Horn mountains of Wyoming, heading for Lake Yellowstone Hotel at Yellowstone National Park to stay overnight.

We continued to Old Faithful Inn, where the girls encountered a brown bear at the vending machine. They were scared at the time, but after leaving the park, they thought it was a "cool" experience and often talked about it. The three of us hiked around Yellowstone, taking in the entire geothermal experience, while Steven shopped at the lodge. He discovered some beautiful masks made by Native Americans to complement our collection at the lake house.

Steven asked me to join him to see the Native American pieces. The "Prayer Pipe" enamored me, and the shopkeeper explained that the ceremonial pipes were used for prayer and meditation. It was said that these pipes would give the keeper great powers, as long as he lives an honorable life; if not, the powers will leave. As the smoke tendrils rise upwards, the prayers are delivered to the creator. The shopkeeper explained that one does not own a pipe, but instead is the keeper of the pipe, thus reflecting the native belief in responsibility rather than ownership. Steven wanted me to choose several for display at the lake house. After the shopkeeper's explanation, I selected one to keep. I never smoked from it but did place it in a prominent place on our glass shelves.

We were awed when Old Faithful Geyser shot its contents more than 180 feet in the air. We hiked around colorful, bubbling mud pots amongst the backdrop of the dramatic Yellowstone Canyon and drove through the picturesque Grand Tetons National Park, and then stopped for lunch. We headed for Jackson Hole, Wyoming and stayed at the Jackson Lake Lodge.

While the tour is a wonderful way to see all of the sights, rest is hard to come by, if you take all the side tours, which the girls insisted on doing. I happily accompanied them. Steven went off on his own and found more masks for the lake house at one of Jackson Hole's upscale shopping areas. He excitedly described the masks to me, but I did not get to see them until after we got home. That Federal Express account came in handy.

Celeste

I love all animals, as do my daughters, but this kind of love does not explain my love of real fur coats. Steven liked this contradiction, although I felt terrible when strangers hollered obscenities at me when I was wearing fur. I enjoy the softness and warmth that faux fur cannot provide. It was a beautiful experience to see all of the moose, bison, and antelope in their natural surroundings and not in a zoo. While in Wyoming, I was able to convince my husband to join us on a rafting trip down the Snake River. When he said that he had a good time, the comment pleased me immensely. He did decline the invite for horseback riding; his back was very tight, and he was suffering in pain. We took many photos of the spectacular mountain scenery, while on horseback trips. Steven was again feeling the effects of higher altitudes with his chronic asthma.

Our last stop was Salt Lake City, Utah. The city was already preparing to host the 2002 Olympics, and we bought many souvenirs, even though the Olympics were five years away. We stood by "This is the place," a monument erected by Mormon pioneers in 1847. We tried to trace our family history at the Family History Library but were not successful. After returning home, we were bombarded with visits, telephone calls, and mail from the local Mormons. Steven was furious because he accused me of passing out our personal information when I searched the Family History Library with Jennifer and Kristina; I never did that again.

Steven said one of his greatest joys was shopping for my apparel. How lucky for me! While in Salt Lake City, Steven went shopping at Nordstrom's and loaded up on shoes and purses for me. He explained to me that the department stores carry different merchandise depending on the region or state of each store's location. He had excellent taste, and we loved the same brands. He knew how to coordinate an outfit to perfection. At my trial, I was portrayed as a shopaholic; the majority of my massive shoe and purse collection was gifted to me from Steven. He loved accessorizing my wardrobe.

Steven never shopped in a mall, only the high-end flagship stores that had an entrance directly from the parking lot or garage. In Dallas, he loved the valet parking at Neiman's. He went to a department that sold Chanel, St. John's, and other designer goods he was interested in seeing. He sat in a chair, while the sales clerks brought their merchandise to him. He had difficulty walking and insisted on being treated in a manner compatible with the tens of thousands of dollars he spent on my gifts. The sales clerks always enjoyed Steven's humor, flirting, and of course, his generosity. While he shopped, we took a helicopter ride over Copper Canyon and Great Salt Lake basin. We were amazed at the size of the tires on the heavy equipment, far taller than a two-story house. We ended our guided tour at the Salt Lake Temple. The bus tour was exhausting, but exciting and educational for us. We stayed an extra two days to relax before flying home.

During our flight home, Steven decided that we needed to use only wooden hangers and wanted every hanger in both houses exchanged for the high-quality type. He ordered the hangers after we counted how many pants, dress, coat, and shirt hangers we needed. It was in the thousands. He ordered hundreds of extra hangers so we would never run out.

The time came to plan our 1997 Christmas vacation. Steven wanted input from me, since his chosen trip that ended in St. Thomas had, again, been ruined by the president's entourage. I knew he wanted the sun, so I suggested we cruise the Mexican coast and the Bay Islands in Central America. I had seen an advertisement that cruise ships were leaving out of Galveston, Texas. We could make the four to five hour drive to the pier and not have to fly to a port-of-call. He liked the idea and booked a

Christmas Cruise aboard NCL's "Star" to Calica, Cancun, Cozumel, Curacao, and Roatan.

At the time of our booking, the Star was the first and only full-time cruise ship using the Port of Houston. Steven booked our stay in the best suite on the ship, the Owner's Suite, and a cabin for the girls on another floor at the opposite end of the ship. The cruise became a nightmare. Not long into our trip, the Houston Chronicle dubbed it *"The Cruise from Hell"* and *"Voyage of the Damned."* Steven was calling CNN and other media outlets from his cell phone, begging them to rescue us. The air conditioning failed, leaving us sweltering and forcing us to sleep on lawn chairs on the open decks. Lack of air conditioning caused overheated waiters to drip sweat in our drinks and on our food. Sewage backed up on the same floor as the girls' cabin. The brackish and undrinkable water forced NCL to ration the bottled water on board the ship. It was a total disaster, but the girls had a blast. They were able to run around the ship, unsupervised, with a group of teenagers also traveling with their parents. They stayed up all night long practically every night.

Steven was so disgusted with our "bad luck" concerning the Christmas trips; he drank non-stop. The embarrassing part about his drinking was that he wore only his white BVD underwear under his robe that rarely stayed closed because of the high winds on deck and because of his sizable girth. He became loud and belligerent and urinated under the stairwell because it was too much trouble to get to our suite. All I could do was stay in the lounge chair next to him in my pink pajamas, praying that he would not fall and injure himself. Some of the other passengers thought we were nuts; I thought so, too, so their remarks and facial expressions did not bother me. Luckily, Steven could not hear or see them, or I am sure he would have verbally accosted them.

One of the four main engines failed and combined with the strong headwinds blowing, the ship was so far behind schedule that our first stop to Calica, Mexico was canceled. By the time the ship limped into Cancun, we were anxious to get off. Steven was so upset that he stayed on board. This was the first time I had seen Steven remain drunk from dusk to dawn. He was difficult to be around those few days.

Cancun is one of Mexico's most famous beach resorts with ancient Mayan ruins nearby. Tulum is a half-hour drive southeast of Coba. The girls and I took a bus trip to see the Chichen Itza pyramids, an archeological site built by the Mayan civilization. During the spring and fall equinoxes a shadow is cast by the angle of the sun. The edges of the nine steps of the pyramid combined with the northern stairway and the stone serpent head carvings create the illusion of a massive serpent descending the pyramid.

It was an exhilarating experience to climb the El Castillo pyramid and explore the inside chambers with my daughters. The El Castillo pyramid served as a temple to Kukulcan. The ninety-foot-tall pyramid was built between the 11th and 13th centuries directly upon the foundations of previous temples. The architecture of the structure encodes precise information regarding the Mayan calendar and is directionally oriented to mark the solstices and equinoxes. Each face of the four-sided structure has a stairway with ninety-one steps, which together with the shared step of the platform top added up to 365, the number of days in a year. The girls wanted to climb up and down every step and I tagged along. We did not know how fortunate we were to be able to do this at the time; a woman fell to her death in 2006, now no one is allowed to climb or explore inside. The site also contains many beautiful stone buildings in various states of preservation. The structures were formerly used as temples, palaces, stages, markets, baths, and ball courts. It gave me immense joy to be able to share all of this beauty and history with my daughters.

Some of the passengers flew home from Roatan on Christmas day. Roatan is one of three in a group of islands found just off the coast of Honduras. The primary languages are English and Spanish as the islands are owned by Honduras. Steven said we were better off on a sinking ship than trying to fly home from South America during the holidays without preplanned arrangements. I did not share this comment with the girls because they would have taken the sinking ship comment literally. Even I was not so sure, but did know I wanted to remain with Steven. He continued to drink. And drink.

We docked in Willemstad, Curacao and Steven again stayed aboard. The port reminded me of Old San Juan, Puerto Rico with its historic districts and street life. We spent the majority of our time shopping their high-end retailers. We also took photos of the vivid sherbet-colored buildings that showcase the Dutch colonial architecture, structures that will not be found anywhere else outside of the Netherlands.

While we were there, we stocked up on genuine Curacao liqueur that is produced in a 17th-century plantation house. Our friends, Jim and Dawn, loved to add the blue liqueur to their vodka, so it was purchased for them.

Cancun is richly filled with Mayan history. The Kukulcan Boulevard was surrounded by water, the Caribbean on one side and a lagoon on the other. Kukulcan was also the name of the 13th ruler of Chichen Itza, who sacrificed himself to the rain gods by being cast alive into the 20-meter-deep well.

On a visit to El Rey, the main archeological ruins in Cancun, we walked among the stone plazas that made up the ancient fishing village inhabited from the 10th to the 16th centuries.

On the return to Texas, one of the ballasts broke causing the ship to become lopsided. Steven was furious, that again, another Christmas vacation was a disaster. The cruise made me seasick. Daily, I required two shots of Phenergan to keep from vomiting and was grateful to dock and get home. All we could do was laugh to keep from crying.The whole mess reminded us of Chevy Chase in National Lampoon's *Vacation*, only worse!

Jennifer and Kristina wanted to graduate in 1999 instead of 2000. We had to find other ways for them to earn credits for their diploma in addition to the courses they were already taking at Westlake High School. Unbeknownst to my husband, I was paying hundreds of

167

dollars in cash to college students to complete their high school course work. Steven inquired about our options when he called the Superintendent of the Eanes School District, who referred us to the Austin School District, which directed us to Anderson High School. We were then able to enroll the girls to participate in the school's trip to Hawaii to earn a geology credit. Steven could hardly wait for spring-break to arrive when the teens would be gone and it would be just the two of us.

When the girls returned, I paid a University of Texas student $200 to complete their extensive reports that were due.

While the girls were away, Steven and I took off for a week in the Bahamas. He originally wanted to go to Fiji, but then changed his mind and booked a trip to the Bahamas. I mentioned to Steven that I wanted to travel to Australia someday. He said when we did visit Australia we would stay a few days in Fiji on the way to and from because it was a 24-hour flight and he would go stir-crazy being on the plane that long.

Our new neighbors at the lake house were from Australia, and when the wife described her country, I knew someday I would want to travel there. Steven said he did not want to go to Fiji twice, so we headed for the Bahamas.

There are over 700 islands of the Bahamas sprinkled over 100,000 square miles of ocean, starting just 50 miles off the coast of Florida. That area also boasts the most transparent water on the planet with a visibility of over 200 feet.

We decided on Nassau, as Steven wanted to dine at Graycliff because of its five-star status. He knew the restaurant was in a historic mansion and boasted a wine cellar that housed over 200,000 bottles from more than fifteen countries. I asked my husband if he wanted to try a bottle, but he declined, saying he would stick with "Wolfy." We discovered another restaurant, Humidor, which Steven enjoyed. He liked their prime-cut meats, cooked Brazilian style, on giant rotisseries, and served in a seemingly endless progression. He ate his money's worth there.

I took a side-trip to the nearby island, Bimini. I wanted to see the pay phone, where Hannibal Lector called Clarissa in the last scene of *Silence of the Lambs*. I also wanted to buy the fabulous Bimini bread, which is slightly sweet and very soft. Our Toro Canyon home was selected for the annual American Institute of Architects Homes Tour. Steven had no intention of being present for the tour, so we flew into Hong Kong three days before the viewing was to take place. My husband wanted a specific tailor in the city to make a new wardrobe for both of us.

Marveling at this sparkling city of glass skyscrapers, I shopped in Stanley Market alone, as Steven was too weak to walk even the short distance from our limousine.

In Kowloon, I purchased jade, silks, lacquerware, cloisonné porcelain, and embroidery. I went to the local fish market and wandered through the hidden shops. Steven had given me a list of over 30 people to whom he wanted to give a jade "chop." The chop was a jade figurine on top of a "stamp" that had the last name of the recipient carved on it. This unique figurine could be used as a stamp with ink or a seal with wax. The chops were extremely heavy for their small size of less than 6 inches tall. The shop owner said he would carve the names in each one and hold them until we returned to Hong Kong.

When I took a closer look at the chops, I was genuinely pleased with their beauty. When Steven saw them, he raved about my selections! Since most of the receivers lived in Austin, I assumed we would both hand-deliver them. Steven said he did not want me running all over town when we could take them to The Box Store and have them packaged and delivered by UPS. This was just another example of Steven flaunting his wealth. Having to fill out all of the packing slips, I may have grumbled a bit, but I did not mind because my husband asked so little of me.

While waiting at the Hong Kong airport for our flight to Beijing, Steven made himself a cocktail and bought me an egg roll from one of the fast-food stands. Steven did not eat, as he usually did not mix food with his alcohol. He said it slowed down his drinking. Twenty minutes into the flight I became severely ill and spent the entire two-hour trip in the tight quarters of the airplane's restroom.

I was embarrassed to be so much trouble. We had joined our tour group at the airport to travel with them. I had no choice but to go back to my seat before we landed. I could not stop retching, even though nothing was left in my stomach; my sickness was compounded with painful, loose bowels. It was apparent to the flight attendants that I needed to stay in the restroom, even though this was against regulations. Steven was becoming loud and boisterous, because he wanted them to render me immediate medical aid, which, of course, was impossible on the plane. Thank goodness we were seated in first-class. After landing, I was able to run off the plane to the first available restroom. The flight attendants had already prearranged for a wheelchair and an assistant to meet us at the gate for Steven.

I reached the first bathroom stall and was in shock. The toilet seat was flat on the floor! All I could think was "What the hell?!" I was too weak to squat, so I had to sit down with my legs splayed straight in front of me. It was utterly disgusting to sit on the floor where others sat before me. I could hear Steven insisting the airport employee wheel him into the ladies restroom to check on me. I was feeling so sick; I didn't even care. All the ladies in the restroom scattered when my husband entered. I begged him to tell the tour to go on without us and hire a car to drive us to the hotel when I could make it to the car. The employee called another to stay with me while, he wheeled Steven to the baggage claim, secured a car and driver and loaded our luggage into the limo.

By now, our tour group was long gone. It seemed like I sat on the floor for hours, but eventually, I made it to the limo, where Steven was utterly besotted. Bless his heart. He was beside himself. So used to me doting on him during our travels, he was not prepared for me to fall ill. I hardly remember the drive to the luxurious Peninsula Hotel and was glad the hotel doctor was waiting for my arrival.

Celeste

The doctor surmised that it was food poisoning
from the egg roll because that was the only food I
consumed that Steven had not. When my husband heard
this, he suggested, " Start drinking with me instead of
against me." I declined. Steven always transformed and
became mean after a few cocktails. If I were also drunk, we
would argue. When sober, I knew how to keep my mouth
shut, as I am a happy drunk. I knew that to put up with
Steven's drinking; I had to remain sober; it was the least I
could do since he put up with all of my goofy antics. Our
marriage was equal give-and-take.

Steven enjoyed having me confined in the hotel
suite with him. I slept most of the time, as the doctor came
every few hours to give me a shot. He watched a lot of
television and had at least one massage every day by a
masseur who came to our suite. Steven always insisted on
being massaged by a man, claiming that the females were
not strong enough to give him a deep-tissue massage. I
preferred a female masseuse, as the men were too rough for
me.

By the fourth day, I felt well enough to venture
outside. The first thing I noticed about Beijing was the
smog, a thick, gray soup that engulfs the city most of the
year. The hotel doctor gave us surgical masks to wear when

we ventured outside. Masses of people wore masks, especially the natives. It is a peculiar sight to see the majority of the population donning surgical masks. It was a relief to know that we had brought Steven's oxygen, nebulizer, and CPAP machine. His lungs could not take the pollution. Tiananmen Square was my first stop and I was surprised that it was small in comparison to how immense it looked on TV. I was struck by the image of Mao Tse Tung that is forever enshrined high above the square. Stepping through the Gate of Heavenly Peace into the Forbidden City led me to tour the 15th-century palace, where emperors ruled for nearly 500 years.

In Beijing, families live, as their ancestors did, in courtyard-style houses that sit in the shadows of towering, modern skyscrapers. Hutongs are the narrow alleyways lined with the courtyard-style compounds that date back to the 13th century. We were fortunate to hail a rickshaw to take us to Ritan Park. In the park, seeing men taking their caged birds out for walks intrigued me. There was also a multitude of children, of all ages, flying oversized kites.

I accepted an invitation to a local's home, where we had tea in a typical household. Unable to speak each other's language, we communicated a lot with hand gestures. I was curious about the inside of their homes.

Arriving back at the hotel, I excitedly narrated to Steven how I had spent my day. He became angry, saying that I was a lunatic for going into a stranger's house in a Third World country. I said that he was ridiculous because Beijing is modern and we were staying at a luxury hotel, so it could not be considered Third World.

I tried to explain to him my complete ease and lack of nervousness. Throughout our trip, I had been stopped multiple times by the locals pushing their children in front of me. They also could not speak English, but through their gesticulating, I understood that they wanted to take a photograph of me with their children. I was not sure if it was because I was tall and blonde or if it was because they thought I was a celebrity. Steven said it was because I was beautiful. That experience was funny to me, but irritated my husband; he claimed that the Chinese were the pushiest people he had ever met.

I walked part of the Great Wall of China, by myself, and rode a cable car to the highest point. Steven had to be carried in his chair arriving and leaving the cable car. The people there were very accommodating. I could not understand their remarks regarding Steven's weight, but their eyes widened big, and they began to talk loud and fast when they saw him. They probably thought he was

Buddha! Steven basked in all the attention he received.

I toured the magnificent Summer Palace, once a retreat for the Forbidden City emperors. The temples, shrines, ceremonial halls, bridges, and extensive gardens were breath-taking. I climbed aboard a dragon boat for a peaceful cruise on Kunming Lake to enjoy a view of the palace from across the water. Taking many photographs, I missed Steven's company, wanting, as always, to share my discoveries with him.

Steven did join me on a cruise down the Yangtze River; it boasts of being the third largest river on the planet. We were amazed at the beautiful mist-covered mountains, feeling the surrounding mystique of old China travel. I was not expecting to see the many dead bodies we saw floating down the river. What was creepy was the indifference shown by the natives; he said this was because China was so overpopulated that death was something they were accustomed to seeing. The thought of this cultural reaction was macabre and sent chills down my spine. We saw the world's largest dam, Three Gorges Dam, surrounded by some of the most dramatic scenery in all of China.

We traveled on to Shanghai, a very cosmopolitan city. I met students at the Children's Palace, an art, music, and dance center. I purchased a beautiful nude painting for Steven; one that was rather large, but the honesty depicted by the artist was outstanding. The woman was painted without a flat stomach or perky breasts in a perfect lifelike manner. When this unusual piece of art was unveiled to Steven, he was thrilled. The sales clerk kept insisting that I take the frame. When paid his asking price, he removed the frame and rolled up the art piece. No doubt he thought not wanting the frame was on my part to reduce the asking price.

One day we took a cruise on the Li River, and that night I strolled alone by the silk stalls at Guilin's colorful night markets. I found the 18-inch, square linen handkerchiefs which Steven was always unsuccessfully searching for, as he preferred the larger size. I bought 50 of the linen pieces, and my thoughts of him truly touched him. Later, at home in Austin, I had his monogram embroidered on all of the handkerchiefs. After Steven's death, I kept one in my purse. I could smell him and hear his voice when I held the keepsake to my face.

My absolute favorite tour was in Xi'an, a viewing of the more than 8,000 Terracotta Army of the ancient capital. This incredible collection of terracotta sculptures was discovered in 1974 by a group of farmers digging a

water well. The figures vary in height from 6' to 6 ½'
according to their military roles, the generals being the
tallest. The life-sized figures include those of warriors,
chariots, horses, officials, acrobats, strongmen, and
musicians. The Terracotta Army is a form of funerary art,
buried with the First Emperor of Qin in 210-209 BC. The
figures were placed in the pits in precise military formation
according to rank and duty, varying in height, uniform, and
hair style. In accordance with rank the individual facial
features, weapons, and armor from battle used in
manufacturing these figures created a realistic appearance.
Each statue was unique, making the existence of these
figures to serve as testaments to the amount of labor and
skill involved in their construction. These statues also fully
reveal the power the First Emperor possessed, enabling him
to command such a monumental undertaking.

From China, we flew to Bangkok, the capital of
Thailand. This city is referred to as the "Venice of the
East," because of the number of canals and passages that
divide the area into separate patches of land. We stayed at
the spectacular 5-star Mandarin Oriental Hotel. Steven
bragged that this hotel was known as one of the most
outstanding for grandeur in the entire world, a pure
paragon of luxury, and rich in history. While dining, I

noticed the magnificent recessed ceilings in one of the many dining rooms and asked Steven if we could copy it for our living room. I took several photos and when we returned home, our carpenter, Doug, recreated these ceilings in our immense living room. It looked terrific, and my husband was thrilled with the idea.

Many of the canals, called Khlongs, in Bangkok still exist. People reside and operate markets along the canal's banks. These canals are dangerously polluted with sewage. Bangkok seems to be one of the worst cities in the world for traffic, with massive, day long traffic jams. It took us more than three hours to travel just two miles by taxi. Travel by foot is faster, but Steven could not manage that distance.

Bangkok has severe environmental issues because of air pollution, primarily caused by the traffic and dirt left on the streets from never-ending construction projects. Bangkok's mold growth is ubiquitous, as the wet, tropical climate causes it to grow, and many residents merely ignore it. I was regretting Steven traveling in this area with all of his breathing problems and I was always worrying about his health. Fortunately, he wanted to stay inside the hotel and schedule private massages, TV time, lots of room service, and plenty of drinking.

Celeste

I found the visit to the Bang Khu Wiang Floating Market interesting because sellers sold natural goods and vegetables. I saw monks' rowing boats seeking to collect alms. The market was not at all commercialized, and I enjoyed seeing one of the few places left where it is possible to view their traditional way of life. I was not brave enough to buy any of the vegetables after my food poisoning experience in Hong Kong. Flies converged on the produce at the outdoor markets, furthering my desire not to eat anything. Unrefrigerated fish were stacked in moldy crates that were swarming with flies. I gagged at the sight and wondered how the natives survived such unsanitary practices when I could barely survive eating one egg roll.

Thailand has a variety of shopping experiences from street markets to world-class, luxury malls. Water markets are gradually disappearing, but remain steady tourist attractions. Many tours are offered and I was fortunate to experience all three types of shopping markets.

I visited temples with gold ceilings and walls inlaid with rubies, emeralds, and sapphires. Seeing this makes it difficult to realize that most citizens are poverty-stricken. I purchased a couple of paintings at one of the art galleries. The artwork was restricted to rural motifs, but the artisans were naturally skilled.

I decided to cut our visit short because Steven was having too many breathing problems that reached the point where he would not even go to any of the hotel restaurants to eat. He wanted only room service, saying that he was too tired to leave our room. He wanted us to stay in the suite and spend quality time together. I would have gladly complied, but I was too concerned about his health.

We traveled to San Juan and Aruba for our annual Christmas vacation. Steven gave the girls and me two sleeping pills each after we took off. We were rested upon arrival in San Juan, but Steven was intoxicated. Thank goodness he had a car and driver waiting for us on arrival! He was so good to us and always thought of everything, even if he was a drunk.

San Juan is known as the shining star of the Caribbean. The Bacardi rum factory on the island is the largest rum factory in the world, and the city is magnificent. Bioluminescence Bay is one of the few places in the world considered a wonder of nature, and El Yunge the only tropical rainforest in the United States territory. I enjoyed learning about Puerto Rico's history and architecture as the girls and I strolled through the streets of Old San Juan. We stayed at the El Presidenté Hotel, both a beautiful and world-class hotel. The highlight in San Juan for the girls was purchasing t-shirts at the Hard Rock Café for Jimmy and all of their friends.

We traveled on to Aruba, located north of Venezuela. I liked the island's motto, "One Happy Island." The dry climate and forests of cactus felt like we were back in Arizona instead of in the Caribbean. Steven spent his days imbibing by the hotel pool.

The girls wanted to go to Carlos and Charlie's, a popular bar and restaurant because of its reputation for fun. They had heard that they played retro music to an always-packed house. Steven was intoxicated and did not want to go with us, so we planned to go there for lunch. While there we ended up in the midst of a rowdy group, singing the popular song "YMCA." I was delighted to see my daughters have so much fun. I hope they remember those fun times we spent together.

To celebrate graduation from high school, the girls and I went to Australia. In Melbourne we admired the city's Victorian architecture while traveling through historic districts. In Sydney, the largest city, we attended a cocktail cruise on a private boat. We took a behind-the-scenes tour of the Sydney Opera House. It is an architectural masterpiece with the billowing sail-roof design that has been seen in numerous publications.

We visited Taronga Zoo and saw koalas, dingoes, wallabies, Tasmanian devils, and emus, to name a few. The girls took a photo of me hand-feeding a kangaroo at the petting zoo. We were fortunate for the opportunity to see aboriginal life and traditional ceremonies in a cultural park along the beautiful coast of the Coral Sea. We were awe-struck while exploring the Great Barrier Reef. Our trip included a ride on a high-tech catamaran; we enjoyed the magnificent coral formations, visible through the clear water.

In Auckland, New Zealand, we rode a moving walkway in a transparent tunnel that passed through the reef fish tank and the shark tank. Also on the agenda was a visit to a working dairy farm and a hands-on look at sheep-and-cattle farming. I was thrilled to try my hand at milking a cow while wearing a fur coat.

Jennifer and Kristina especially enjoyed the Whakarewarewa Thermal Reserve featuring bubbling mud pools, geysers, steam vents, and hot springs. We cruised the crystal waters of Milford Sound with its sheer cliffs, glacier-carved inlets, waterfalls, and snow-capped peaks. I hope my daughters remember those times and how much love we shared.

Celeste

We took a gondola ride followed by an aerial tour of Queenstown and the Remarkables Mountain Range. The girls' favorite part of the trip was the Shotover Jet boat ride in Queenstown. Sitting in front, we skimmed past rocky outcrops at close range, as the boat twisted and turned through narrow canyons at breath-taking speeds. We held on tight, as the boat made the world-famous Shotover Jet 360-degree spins. The girls were thrilled, but I was scared speechless. When we got off the jet boat, I could hardly wait to call my husband. He always enjoyed listening to my stories of our trip, and I loved telling him everything we did. Forever grateful, I thanked my husband for providing such opportunities to us.

My husband wanted to travel to Europe at the beginning of October, 1999 to solidify our marriage. Being Steven, he took over the travel plans for our vacation. What initially started as a romantic vacation to Germany for a cuckoo clock, the trip culminated in his arranging for a $60,000 limousine ride from Frankfurt, Germany all the way to London, England, via the Channel Tunnel through the Strait of Dover.

Steven had our travel agent arrange our upcoming 1999 Christmas holiday in Cuba, instead of our usual two weeks "somewhere" in the Caribbean. Americans are restricted from traveling to Cuba, so Steven had our travel agent make all the arrangements with cash, including getting into Cuba through Mexico. I was worried about the Cuban Immigration Services stamping our passports upon arrival in their country. Steven was instructed to have a blank piece of paper inside each of our passports so that when we arrived, Cuban Immigration agents would stamp the paper and not the actual page in the passport. Once we returned to Mexico, we were to throw away the paper, and our passports would remain "legal."

We had no intention of throwing away the stamped papers, but planned on having them arranged in a custom frame to proudly display in our office at home. Steven did not want us to have "any old piece" of blank paper; even though he was assured that the Cuban government did not care what they stamped. He took the passports to our printer and had the paper color matched and cut to the correct size of our passport pages.

Over the years, Steven had paid the IRS millions of dollars in taxes and felt that this payment entitled him to travel anywhere in the world, primarily since it was the United States government that forbade travel to Cuba. For this reason alone, he appeared more excited about the trip to Cuba than about our trip through Europe, but I knew that was not so.

The trips in this chapter are a sampling of our travels. I went on safaris in Kenya and Tanzania, I gorilla trekked in Uganda. I have skied throughout the U.S. and Canada. The only continent I did not step foot on was Antartica. I have been blessed to experience the diverse offerings of the world.

Our terrific traveling times were the highlight of my life. I fondly and vividly recall our trips when I am feeling depressed. I whisper a solemn "thank you" to Steven in heaven.

7

Decorating Toro Canyon

Late in the fall of 1995, Steven and I continued working together on the building of our dream home in Austin. He wanted to dictate the outside specifications to include our water gardens, landscaping, and the long cobblestone driveway. He asked me to take over everything on the inside, including all the fixtures and furnishings. Steven had hired a decorator to collaborate with me when we built the lake house. I now felt competent in my ability and asked that he allow me to decorate this house without the assistance of a decorator. I was thrilled beyond words when my husband gave me carte blanche and proclaimed that he had more money than I could spend. Naturally, I took that statement as a personal challenge!

I began by purchasing the furniture. Once the construction was completed, I wanted to be able to furnish the entire house at the same time as our official move-in date. I didn't want to be continually shopping for art and furnishings as we did with the lake house. Thank goodness he agreed with me.

I took a copy of the plans with me on several visits and purchased most of the furniture from the upscale store, Louis Shanks. I spent close to a million dollars decorating and furnishing, excluding the fine art and antique collections I'd started. Even I was surprised at the tally. Regardless, we both were still thrilled that everything was ideally suited to our tastes and styles.

After paying for the furniture, Steven decided that I could easily spend more money than was readily available. The dog bed I commissioned was hand-carved to match our bed and cost almost $6,000. Steven was more than happy to pay for the purchase, but not without sternly suggesting that I slow down so that he could catch up with my spending. He did state that the "little asshole" would never appreciate such an elegant bed, and he was correct. She never spent a single night sleeping in the bed, a fact about which Steven always reminded me. I then asked him if I could use the $500,000 he had given me the previous year to purchase artwork. He said he thought I should save the money, but if it was that important to me, I could do with it as I pleased since it was mine. Of course, the State never mentioned any of these facts during my trial.

The furniture I picked was made and carved from dark woods, both thick and dense. My favorite manufacturers were Baker, Henredon, and Thomas. As a contrast, it was my choice that most of the fine art be antique and in pastel colors, and I wanted to pay for it with my money.

Steven had the carpenters construct a rudimentary stool in every room in the house, so he could sit and observe the construction without having to drag his chair around. We agreed that the construction would commence at $1.1 million. This was the second home we built together, and we were aware that change orders can be costly. My husband felt that his presence on the site every day was required, even though we were paying for a construction foreman. Steven did a magnificent job, and I regularly told him how proud I was of his efforts.

The construction put a temporary halt to our overseas travels. I was looking for specific pieces of art for my collections, and I made several trips alone. I remembered seeing some beautiful porcelain in Italy when we purchased the white Carrara marble for the vanities in the lake house. I was quite proud of the lake house, decorated with loud; vibrant colors intermingled with artifacts from Africa and Asia with an eclectic mix of antique Mexican, Mayan, Mesoamerican, and Native American pieces. The lake house was "fun," according to Steven. I wanted our new residence to exude calm, peace, and tranquility; the colors I chose were muted, and the central theme was floral. I wanted flowers throughout the entire home. Steven also loved flowers and had them planted everywhere outside on the 2 1/2 acres of formal landscape. He surprised me at least once a week with a beautiful bouquet of fresh pink flowers. In turn, I surprised him once a week with one of his favorite desserts. Each of us had a sweet tooth.

I fell in love with the Majolica porcelain that we came across while touring museums in Europe. Majolica's earthenware is decorated by applying colorants with a brush on the raw, glazed surface. The thickness of the antique glaze melts, giving a glossy surface, maintaining the line quality of the surface decoration. Antique Majolica derived its name from the Spanish shipping port of Majolica in the 13th century. The vases, plates, and pitchers were elaborately decorated with flowers. In my hunt for antique Majolica, I discovered Barbotine in an Austin high-end boutique that boasted of specializing in exquisite home furnishings and décor for the "discriminating buyer." Steven just loved the wording of their ad campaign. I purchased several massive Barbotine jardinière vases that weighed over 20 pounds each. The vases were several thousand dollars apiece; Steven suggested I try to locate some in France. He wanted me to keep what I had purchased because he thought they were magnificent. He told me that my $500k was not going to last long and I could add to my collection by buying directly from the source at a lower cost, and they would have a more significant selection. France is where I first headed. Surprisingly, Steven suggested I go to France because he detested the French natives as a whole. He believed that they were rude and arrogant and just pretended to like Americans. He was adamant that they disliked us and told me, when in France, to tell the shop owners that I was born in Canada. He claimed they would charge me more money if I admitted to being an American. I never did confess, as everything was to be shipped to Texas.

I was overwhelmed by all the quaint shops. While in Paris, I did purchase a Chanel handbag or two with coordinating shoes, but did promise Steven that the majority of my time would be spent acquiring antique accessories. I felt all grown-up, for my 33 years of age in taking such a critical buying trip, but it was lonely. I must've called my husband dozens of times a day to get measurements for specific pieces and to question him about fitting the chosen pieces in different areas of our home. I also wanted his reassurance that I pleased him. He kept repeating he was proud that I was turning our home into a showplace. He never minded that our combined telephone bills averaged over $1,500 a month. He loved talking on the telephone, especially after a few cocktails. Sometimes, when at home, I hid the cordless phone, so he would not start making calls while intoxicated because he would be obnoxious after a few drinks.

The Barbotine vases intrigued me because of the stylized plant motifs, including flowers and tendrils that were not applied as an even layer, but in the form of thick incrustations in patches and trails. Most of the vases I bought had bouquets of flowers on them, where the impressionistic style could be seen in the enameled flowers. My favorite vases were gorgeous and painted in pinkish tones of brown and mauve with shades of cream. The ones I purchased were dated from the 18th and 19th centuries, and I had several dozen in my collection.

I noticed an enduring symbol everywhere in France and learned it was the "fleur-de-lis." This unique flower looks like a stylized lily, and I especially liked that the three leaves represented the medieval social classes: Those who worked, those who fought, and those who prayed; to me, that description was dreamy and romantic. When I drew an example for Steven and explained the meaning behind it, he had the flowers painted on the massive stone arch above the chef's grill in the kitchen. We also had it carved into the key of our limestone fireplace mantel.

While searching for Barbotine, I came across a magnificent and delicate antique Limoges trinket box. I thought that a collection of these boxes would be impressive as accent pieces for the bookshelves that lined the entire wall of our master bedroom. I traveled to Limoges, even though I was warned that it is not a city that calls for an extended stay. For me, my visit was worth the trip. I purchased dozens of trinket boxes and candy dishes all from the 18th century, being assured that they were some of the finest china pieces ever produced. I also purchased an antique Limoges Chocolate Pot. At the time, I did not have a specific place in mind to showcase it. I could not resist the pink tulips painted around the delicate pot because tulips are my favorite flower and pink is my signature color. Soon, I began noticing chocolate pots in all of the antique shops, making them another vast collection that I displayed in the large arched alcove in the butler's pantry.

My next stop was Dresden, Germany, whose rich cultural heritage makes it a popular tourist site. My primary interest was their antique porcelain. I purchased many Dresden pieces marked antique: porcelain figurines, urns, vases, and figural compotes. Shopkeepers could not believe that my purchases were not bought for a business purchase. They could not fathom the vast amount of my purchases being for just one home.

My last stop was in England, the Staffordshire district. I was told that it was the center of the English pottery industry, and my weakness was for the Staffordshire Spaniel figurines. The Spaniel breed of dog has always been my favorite. The charming canine figurines were created between 1840 and 1870. All decorated by hand, no two figures are exactly alike. With my sizable budget, I was able to purchase high-quality pieces. While amassing pairs of dogs, I became captivated with the antique Staffordshire inkwells, humidors, tobacco, cigarette and figural watch holders, vases, platters, pugs, whippets, cats, shepherd's dress, lions, lambs, and lidded bowls. The inkwells, humidors, cigarette and tobacco holders were displayed in our bar while the dozen or so pairs of dogs were arranged by our floral designer on top of our gigantic entertainment center. The other small and delicate pieces were displayed in the four locked glass cabinets in the formal guest bathroom and its adjoining entry area.

When I arrived home, Steven asked me to watch the movie, *The War of the Roses,* with him. I enjoyed the black comedy about a wealthy couple with a seemingly perfect marriage. He could not wait for me to see how their material possessions, Staffordshire pottery, became the center of an outrageous and bitter divorce battle. I asked him if that is what he thought was going to happen to us. He almost fell over laughing, and then asked me, "Darling, don't you understand? We have what most people would kill for." Just thinking about how true that statement turned out to be, sends chills up my spine. Steven boasted, to all who would listen, that we had the most extensive Staffordshire collection in the entire southwest region of the United States.

I traveled on to London to find additional Toby mugs and jugs for the bar. I was also captivated by Wedgewood's antique stoneware biscuit barrel or cracker jar. The barrels are about 6 inches high, and about 5 inches in diameter; the pieces I purchased had sterling silver bottoms, with button feet and sterling silver top rims with handles. The barrels were embellished with intricate beadwork in silver around the edge of both the top and bottom and the handles had a silver finial in the center. The pale-blue stoneware has an unglazed matte finish. The jasper dip designs around the base of the jars had scenes such as "Sacrificing Figures," "Cupids," and "Romanesque Motifs." I proudly displayed these jars on the shelves of the bookcases in our master bedroom.

While in London I also purchased many chocolate pots and antique trinket boxes. The porcelain boxes had long ago been used to store jewelry or other fine vanity items. When I called Steven earlier that day, he suggested the alcove in the butler's pantry as a perfect place for the chocolate pots, recommending that I start with at least 20 to 30, since the area was extensive. Every time I called home, he sounded like a kid at Christmas opening FedEx packages and freight containers filled with all of my purchases that I had shipped home ahead of me. Once in a while, he gently chided me for my clothing, shoes, and purse purchases being charged to his Visa instead of to my American Express card. I know it sounds silly, but I answered him by reminding him I was spending "my money" on the décor and "his money" on me. He seemed satisfied with my explanation and always remarked how beautiful I looked in Chanel, Burberry, or Christian Dior – my favorites and thankfully his favorites, too!

Arriving back in the States, I had to go through Customs in Miami. Steven was feeling restless and on edge, having been the sole caretaker of a moody teenager while I was off globe-trotting. He made arrangements to meet me in Miami, and together, we relaxed. The Florida Keys was a perfect place, as he wanted to sport fish and I wanted to try my hand at scuba diving. We spent a couple of days looking at condos to purchase.

Steven liked the Florida Keys because it gave him the feeling of being on a tropical vacation without leaving the U.S. The Florida Keys span about 110 miles and are connected by bridges and causeways. I liked Marathon the best because of its location in the middle and offered many relaxing vacation resorts. His favorite was Key West, also known as the Last Resort; he said it was like eating the last piece of pie.

Steven wanted me to decide if I wanted to own a condo in the Keys or South Padre. He enjoyed the lake house, but not nearly as much as I did. Living at that house, while building our dream home, took the "fun" out of it for him; he said he was too old to live in such close quarters with a temperamental teenager and two dogs and a cat that did not respect or listen to him. I made him promise that he would not buy a condo until we were settled in the new house for at least a year. The thought of having to decorate another residence was a daunting task that I was not ready to take on.

We arrived back in Austin rested and happy. After moving into our home, we enjoyed many happy times together in both of our homes. At my insistence, Steven dropped the third-residence idea. He then diverted his attention to planning a $600,000 mausoleum with an elaborate bronze gated entry and massive stained glass rear window. He ordered our caskets and had an artist make a drawing of what the finished resting place would be like. I could not fathom Steven's wanting to purchase a mausoleum that cost as much as the construction of our entire lake house. When I questioned him, he said that he grew up dirt-poor and wanted to leave a lasting legacy, claiming that he could not think of a better way to prove his success. He was so convinced that the homes and business ventures could always be sold, but the mausoleum would last forever.

Once our dream house was ready to be shown off, my husband began planning an elaborate, formal house-warming party inviting over 250 guests. He met with the caterer, valet parking company, printer, and florist and personally supervised every detail of the affair. He boasted that he spent over $15k just on the caterer, and I know that the entire party cost more than $35k. I told Steven when the girls married that I expected an affair just as elaborate for each of them. He did not care about expense, being the consummate host, who enjoyed showing off. I was just happy that he was generous and not a penny pincher. Our excesses came back to haunt me during the trial; had I testified on my behalf, the jury may have had a better understanding of my lavish spending, for which Steven was equally guilty. He had always encouraged me on every shopping trip to spend whatever I wanted. The predatory press crucified me on the front page of our local newspaper after the twins sued me for Steven's estate because I flaunted wealth.

Our Toro Canyon home in Austin was selected for the annual American Institute of Architects Homes Tour, Austin Chapter. This honor thrilled Steven immensely. Being flamboyant, he wanted everyone to see our home. He enjoyed being flashy and telling stories about the fine art we acquired while traveling and the memories each represented. The tour occurred over a weekend for about 8 hours each day. The purpose was to showcase the work of local architects so that the general community could see the value of their designs. I agreed to allow the home tour because a strict set of rules must be adhered to before entering private homes. Tickets for admission are sold to cover the cost of the American Institute of Architect's expenses, such as security. We personally contracted off-duty sheriffs to provide additional security.

Steven did not want to be home when the tour was scheduled so we traveled to China during that time. Steven had a magnificent surprise waiting for me when we arrived home. He had Ian, our mural painter, paint a beautifully detailed Romanesque scene in the recessed ceiling above the bed in the master bedroom. It was indeed a work of art. I loved staring at it before falling asleep for a nap. He had arranged for the painting to be done while we were in China. My husband was always trying to outdo his last gift to me. At Steven's instruction, Ian finished the painting before the AIA Home tour began.

8

Meeting Tracey Tarlton

I first sought help for severe depression in early March 1999, at The Pavilion Psychiatric Hospital in Austin, Texas. People could not understand why I was suffering from depression. They said things like "What could she possibly be depressed about?" I had a loving husband who provided us with two magnificent homes, which were furnished and decorated with top quality items from across the world. I had a jewelry collection that rivaled royalty, and a wardrobe that included fashion and accessories from many top designers. We were always globe-trotting on vacations, and so much more; the list was endless. What people did not realize was that I suffered from post-traumatic stress disorder, PTSD. This disorder was a direct result of years of abuse beginning when I was just a little girl. It took years of counseling for me to understand that I did not cause this; I was a victim. No matter how beautiful my life was, the depression was always lurking in the shadows, waiting to rear its ugly self. My marriage to Steven had nothing to do with my depression. It was my husband who was diligent in seeking the proper help I needed.

At the time of my first admission into The Pavilion, I was collecting donations for a silent auction to generate funds for the Montessori School, in Briarcliff, owned by Willie Nelson's daughter. Steven and I were well known in the community and spent vast amounts of money at different establishments. Our popularity helped me gather sizable donations of art, furniture, furnishings, and gift certificates to be auctioned off. To honor my obligation to the school, I depended on the twins to help finalize the donations while I was at The Pavilion; the school was depending on my participation.

This arrangement entitled the twins, for the first time, to have complete and unsupervised access to my Cadillac and my SUV. Before my hospitalization I did not allow them to drive my SUV, because of worry about their safety; they tend to roll over easily, and the girls were not experienced drivers. Needing their help to fulfill my commitment, I gave them the "keys to the kingdom." Steven and I had donated $5,000 for a table seating ten at the auction. He wanted to be prominently seated up front and center during the event. He surprised all three of us girls with stunning gowns purchased from St. Thomas, an exclusive women's clothier in Austin. I ended up loaning my new gown to my friend, Dawn, as she was going to the auction, so the dress would not be a complete waste of money. I gave four of the seats at our table to the twins and their boyfriends as additional payment to them for helping me. They wanted to see Willie Nelson perform up close and personal. I treated them to a day of pampering at the pricey salon in our new shopping center. The other six seats were given to Jim and Dawn and other friends because my husband did not want to attend without me. To show appreciation for my help, Willie wrote a song for me titled, "We Sing for Celeste," displayed in the auction events catalog. Willie signed a CD, expressing his gratitude and gave it to the girls for me. My daughters enjoyed the attention they received that evening and reportedly beamed throughout the gala.

When they moved out, they stole my framed, autographed CD. They also stole the framed Fox 42 and KBVO TV license plates that were from Steven's and my Cadillacs.

The next day the girls complained to me at the

hospital that I was a terrible mother for asking them to run errands for me. Their complaining made me feel like I was treating them as indentured servants. I cried and did not sleep at all that night. I did not tell Steven what they had said, knowing that would add a note of querulousness to their already-fractured relationship. Instead, I continued to try to bring peace between the three of them in any way possible.

When I first met Tracey Tarlton at The Pavilion in early March 1999, she was unable to tie her shoelaces and her appearance was disheveled. She had difficulty venturing outside the hospital to smoke. She told me that her medication was disabling her and that she could not wait until it stabilized in her body. I did not know it at the time; she was being treated for alcoholism, drug addiction, aggression, and schizophrenia with delusions. She led me to believe that she was undergoing treatment for a bipolar disorder, directly related to her violent childhood abuse. I found out at my trial the documented reasons for her stay at The Pavilion.

My first feelings for Tracey were of sadness and sympathy. My daughters urged me to befriend her, as her condition also tugged at their heartstrings. They met her during a visit with me and eventually began doing things for her, like helping to tie her shoes, holding onto her as she walked to the smoking area, and helping her light her cigarettes. They spent endless amounts of time sitting with us, while she and I smoked on the outside patio at the hospital. Over time, my daughters grew close with Tracey.

It was not long before my daughters and I became involved with the other patients on my floor. It seemed the more that I focused on other people's problems the less I felt the pain of my own. I had my daughters bring fast-food or pizza to the patients on my floor on a daily basis. When I discovered that one patient had no clothes to wear upon release, I had the girls purchase a week's worth of clothing for him, including underwear and socks. I wrote checks for patients' bills and also paid back taxes they owed. I even bought some of the patients' artwork, knowing I would never display it. I tried to help anyone with whom I came in contact at the hospital, not just with Tracey. It was a good feeling to help others. I treated the staff to lunches and dinners and often sent fresh pastries and baked goods to their break room.

Due to my desire to be needed, Tracey and I became close friends. A trauma bond between us surfaced; she and I had experienced similar childhood situations, which included years of sexual molestation that began when we were just young children. My abuse was brought upon me by my adoptive father and later by my brother, Cole, when I was a preteen. For Tracey, it was her mother who molested her repeatedly. She understood the anguish and the shame that accompanied us into adulthood. It did not matter to me that she was a lesbian; I had finally found someone to whom I could "open-up" and not feel uncomfortable in her company. She understood the humiliation I felt about being abused. We both understood the feelings of disassociation, of not wanting to be touched, or to allow ourselves to be close to other people. The violence in our lives helped us to connect on a deeper level.

Tracey is one of the most brilliant people I have met in my life. As her genius like intelligence impresses me, conversely, her grandiose thinking is a mystery to me, especially regarding her perception of our friendship. She later testified at my criminal trial that I flirted with her and "wanted her" from the moment I had laid eyes on her. Tracey wrote in her journals, "Celeste only wanted to be friends" and my defense attorney presented it to the court, but the jury ignored it. In truth, all I wanted was a friend who liked me for me, good or bad. I found it comforting that she did not expect me to give her anything but my time and friendship. I did not realize that all the time I gave her, as a confidant and friend, would be the green light she needed for her to become obsessed with me; her motives were psychological. In her mind, she saw moves and loves that suggested and fed her lesbian bias.

For this reason, people give her a pass for her bad behavior, because her preference is something she cannot help. People think I manipulated her, when in all truthfulness, I wanted Tracey's friendship, not to be a sexual partner in her life. Written in her journal as her truth and reality, and retained as evidence, it is clear Tracey imagined a nonexistent relationship, "It gets hard to pretend that I have a girlfriend who wants to see me."

Towards the end of our friendship, my inner voice did tell me that she had more than a platonic friendship in mind. I was in denial, telling myself, "It's not all about you, Celeste." I called myself an egomaniac, thinking to flatter myself by imagining she had romantic feelings for me. I scolded myself for not being a better friend to her. I also wanted to prove to everyone, especially to myself, that I was not homophobic.

Eventually, Tracey and I were released from the hospital. My release came first while waiting to enter a hospital that had a program specializing in post-traumatic stress disorder. Steven was flying all over the country, personally researching various hospitals to continue my treatment.

When visiting Tracey at The Pavilion, the patients were not always supervised when outside in the courtyard smoking. Sometimes, we piled into my car and went to a nearby park with some of the other patients. I do not understand why we felt compelled to leave the area. We were not doing anything other than visiting with each other and smoking cigarettes. I guess we thought it was against the rules and no one was around to tell us otherwise. We made these short trips a few times, stopping at a convenience store along the way for sodas, snacks, and cigarettes.

I visited Tracey at The Pavilion on a daily basis, and sometimes, Kristina went with me. Tracey, too, was waiting to go to another treatment facility. I did not realize that she could not be released until she found a long-term treatment center. Her suicidal tendencies, aggression, and addictive behaviors had not improved. I assumed she had not decided on where to go since Steven had not yet decided where I was going. Tracey was eventually escorted to the Menninger Clinic in Kansas by a friend of hers.

Steven decided he wanted me to go to the Timberlawn Psychiatric Hospital, in Dallas, Texas. He playfully teased me that after he had traveled all over the country the best place for me was in our backyard. He always tried to do the best for me, and I loved him for that.

When Tracey found out that I was going to Timberlawn, she made arrangements to transfer there. Out of friendship, I wanted to help her; I asked our travel agent to book the necessary flights. Tracey paid for all her expenses with her credit cards. Her mental faculties were so deteriorated that she had to be escorted by a nurse from Menninger. Her medical records were presented to the court, and it was written that she had severe hallucinations on the flight. She saw "little green men" on the backs of the airplane seats. I knew none of this information until my trial.

During my civil trial, the twins told their attorneys that I had paid for Tracey's ticket, which I had not. The girls did not know that I had discussed her travel with Steven. He said I should help her arrange the flight, but Tracey should be responsible for paying her fare.

I was admitted to Timberlawn Hospital a few days after Tracey's arrival there. At first, we were roommates. The prosecution was relentless in court over the fact that Tracey gave me a back massage during that time. I had no idea that anything could or would even be construed by

what I thought was an innocent gesture. For years I had
paid for professional massages on a weekly basis, so I
never thought there was anything sexual about it. On many
vacations, Steven and I received daily massages, always
done with us being completely nude. I never felt
uncomfortable or uneasy about our nudity. When Tracey
massaged my back, I kept my underclothes on because she
was gay. Feeling nothing sexual about it and having a stiff
back, I thought only of my relief. I was having spasms in
my back from carrying the luggage to the room; I had not
packed lightly. I did not care if the place thought I was a
tourist.

Our cohabitation was short-lived. Tracey
participated in the same group therapy sessions I attended.
This unfortunate coupling led her to become antagonistic
towards my husband because she heard some of my marital
issues being openly discussed. It was easy for me to blame
someone else for my problems, especially in a group
setting with a bunch of women who were just as eager to
"husband-bash."

Tracey and I became involved in a disagreement. I
did not like how she took it upon herself to advise me to
divorce Steven. She knew very little about him and me.
Her forcefulness with the issue disturbed me. She was

transferred to the adult psychiatric unit, where she was housed with other patients who were suicidal, and had drug and alcohol issues. Tracey blamed Steven for her move, even though I told her that I was the one who had requested the move to a new room. She became enraged and paced with clenched fists.

During the trial, I found out that she had told her therapist, "If he (Steven) hurts her (meaning me), then he'll meet with an untimely death." Another similar statement was made in a therapy session, "This would be solved if certain people met with untimely deaths." This comment had never been reported to us; I had no idea she wanted him to die. Had I known her awful thoughts, recorded by her therapist, I would have immediately ended the friendship, and we probably would have filed a Protective Order against Tracey. I am sure the hospital did not tell us, knowing that I would leave, taking with me the large sums of money Steven was paying them since our health insurance did not cover my treatment.

I did not know that Tracey wished Steven harm, and eventually she and I became friends again. She stayed in a local motel down the street from Timberlawn, while attending as an out-patient with the group therapy sessions. I felt comfortable around her. She knew all my feelings,

211

deep, dark secrets, emotional turmoil, and character flaws; every issue that I was forced to confront in my group therapy sessions. She gained my trust and knew so much about me; she seemed genuinely concerned about my well-being. I believe this was the reason I so readily disregarded her attention as nothing more than platonic friendship.

When Tracey's medical insurance ran out, she was forced to move back to Austin, where she continued her weekly therapy with a private psychologist.

Steven continued to visit me every Thursday at Timberlawn, where we participated in private marriage counseling sessions. After a couple of months, I graduated to out-patient status. Steven rented a hotel room for me in the Galleria area of Dallas, about a 30-minute drive from Timberlawn; he said the hotels closer to Timberlawn were in rough neighborhoods and worried about my safety. He always thought about every detail.

Steven rented the room by the month, even though I drove home to Austin on weekends to spend time with him and the girls. He also stayed in the hotel room for his Thursday visits and counseling sessions. He did not want me to have to pack and unpack every week. I was heavily medicated with anti-depressants, and I drove the five-hour, one-way trip, back and forth between Austin and Dallas, which resulted in my being involved in several minor car accidents. I had visits from Tracey during my weekend visits home.

I was at Timberlawn from late March 1999 to June 1999, at which time I had been making progress, and for a period of time, was feeling better. I was released as an out-patient. The condition of the release meant that I would be an in-patient at Timberlawn at the end of nearly every week. My visits home to Austin were limited to one or two weekends a month. April was the first month of my out-patient status, and May was a difficult month for me, so these visits were more restricted than those toward the end of my treatment. The prosecution made it appear that Tracey was a routine visitor at my home, and that is not true. If she had been a regular visitor, she would have known all the doors were on sliders, not hinges. During visits to our house, she spent time with Steven, because he likes to drink and likes to have a drinking companion. I could not drink alcohol, due to the severe interaction, when mixed with the medications I was taking. I thought their drinking together would solidify a friendship between them. I still had not known that she was an alcoholic and a drug addict. She kept this information well concealed from me. All her interactions with Steven involved abundant amounts of alcohol.

During the week, both of my girls spent time at Tracey's house; she often helped them with their homework assignments. I helped them, too, after Steven had my computer system installed in the Dallas hotel room.

Tracey and I helped Kristina write a book report on Dr. Jekyl and Mr. Hyde, while we were on a 3-way conference call that lasted past 2 a.m. The hotel front desk clerk sent and received numerous faxes with edits and corrections so that Kristina could claim the paper as her own. She did not bother to read the book, which made the task incredibly frustrating. At that time, I was unfamiliar with sending and receiving documents via email; our telephone bill was astronomical, due to the many faxes and conference calls. Steven was angry when he found out why we were on the phone so late. When he came to the hotel, the desk clerk informed him about the late night faxes which were numerous and disruptive. He was livid and embarrassed when he learned the hotel knew we were helping Kristina cheat. He was furious because the fax machine was located in our home office, he did not want the girls in our wing of the house. He was adamant that he did not want them using our computer or our fax machine. I was mad at myself for making Steven mad at me; I should have done the right thing and told Kristina to read the book and write the report. I was ashamed that I again disregarded one of his few requests that he ever made of me.

Tracey and the girls became close. She spent much more time with them than I was able to, due to me being a patient at Timberlawn. I encouraged their spending time together, just as I had made Tracey's friendship with my husband even closer.

There was a time when I was staying at the hotel, Kristina called and said Tracey was suicidal. At my urging, Kristina drove to Tracey's house in the middle of the night, as Steven had long been passed out. Kristina found Tracey enraged, pacing, and acting paranoid; she confiscated Tracey's handgun and turned it over to the Austin Police Department. I later learned that she had left Tracey at home with her 20-gauge shotgun. Kristina was a senior in high school at the time and naively thought that a person could not kill themselves with a long-barreled gun. I regretted that I had encouraged the friendship by allowing my teenage daughters to become enmeshed in Tracey's unstable lifestyle. To this day, I am very grateful they suffered no physical repercussions, and can only pray the mental anguish to which I had exposed them is now just a bad memory.

Celeste

By April of 1999, Steven was at the end of his rope regarding the twins. He had discovered that they both were caught cheating on their History and English correspondence courses at the University of Texas. This cheating was especially embarrassing to him because the call letters to his television station, KBVO, were named after the university mascot, a Longhorn named Bevo. Steven was well known in university circles. The girls turned in identical work for each subject, not thinking that the same person graded both papers. Justin completed the same history paper for the twins and Christopher completed the same English paper for them. Why they would assume that each student would have a private grader is a mystery to me. A school administrator called Steven regarding this unfortunate situation, so there was no way I could cover for them.

These two classes were all the girls needed to complete to graduate with the class of 1999. I had retained both girls in 2nd grade, so they were always a year behind their cousin in school, though there was only a two-week age difference between them.

Steven was furious about the academic cheating, and I was shocked by the depth of this wrath. I cannot imagine what would have happened if he discovered I paid college students to complete the twins assignments. He told me I was no longer to cover for the girls. To allow them to graduate on time, he enrolled them in a summer-school program in another public school district in Austin. The tension between them was so thick that Kristina left the Toro Canyon home and moved in with my ex-husband, Jimmy. Again, Kristina claimed that she was being abused, but this time said that it was Steven who was verbally and emotionally abusing her. I was angry and disappointed with Kristina for "crying wolf" to curry favor; she never knew what abuse was and to say she was being abused to manipulate people hit a sore spot with me. Jimmy drove her to the other side of Austin every day to and from school and also tried to help her "get her head on straight," as Steven had requested.

With encouragement from my husband, on one of my weekends off from Timberlawn, I went with Tracey to Atlanta to attend her niece's wedding. Before the trip, we went to two of my favorite clothing stores in Austin to buy outfits for the wedding. The prices were a little steep, but Tracey did pay for her purchases with her credit cards. In Atlanta, we shared a hotel room, but not a bed; it was not unusual for me to travel this way with friends or my daughters. I did not want to be alone, I do not like to be alone.

Anytime I left Austin to go on shopping trips with my other friends, we always shared a room. My friend and Maid of Honor, Ana, and I shared a room in New York for a week. My other friend, Dawn, and I shared a room in Seattle for over a week and slept in the same bed. I shared a room, but not a bed, with my female friend Kyle, when we went shopping in Dallas. Another friend, Dana, and I slept in the same bed at her sister's house, while on a trip to Houston for haircuts. Kristina and I slept in the same bed until she was 19 years old. Women often do sharing of this sort. Being afraid to be alone was the reason why I like sharing a bed. Many times I slept with my mom. Later, when mom worked, I stayed with friends, rather than being alone. My mom worked late and left early in the morning. Of course, prison has cured me of this habit. I have never felt more alone than I do in prison. However, this was another area in which the prosecution honed in on during my trial to make it appear that I was an "undercover" homosexual.

Tracey was a manager for a large, upscale bookstore and wanted to host a party for the employees. She asked me if I had any ideas where she could have the party. I prided myself on the ability to be the perfect hostess and party planner. I had extensive experience with throwing and hosting parties for my friends at the country club and elsewhere, including the numerous parties my husband and I held in both our homes.

Since Tracey's house was in shambles due to remodeling, I volunteered to give the party for her at our lake house. I initially offered to throw it at our residence in Austin, but she was afraid the bookstore employees would be intimidated by our opulence. I did not tell her that I had invested over $750,000 in the lake house because I was afraid that would also intimidate them.

The theme was "A Fashion Victim Party," because I felt everyone would be more at ease and have fun and not worry about being perfect. Everyone was to dress in their worst fashion reject. I bought material in my signature pink in a crazy paisley pattern and had my tailor make a pantsuit for me. Everyone thought the party was a hit and Tracey's companions had a good laugh at my crazy outfit.

Someone from the bookstore made marijuana brownies. I ate quite a few bars because they were delicious. I must have been "high," because the next thing I remember was being awakened on the front lawn by the automatic sprinklers coming on at 3:30 a.m. I staggered into the house and went to bed in my wet clothes. Kristina and Justin came over early the next morning in the guise of wanting to help clean up because it was Sunday, the maid's day off. I should have realized something was up because they had never before volunteered to clean anything, especially Justin.

During the trial, the prosecution produced photos of the marijuana brownies, rolling papers, liquor bottles, and the complete disarray including over-flowing ashtrays. Unbeknownst to me, the teens bought a disposable camera and had taken pictures of the mess before waking us. I question why they bought a disposable camera when they both owned top-of-the-line 35mm cameras. I had no idea they had even taken the photographs and can only surmise that they were planning on blackmailing me with them. Everyone knew Steven's private photographer had been hired to take the pictures at Tracey's party. It is clear to me now that the kids had ulterior motives back then. I often wonder about their secret discussions and the plans they were conniving against me and why.

The prosecution focused significantly on my planning and hosting of the party for Tracey's employees. Held during the first week of July 1999, the photos had not surfaced until 2002. The girls testified at my trial that Steven was unaware of the parties that I gave, which was not true. I charged everything, and he religiously reviewed all bills before making payments. I had nothing to hide and told my husband all about the parties and how much fun everyone had. He scrutinized everything in his world, as he had not reached his station in life by being ignorant or careless. He was well aware of the fact that I often threw parties and he indulged me by showing interest in the various themes I planned for them. He was the one who suggested a "vulgar" paisley pattern for my pantsuit. He attended several of the parties, but not all. I always hired the same vendors Steven used, because he insisted that our loyalty repays good quality service.

I had thrown a surprise party for Dana's 40th birthday, a surprise party for Dawn's 30th birthday, a graduation party for Dawn, a "lot party," when we bought a piece of property, an elaborate baby shower, parties for our investment clubs, and Bunko games. Steven had attended only a couple of the parties and stayed briefly, long enough to say hello and visit with a few of the guests. He never minded paying for all the parties and preferred to remain at home sipping his "Wolfy."

Steven held a small dinner celebration for the girls at the country club following their graduation ceremony. In attendance were Steven, Jennifer, Kristina, Tracey,

Christopher, Justin, and his mother, Mrs. Grimm, Jimmy
and myself. Jimmy attended the graduation ceremony, but
did not join us at the club for dinner, even though Steven
did invite him. Since Steven and Tracey had several
cocktails at the club, she came home with us. When they
continued drinking on the front patio, I realized that this
was the only time I had ever seen my husband have a
cocktail after dinner at our home.

Later, I was sitting in one of the rocking chairs on
the right side of the patio. Tracey had been sitting next to
Steven in one of the rocking chairs on the other side. She
got up, staggered over to me and placed both her hands on
each arm of my chair. She leaned close to me as if wanting
to kiss me, which made me feel incredibly uncomfortable.
She was totally in my space, which I detested. When I
pushed her away, she became angry and belligerent and
started arguing with Steven when he returned from the
bathroom. Ultimately, she wanted to go home but was far
too intoxicated to drive. Jennifer's friend, Christopher,
drove Tracey home in her car and Kristina and I followed
them in my car so that Christopher would not have to take
a taxi back.

I found out later, after Tracey shot Steven, she had
taken off her clothes that night in front of my daughters and

222

Celeste

Christopher. Completely nude, she rambled on about how she was "in love" with me. Had I been told of this "little act," Tracey would have never been allowed to attend the graduation party at Jimmy's house. Christopher told me, after Steven recovered from the shooting, that he had been horrified to see that Tracey was extremely hairy. I was repulsed to hear him say that her pubic hair grew from her navel to her mid-thighs and she had many long hairs around her nipples. I had not known these details that later added to my disgust of her.

The following night was Jimmy's graduation party for the girls at his house. Tracey had since called and profusely begged for forgiveness, blaming the previous night's incident on the alcohol she had consumed. Steven did not attend, saying that he had no intention of going to "that side of town." At the party, everyone had too much to drink, including the girls. Jennifer was so drunk, she fell on her face and received, what I later called "road rash," a scrape on her forehead and chin. I had a few cocktails, against my better judgment, and foolishly combined alcohol with my medication. I was light-headed and got sick to my stomach. I went upstairs and passed out, fully clothed, on Jimmy's bed.

I do not recall waking up until mid-morning the

next day. The following events were relayed to me by Kristina and Jimmy: Kristina said she went upstairs and saw Tracey kissing me, while I was unconscious. She went downstairs and asked Jimmy to help. He told Tracey to leave and then locked me inside his bedroom, placing the door key above the door. A short time later he returned to check on me. Again, he found Tracey was trying to kiss me. He said that I told him; "She is trying to make me a lesbian, and I don't want to be one." I did not realize until my trial that Tracey was an erotomaniac. Later, when she left, she was arrested for drunk driving not far from Jimmy's house. Her car was impounded, and she was taken to jail. During my trial, Jimmy's account of what happened was entirely disregarded by the prosecution.

The twins drove me home around 11:00 a.m., shortly after I woke up. I found out from Steven that Tracey had been calling the house all night from the jail. He was furious and told me to get her out of jail and that I was never to see her again. He told me to blame it on him that she was not welcome in our life anymore; he was concerned about her unpredictable behavior and wanted us out of harm's way, especially after spending the night in jail. The girls and I went to the jail and helped arrange bail. We picked up her vehicle from the impound yard and delivered it to her house. Kristina and I returned to the jail and waited for her to be released. All the way to her house I blamed Steven for breaking up my friendship with Tracey. It was easier for me to hide behind my husband than to face her wrath in the car; I was not sure what her reaction would be. I was a coward and I should have told her that I was also tired of her and her shenanigans. Tracey called him a "fat fuck" all the way to her house. I live with deep feelings of guilt, and I admit that I never offered a favorable word on my husband's behalf, but just kept my mouth closed like a timid child. From the time Kristina and I dropped Tracey off, after picking her up from the jail, until after Steven was shot, I never saw her. She continued making excessive calls on all our phone lines, wanting our friendship to resume. I felt like she was stalking me. The girls told Tracey I was unavailable when she called.

Tracey was a loose cannon. Traits of Tarlton include numerous attempts at suicide; many times sought psychiatric treatment; was diagnosed as delusional; was bipolar, had both auditory and visual hallucinations; was admitted to several mental institutions; and was obsessed with trying to build lesbian relationships with married women, especially me. It is difficult to accept this unstable person confessed to shooting my husband and was able to make a plea bargain with the State for a reduced sentence.

One time Tracey picked up a complete stranger, Reginald Breaux, outside a convenience store. They drove around drinking beer, and an argument of some sort ensued. Tracey pulled a knife on the man, ordered him out of her vehicle, then tried to run him over. She was arrested and remained in jail for several days before the charges were dropped.

I was looking forward to an upcoming trip Steven and I had planned. The trip was to be extended, one that I was sure would get rid of Tracey, once and for all. We were to be away for almost two months, so she would have no way to call or reach me. My mistake was in letting her know the dates we would be traveling.

We were to leave on October 3, 1999, and planned to pack for the trip the day before. Instead, Tracey shot my Steven at 2:30 a.m. on October 2, 1999. I did not know at the time, but the girls had secretly continued to see Tracey at her house on a regular basis. A neighbor who lived across the street from Tracey talked with my attorney, Catherine Baen, and planned on testifying, on my behalf, in regards to seeing Jennifer and Kristina spending a tremendous amount of time at Tracey's house, especially just before the shooting. Kristina, not me, had keys to

Tracey's house. Our cars, and those of the girls, were noticeable in her neighborhood. Tracey's neighbor, who would have testified, died from breast cancer days before my trial began. Catherine spoke with the neighbor at length and those discussions were not permitted in the trial. At the trial, the girls were less than truthful and claimed they rarely talked with her. Tracey's friends and employees testified that they never saw me with Tracey after the graduation party. The prosecution also disregarded this testimony and twisted the facts to tailor to their theories.

In 2006, when I was at Mt. View prison, a fellow inmate, Wanda White, approached me, while I was sitting on the bench. Her sworn statement, "Tracey had told me this on the rec field. She told me that she killed Steven because she wanted him out of the way because she was getting too obsessed with Celeste, but that Celeste didn't know she had feelings for her. Celeste just knew her feelings were of friendship. But after she got rid of him, she was going to approach Celeste and admit she wanted to be with her as a lover."

In 2002, the front page headline and an accompanying article in the Austin-American Statesman read, *"Tracey Tarlton pleaded guilty to the 1999 shooting of retired television executive, Steven Beard, Jr., and agreed to testify against Beard's widow in her Capital Murder case.* " Tarlton received a plea-bargained sentence of 20 years for her testimony. She was released on parole in mid-2011. To avoid a possible death sentence or life in prison, she had a motive to testify against me.

Tarlton spun a tale of meeting with me on Friday, October 1, 1999, for a walk-through at the Toro Canyon home, specifying what door to use and where to park. The Beard family planner and my planner showed appointments. I went to two hair salons and cashed a check at the bank during the time of the alleged walk-through. The maid, along with business personnel and records, provided proof that the walk-through could not have taken place, as testified by Tarlton. Christopher Doose arrived at the Toro Canyon home from San Angelo, neither he or anyone else saw Tarlton or her vehicle anywhere in the vicinity.

A sexual relationship, both at St. David's and at Timberlawn, was part of Tarlton's sworn statement, but I VEHEMENTLY DENY IT. Motels were mentioned, but there were never records produced for any so-called liaisons. The teenagers, with their devious behavior, could not provide any pictures to support their testimony of an intimate situation with Tarlton.

Celeste

Her recount of activity was given over two years after the shooting and contradicted reality in many ways. It was all hearsay.

Tarlton gave a timeline for the prearranged walk-through of the home when I had an ironclad alibi documented by business records.

She stated she let herself into the Beard mansion through "hinged doors." All seven sets of doors were on sliders. A proven fabrication.

Tarlton testified that the security gate at the entrance to the enclave had been left unlocked for her access on the night of the shooting. The massive gate had been removed several months before the shooting because another house was under construction. The gate was to be reinstalled after the construction was completed; as of the time in question, the gate was nowhere in sight. A proven fabrication.

She said that she climbed stairs inside the home to enter our master bedroom from the patio. No stairs exist where she claimed to have been. A proven fabrication.

She testified that I made botulism and we allegedly covered Steven's head with a plastic trash bag. Documentation from the hospital to support the theory of poisoning or asphyxiation were not submitted as evidence because no such records existed. On the day in question when she said we covered Steven's head with a trash bag, I was with Jodi, Marilou's granddaughter, school clothes shopping. A proven fabrication.

The stories about sleeping pills, to which the pharmacist testified, stated that there was no "overuse" of sleeping pills. The bottles of sleeping pills taken into custody by the police were hardly used. Only Steven picked up our prescriptions. A proven fabrication.

Tarlton's confession confirms what the police wanted to hear: I was somehow involved. The trial proved, beyond a reasonable doubt, that Tarlton shot Steven because she wanted to be with me and that alone.

9

Kristina and Jennifer

Jennifer moved in with us after Craig died. It was then that I suspected my daughter was a lesbian. It was more than her tom-boyishness, similar to Tracey's in looks and nature, which influenced my thinking. I just knew these truths in the pit of my stomach. When trying to discuss this matter with Steve, he became angry with me. He claimed that, by my thinking that way, and not exposing her to "girlish things," I would cause her to become a lesbian. He did not understand that people are born that way and believed it was caused by factors such as life experiences and upbringing.

Steven had a plan and enrolled both girls in etiquette classes. He was sure that instruction in manners, meals, and social graces would be all that Jennifer needed to point her in the right direction. He said the classes would help Kristina brush up on her social skills for formal functions later in life. He said both girls needed to learn correct dining etiquette.

As time passed, I expressed my feelings about Jennifer's sexual orientation with my friends, Marilou and Dawn. When Jennifer began dating Christopher Doose, Steven was happy, satisfied that his plans were successful, but I was not so sure. Christopher was so effeminate that I always suspected their dating was a cover-up. I never once considered them engaged in a sexual relationship. After my trial, they parted company. Several years later, my jeweler told Spencer that Jennifer had come into the store to purchase wedding rings for herself and her soon-to-be wife.

I am surrounded by homosexuality in prison, which does not bother me. I believe each person is entitled to live their life as they are and not conceal their true identity. I accept that my daughter has chosen this lifestyle. I love her.

I recall a vicious argument I had with Kristina when she was in her late teenage years. She was screaming hurtful things at me, her anger was boiling over. I wanted to hurt her more than she was hurting me and screamed back at her the dirty truth about my deep rooted shame, "Well, at least you never had a big nasty dick sticking out of you when you weren't even in kindergarten yet!" I was taken back that I said this aloud. I kept that dark, evil secret from my daughters all through the years. We both stopped yelling at each other. Kristina was mortified at the reality of what I said. We hugged and cried.

When the girls graduated from high school, I offered them a trip to any destination in the world to celebrate their accomplishment. They chose Australia and New Zealand.

Initially, the trip was booked for the entire family, but Steven ultimately begged off, not wanting to be on an airplane for 24 hours straight. He made alternate arrangements for a family trip to Canada in July. On the way back from that trip we planned to stop in Stanwood, Washington at the storage unit so that the girls could search through their deceased father, Craig's, personal belongings in hopes to find mementos.

Steven did not want me to take the girls to Washington without him. He felt that I had no control over them and that I let them take advantage of me. He begrudgingly agreed to allow the boyfriends to go with us and insisted on separate hotel rooms. Of course, behind his back, I told them they could sleep where they wanted, as long as in the morning they would return to their correct rooms before we called them to join us for breakfast.

Purchased primarily for this trip, my husband bought a fully loaded Suburban with a flat-screen DVD-TV and video games with movies galore.

Once we hit the higher elevations in the Rocky Mountains, Steven became erratic, belligerent. His physician confirmed that his behavior was due to a lack of oxygen and ordered it for him.

When we arrived in Seattle, Steven felt much better at sea level. We stopped at the storage unit in Stanwood, as planned. We donated their father's car to a local women's shelter. The girls were very disappointed upon finding that their father's only personal effects were mostly articles of clothing. They still had no photographs of him.

We shipped the clothes back to Texas because I planned to hire someone to make a lap quilt out of them for each of the girls. It was the only idea I had to salvage something belonging to Craig since we had gone through a costly and emotional two-year court battle to obtain the clothes for the girls. I felt that a lap quilt would cover them with a feeling of peace when they thought about Craig. Steven flew home from Seattle because he could not withstand the drive back through the high altitudes and still required prescription oxygen.

After leaving my husband at the airport, instead of

driving straight back to Texas, the teenagers and I headed to Camano Island, a two ½-hour drive out of our way. We knew that Craig's mother had photographs of their father, and Jennifer knew how to get into her house. We stopped at the local grocery store in Stanwood and bought four pairs of kitchen rubber gloves, to avoid leaving fingerprints.

Christopher, Jennifer's boyfriend, refused to go inside; he had aspirations of becoming a future U. S. President and did not want to risk tarnishing his reputation. Funny thing, though, is Christopher did not mind perjuring himself at the trial, and he conveniently could not remember so many details when questioned under oath. How does one forget such information? He had no qualms about the plotting and planning of our mission, and he even volunteered to be the getaway driver. We parked in front of the house because Christopher surmised that being so obvious would make us look less guilty. The remaining four of us went into the backyard and put on the bright yellow gloves. Mine were bright pink since that has always been my signature color. Jennifer climbed into the kitchen through an unlocked window over the sink, after I moved the knick-knacks on the sill out of the way. She let the three of us in through the sliding glass door. We followed her into the living room and removed some of the photos of their father from the albums, but never went into any other part of the house. I rationalized this was not a crime because we were retrieving what rightfully belonged to my daughters.

The burglary took less than three minutes. We left through the sliding glass door, and Jennifer locked it behind us and went back out through the window above the sink.

I elucidated the "breaking and entering," because we had taken only photographs of their father. Not to be greedy, we left more photographs of their father than we took and had put the albums back on the bookshelves, exactly as we found them. I further reasoned the break-in by the fact that what we took had no monetary value. I was focused only on the girls' happiness, not the actuality of illegally entering someone's home. Of course, this "bad act" was never mentioned in my trial because of the girl's involvement, I am sure. I told Steven what we did. For once, he could not even comment, he just shook his head and made himself a drink.

In 1997, the girls went to Hawaii to earn a geology credit for school. A couple of weeks after the girls returned, I hosted a party at the Austin Country Club for the students and their parents. It was a chance for everyone to share photos and watch the video that the instructor took of the group. Steven refused to attend, and at the time I just assumed it was the type of party that would bore him. He had no qualms about paying the expense.

The girls asked me if they could have a pool party with some of the students with whom they had become close friends with on the trip. I thought it was a splendid idea and the next weekend our house was full of teenagers. I had the local deli cater the party so that the kids would have plenty to eat and drink.

I cannot remember where Steven was at the time. He would usually stay at the lake house by himself, especially when the girls and I had company who were not from the country club or were not his closest friends.

We were all standing around one of the islands in the kitchen when we saw Steven driving towards the garage. After he entered the kitchen, there was an uncomfortable silence, so thick it could be cut with a knife. We all turned to see at whom Steven was glaring. He walked right up to a well-mannered black teen and told him to gather his belongings because it was time for him to go home.

I was mortified at his behavior and tried to diminish

his bold act of prejudice by suggesting that the teens end the party because everyone was tired. I asked Steven to allow me to drive him home, but he refused. I cannot even imagine how that boy must have felt being in the back seat of Steven's car by himself on the long drive to his home on the east side of Austin.

When my husband returned, he launched into a diatribe against black people. I could not reason with him. That was one of those times when he was entirely unreasonable. He told me that having that "nigger" in our home as a guest was unforgivable. "We can employ them, but under no circumstances are they to break bread with us," were his exact words. Then he added, "That's how the cow ate the cabbage," and he told me that was the end of the discussion. I shudder to think what would have happened if he had known that the boy and his family also attended the party at the country club. I had never remembered seeing Steven so angry; the veins were popping out of the side of his neck, and his face was beet red. Spit flew from his mouth when he spoke. I thought he was going to have a heart attack.

My daughters began ranting about how much they hated Steven and how they wished he was dead. I tried to calm them, but they just stormed off to their bedrooms.

Celeste

Later that night I explained to the girls that Steven acted that way because he grew up during The Great Depression, an era when black people had few rights. It was wrong for him to feel this way, but Steven was too old to change.

During my trial, the teens portrayed to the jury that I was prejudiced. They put Steven on a pedestal during my trial to sway the jury to think that I was the one who was prejudiced; I believe their characterization of me did not bode well with the sole black member of the jury. This is precisely why I was made to look prejudiced; it was a dirty, underhanded, and an unethical tactic.

There was a time when a migrant camp was set up in a field not too far from our lake home. The settlement had nearly 100 Mexican men, women, and children living in deplorable conditions. It was cold at night, and I saw people huddling around campfires to keep warm. My heart went out to these people. I went to Wal-Mart and purchased blankets for everyone. I bought all the blankets the store had to offer, and every square inch of my SUV was stuffed with the bedding. When I arrived at the camp with the blankets, it was like Christmas for the families! It never felt so good to give from the heart, and I felt fortunate to be in such a position to be able to afford to do this. Due to his racist attitude, and afraid Steven might

239

scoff at the expenditure, I was afraid of telling my husband what I had done. Instead, he said he was proud of me and told me how much he loved my generous nature. Naturally, such acts of kindness were not brought up at the trial. I do not have a prejudicial bone in my body, contrary to my portrayal.

Unbeknownst to me, one month after Steven's death, the twins, along with their boyfriends, began a secret campaign to incriminate me; they wanted the money. There is a relentless pain that comes from knowing that the children you gave birth to and loved for years are trying to hurt you, especially in the name of greed. Looking back, I believe the idea was hatched when I began noticing their suspicious and sneaky behavior.

Another odd occurrence was the girls hiring their criminal attorney, Wayne Meissner. They forged a second $3,000 check from my account to pay his retainer fee. If the girls were as innocent, as they wanted us to believe, then why hire a criminal attorney? I question why he accepted a check with my name on it as the sole account holder.

The State called the twins as witnesses against me. The teenagers claimed that Steven unknowingly drank 190 proof Everclear vodka. They said I poured out his 80 proof

Wolfschmidt vodka and substituted it with Everclear vodka. Steven would have recognized the difference between the two, by taste and by alcohol content. The teenagers identified Twin Liquors, but records of that liquor store, or any other liquor stores, were not allowed as evidence to support my claim of innocence. Everclear vodka was never purchased by me.

The girls testified that I tainted Steven's food by placing sleeping pills in it. The sleeping pills are bitter, and I know he would have noticed that his food was laced with something. The suggestion was outlandish. Our pharmacist disputed this testimony with her records of the family's medication purchases. One of the tabloid trash books written about me said I stopped at the pharmacy and told the pharmacist, "You are going to have to kiss my ass like you kissed Steven's ass." Our pharmacist, Judy Cantu, testified this statement was not true.

The girls said, "My mother was poisoning Steven with botulism before the October 1999 shooting." That claim made no sense because Steven was a gourmand and insisted on preparing all of his meals. He would have noticed if his food was tainted or laced with botulism. The Judge allowed the prosecutors to admit a book into evidence that had a recipe for botulism, copyright dated

2000, because Tarlton said, "It was like the one she supposedly sold to Celeste." The book admitted into evidence was copyright dated <u>after</u> the date of the shooting. There were no receipts for any book purchased, or medical testimony to corroborate their claims.

The girls testified that I purchased dented cans of food at the grocery store. This lie was not well thought out because Steven insisted on doing all the menu planning and grocery shopping.

Included in a one of the many boxes of items the girls took to Mr. Mange was the Beard family planner. I looked everywhere for that planner. When not using it when meeting Steven for lunch, we always kept the planner in the kitchen desk drawer so we could write in it as needed. During the civil trial, Kristina was asked the whereabouts of the planner by my attorney. She did say it was kept in the bottom kitchen desk drawer, but did not know where it was. Later, at the criminal trial, the planner miraculously appeared in the evidence box that was filled with items not used in my trial by the State. Kristina was well aware of the location of the planner; she stole it from me and had no problem lying about it under oath.

During the course of two years, the girls were prepped and polished for trial because the Judge at the civil trial said it was obvious they were not telling the truth. They were instructed by the State on what clothing and jewelry to wear, how to style their hair, and how to respond to questions. They were to remain soft spoken and shed tears for the jury. They were made to appear sweet and innocent and were to behave like victims. Their melodramatic performance reaped a payday of millions of dollars. They continued their façade during documentaries and news broadcasts, to gain empathy. People were conned by their youthfulness and soon forgot the twins were on a law breaking vendetta.

During the limo ride to the funeral, Jennifer and Kristina were more concerned with how much money they were bequeathed than grieving the loss of Steven. I had to tell them to stop behaving in such a manner. Dawn was there and was appalled at their greediness. To this day, no one except my friend B.J. puts flowers on Steven's grave.

On the morning of the Allocution, Kristina was scheduled to address me before the court. The nurse helped me get emotionally prepared with advice on how to handle the stress of facing my daughter. She told me to think of someone I hated and to imagine that face on the witness stand, in place of Kristina. I immediately placed Tracey in that most hated place. The nurse told me to say all the things I wanted to say to her in my mind so that I would drown out the words spoken by my daughter. As a survivor of incest and rape, I had years of practice blocking out traumatic experiences. Having to face the daughter I loved most, while she espoused all the contempt and hate she harbored for me, made me want to die. I mustered up all my courage and pretended she was Tracey as I shot daggers of hatred from my eyes. Mentally, I was screaming, " I hate you, Tracey, for all the pain and suffering you caused my family and for turning my daughters against me!" I must have given a stellar performance because I found out later that Kristina was interviewed by ABC News and she said, " Her eyes were like daggers, they just dig at you. It is hard to sit across from someone who hates you so much."

Kristina ended her phony, teary tirade by looking at me and saying, "Shame on you."

Kristina stole tens of thousands of dollars from me, she raided my computer and belongings to manufacture material to take to the prosecutors, she stole jewelry and the Waverunners, she forged checks, and she feigned respect for Steven in court; the man who adopted her and gave her the world. She took full advantage of me when I was hospitalized, she lied and conspired against me for financial gain. I say, "Shame on you."

10

Steven Was Shot

In the early summer months of 1999, I planned an elaborate
75th birthday celebration for my husband at the club over
the Thanksgiving weekend. His children had reluctantly
agreed to attend, reservations had been made, and deposits
applied for them to stay at the Renaissance Hotel at the
Arboretum. Steven's birthday coincided with
Thanksgiving. I wanted to combine the two events because
I wanted him to have lasting memories of a united family
in his golden years.

We would be home for only a few days after our
Europe trip; I wanted the celebration to be arranged and
finalized before leaving on our trip. I had initially wanted
to give him a surprise party for this milestone birthday, but
realized I could not pull it off without his help. His children
ignored the invitations I had sent them, and I had to enlist
his help to persuade them to attend. They complied, only

when we informed them, we would pay their expenses, including a stay in a luxury hotel. I hired our photographer to memorialize his 75th birthday, and quietly agonized over the perfect gift. Our planned trip on October 3rd was to fulfill Steven's desire to purchase a cuckoo clock from the Black Forest in Germany. With little or no difficulty, I could have found a clock on the Internet, but this was the first time Steven had asked for a specific item he longed to have. I asked him if we could take a trip to Germany together to find the "perfect clock." He was elated with the idea of us spending time alone together since our marriage had recently weathered a couple of storms.

At my insistence, Steven was hospitalized twice in September 1999, because he was incoherent and having difficulty breathing. It was discovered that his blood oxygen levels were low due to his severe sleep apnea. After he recovered, I confessed to him about my affair with Jimmy. I told him that I was feeling guilty and ashamed of my behavior and I wanted him to have my undivided attention on this trip. I was grateful when he forgave me. I let Steven know that I intended to display my gratefulness to him, while we were alone and traveling through Europe. Our attorney, David Kuperman, had asked Steven if he wanted a divorce and he adamantly said, "No, I do not."

David had deep seeded resentments in this area because his wife recently left him for a much younger masseur she had met at a spa in California.

Our plane to Frankfurt was scheduled to leave Austin late in the afternoon on Sunday, October 3, 1999. We spent Thursday, September 30th, dividing errands between the four of us in preparation for the trip. We were making sure Jennifer and Kristina would not run out of anything they needed. We bought ourselves underwear and socks to be discarded every day after use on the trip. We prepaid our bills since we would be gone an extended length of time. We arranged for our four pets to be boarded at the vets. We canceled the newspaper and put a vacation hold on our mail. Even though the twins were 18, Steven did not trust them to stay alone in the house or to retrieve the mail.

Steven and I spent Friday morning, October 1st, together at the salon in our shopping center, each getting a manicure and pedicure. An evening out with Steven always required me to have my hair professionally piled on top of my head, per his requests. My husband made sure that my hair appointments for up-dos and nail appointments for manicures were prearranged and scheduled by the various concierges at the hotels along our route. Steven's portable oxygen tank was delivered to our home in the morning, and he went to the Bank of America to pick up $10,000 in traveler's checks.

We met for lunch at La Madelaine, and both signed the dual-signature traveler's checks at the table while waiting for our meals. On the way home, he stopped by the pharmacy and picked up the medications needed for our trip. We had planned to save the entire day on Saturday for packing. Steven had scheduled to pick up selected fur coats from the furrier storage at our shopping center while I finished packing. I usually color-coordinated my travel clothes, so that only two purses were needed; one for daytime and one for the evening. Thus, I could also limit the number of shoes and jewelry selections.

I had not decided whether to wear black, navy, or chocolate as my theme color on this trip. Discarding our underwear and socks every day always made extra room for purchases that we did not want to be shipped home ahead of us. I especially liked to keep the gifts for the twins and the maid with me, so that when arriving home, I could instantly give them out. It always gave me so much pleasure to see my daughters smile and to make sure that our maid knew we appreciated her.

Earlier in the week, Jennifer had asked me if she

could stay overnight at the lake house with Amy and Christopher. Friday morning, Kristina asked if she could spend the night at Justin's parent's house. I told her no because Jennifer had asked first to stay overnight at the lake house. She was upset, but made plans to go to dinner and the movies with Justin. I asked her to come home after the movie ended. When I ended the affair with Jimmy, my rule was that one of the girls had to be at home with me at night on weekends because Steven usually passed out in the early evening and I did not like being in the house alone.

Steven and I had built a one-story home that was split-level, with stairs in different areas of the house to add distinction. He believed people owned two-story homes because they could not afford the land and the large roof over the square footage of a one-story. The 3900 Toro Canyon house was approximately 8000 sq. ft. with 374 recessed ceiling lights that sat on 2.5 acres of land, so it was big and empty waiting for the girls to return. We had busy lives and traveled a great deal; this requirement for one of the twins to be home at night with me was not every weekend, and they did not mind because we had fun visiting.

The evening of Friday, October 1, 1999, started out

no different than any other night. Steven poured his first cocktail at precisely 5:00 p.m., what he affectionately referred to as a "Whitey Loudmouth." He loved Wolfschmidt vodka so much that he had a full-size replica of a ½ gallon bottle hand-painted on the ceramic tile backsplash in the butler's pantry at our Toro Canyon home. We also had a large, brightly painted, paper-mache`, gargoyle beastiary that Steven christened "Wolfshit" (a name he gave to his vodka) hanging in the lake house living room. We attended an art show held at an acquaintance's house in Austin, where Steven became enamored with this gargoyle (in Mexico called "Alebrijes") and began to call it "Wolfshit" as soon as he saw it. He relentlessly haggled with the artist (known as Cutaneous in Mexico) and ended up paying the original asking price of $1,600. Our host was embarrassed because Steven's abruptness appeared rude. Steven commented on the way home how much he enjoyed the artist not backing down. The artist, Felipe Linares, is from Mexico, and the gargoyle had been displayed in the Paris Museum of Art, making Steven determined to own it. The artist ended up sending my husband an autographed copy of his coffee table book, En Calavera The Papier Mache` Art of the Linares Family, depicting the best pieces of his colorful art. "Wolfshit" was included in the book. Steven told me that each piece of artwork is only worth the price that you can persuade someone else to pay for it. He just laughed heartily and told me this gift proved the artist enjoyed their meeting as much as he had. I read that Felipe's work is now world-renowned and he has exhibited in museums and art galleries worldwide. This news would make Steven very happy.

During my trial, I was accused of switching Steven's vodka with Everclear vodka. Steven would have instantly known the difference in taste and potency. Once, out of laziness, I poured Steven some of my brand of vodka, thinking that his taste buds were no longer distinguished due to his age and drinking habits. He took one sip and demanded to know why I poured him something other than "Wolfshit." Refusing to drink the vodka I had served, he poured it down the sink then made another cocktail. I was always under the false impression that he bought Wolfschmidt vodka, simply because it was cheap, less than $14.00 for a half-gallon. He poured the good stuff down the drain and refilled his glass with his beloved "Wolfshit," proving I was wrong. With Steven, the taste was all that mattered. I did, on occasion, water his drink down with tap water when he was getting too plastered and acting belligerent. Our friend Philip told me

251

Everclear tastes like gasoline.

Tracey Tarlton testified at my trial that she took Kristina, and not me, to buy Everclear vodka, but Kristina denied this. I suspect that with Tracey, having been an alcoholic, is how Kristina learned about Everclear vodka in the first place. It was not an item stocked at the bar in our homes. Getting Steven to bed, while he was drunk, was challenging and sometimes impossible. Many times I had no choice but to leave him where he had passed out, even if it was outside on the patio. On the nights I was unable to put him to bed, I could not sleep because of worrying about his safety, so I kept a close eye on him for the duration. If I did decide to leave the house, it was only on those occasions when Steven was sleeping, safely tucked in bed. He notoriously woke up feeling fine in the morning; seldom did I see him with a hangover. Steven drank the night of the shooting, while, as usual, preparing our dinner. After all these years, I am unable to recollect what he cooked.

I do remember driving to the lake house in my Suburban with the dogs, Nikki and Megan, after putting Steven to bed. I was only able to take Megan on car rides when the back of my Suburban was empty. She could not ride in the middle, because of the captain's chairs and the leather upholstery. Arriving at the lake house, Amy looked lonely, she was usually the "odd man out," so I agreed to let Megan stay with her. Amy was such a pet lover, and Megan adored her. I also did not mind because Megan found comfort for her arthritis by sleeping on the heated bathroom floor. My heart went out to Amy because she was built like a linebacker. The boys in school were not interested in dating her. She did not ask if Nikki could stay with her too; it was general knowledge that Nikki and I were inseparable. I often made late night trips to the lake house, Wal-Mart, or Home Depot. I was used to staying up late, and these stores were open 24 hours. I bought videos and power tools, even though not knowing how to use either, but wanted to have a stockpile in case we needed one. Watching television, I had to ask my husband or the girls to operate the remote for me.

I did not stay at the lake house long, it was a pop-in visit to see what the teenagers were doing. I returned home with Nikki knowing the next day would be busy getting ready for our European vacation. Jennifer called me on my cell phone to make sure I had made it back safely. Arriving home, I checked on Steven to make sure he had not turned off the CPAP machine or pulled off his breathing mask. As usual, he had removed the mask, so I put it back on him.

He woke up long enough to give his general pleadings for why I should allow him to keep the mask off for the remainder of the night. I kissed him on the forehead and said good night.

I went to Kristina's bedroom to see if she was still awake, she was on the telephone with Justin, so I went into the bar for one last Diet Coke, and went outside by the Koi pond with Nikki to smoke before retiring for the night. I never smoked inside of our home. It was about midnight when I went to bed in Kristina's room.

Nikki slept on my pillow like an exotic cat. The cats usually bed with me, Luci on my right side and Ollie on my left. Megan normally slept in the master bath on the heated granite floor because of her arthritis. She was hard-of-hearing, and on the mornings she slept in that wing, I had to shake her to wake her. Megan was a deep sleeper, which I believe contributed to her incontinence, and because of this, Steven was always badgering me to put her to sleep, but I could not do that. It was not as if we were not able to replace anything on which she had an accident. One time I argued, "You wouldn't put a family member to sleep just because they'd become troublesome." He assured me, "Yes, I would!"

Steven once told me how he had begrudgingly paid

for his mother-in-law to be cared for in a nursing home for over 20 years, even after the death of her daughter, Steven's first wife. I remember listening on the speaker phone to a conversation he had with an administrator at the nursing home regarding her care. She had called him because she was reviewing the file and wanted to confirm the "Do Not Resuscitate" order. I heard Steven say, "Hell, yes! I want that order! That woman's been on my back for over 40 years." He ended the conversation with, "Are you sure there isn't any way to speed up the process?" The woman was shocked and abruptly hung up on him.

It tugged at my heart that this elderly lady was alone in a nursing home never receiving a visit or a telephone call from a family member or friends. I felt it was not my place to visit her, but I did buy her socks, underwear, bras, and nightgowns. I delivered these clothes to the charge nurse for her birthday, at Easter, and Christmas every year, until her death.

Without fail, I took a nap in the master bedroom during the day. Naps are the only time I slept in the master bedroom. Steven suffered from sleep apnea, a life-threatening condition that required him to sleep with a mask on his face that forced a continuous positive flow of air into his lungs. Without the CPAP machine, he would stop breathing hundreds of times a night because his airway was blocked or breathing muscles stopped moving. The unit was very loud, which disturbed my sleep. Steven routinely wet the bed and I had the mattress covered with a plastic zippered protector. This added to my discomfort of sleeping in the master bedroom.

This is why I slept in Kristina's room and kept my casual clothes, such as jeans, T-shirts, tennis shoes, PJs, socks, and cotton undergarments in her walk-in closet. I stored extra make-up and toiletries in the vanity drawers in her bathroom. On a bench seat in her walk-in shower, I had bottles of my favorite shampoo and conditioner, plus a shower cap, and razor. I was diagnosed with Restless Legs Syndrome in 1996, and this diagnosis is my only plausible explanation for my sleeping attire. Ever since I can remember, I have slept with cotton balls between my toes and full-length pajamas (always pink) as opposed to a nightgown. I was unable to sleep if I felt my skin touching anywhere. Even on long car rides, or on an airplane, the cotton went between my toes, regardless of me wearing shoes and socks. I slept wearing a cotton bra and cotton panties. The only time I did not wear a bra was while in the shower. Someone told me at an early age that wearing a bra would ensure I would not look like the saggy breasts that could be seen in National Geographic photos. I usually slept with heavy lotion and cotton gloves on my hands because I suffered from Obsessive-Compulsive Disorder. This caused me to wash my hands so often that they would crack and bleed.

When Nikki and Orly were puppies, they woke me in the middle of the night by pulling out the cotton from between my toes. This is just one of the idiosyncrasies of which prison has cured me. In prison we ration toilet paper, barely receiving enough to do its intended job; I cannot afford to waste any for my toes. This surely proves the adage: mind over matter! Sad but true, in prison, we can get water pills and laxatives, but not enough toilet paper. I wish the prison agreed that, as women, we should not have to fight for our right to wipe.

At about 3:00 a.m. Saturday, October 2, 1999, Kristina and I were awakened by Nikki's barking alerting us to bright lights flashing through the slats of the wooden blinds. We had no idea what was the cause of the bright lights. Holding each other close, we left her room, keeping the animals inside to protect them from the unknown. We made our way to Jennifer's bedroom and called the police. We were told that the police were already at the house.

We headed towards the master bedroom, intending

to meet up with Steven. The seven different telephone numbers in our home were at sixteen separate locations, including our bathrooms and the garage. At this point, I felt that Steven must have fallen and called for help because I knew he had gone to bed drunk. Each security panel in every room was attached to the light switch with an emergency button that could bring immediate help from the security company. Another emergency button was on my bedside table, installed because of Steven's health issues. His CPAP machine had to be on his bedside table, which is why the emergency button was on the other side of the bed.

Kristina and I made it as far as the living room bar when I noticed, through the stained glass, silhouettes at the front doors. As Kristina unlocked the doors, I turned toward the master bedroom to find Steven and was stopped by men coming down the stairs. The men began bombarding me with questions, wanting to know if my husband just had surgery. Their questions confused me because when Steven fell and cut his head open at the lake house in 1996, it did not look like he had surgery. At the lake house, being drunk, he fell off the toilet and hit his head on the baseboard. Steven used to joke that he was Elvis Presley's older brother. I never thought that was funny because the incident scared me. I thought this was another drunken fall incident.

The EMT's tending to him at the lake house that time remained calm, even though they sent him by helicopter to Austin for treatment. Now, these men were anxious and acting excitedly concerned. I repeatedly asked, to the point of begging, if my husband was all right. They would not answer me and would not allow me to see him.

I was escorted out the front door. By this time I was distraught. With all the police and emergency personnel running around, it became clear that it was more than a few stitches needed because of a drunken fall. Our neighbors, Dr. Bob and Bess Dennison, arrived at our house because our private subdivision was lit up like the Fourth of July with the stroboscope of red, white, and blue lights permeating our serene enclave. I asked Dr. Dennison to check on Steven, as nobody would tell me anything. I said to him, "Bob, since you're a doctor, they'll allow you to go in." Hysterically crying, I was both scared and worried, wondering why nobody would tell me what was happening.

While I sat on the front steps, barefoot in my pajamas, Bess had her arms around me. The cotton balls between my toes were gone, but I was still wearing a bra and panties; I had always worn white cotton undergarments to bed, any deviation caused discomfort, and I could not fall asleep. The police made quite an issue about this, questioning everyone if I often wore them. I could not understand the relevance of that line of questioning. Of course, prison has forced me to come to terms with these ridiculous habits. We get three white cotton bras and four white cotton pairs of panties every 180 days, which are cheaply made in Third World countries. If we are fortunate, they will stay held together for this length of time. I rarely sleep wearing a bra, because I have to wash my underclothes in the shower every night and hang them on my bedrail to dry by morning. I do sleep wearing a pair of pants under my state-issued nightgown. I have not overcome the quirk of my legs touching and doubt that I ever will. I am now able to sleep through noise, lights, and bugs without the aids I so desperately needed in my free world.

Unescorted by police and contaminating the crime scene, Kristina went back into the house to retrieve my shoes and a jacket along with my cigarettes and lighter. She also said later that she made a telephone call to Justin, using the cordless phone from the bar.

I remember they brought Steven out on a gurney, and I was able to speak to him. I told him that I loved him and would follow him to the hospital before he was rushed into the awaiting ambulance. From the ambulance, he was transferred to a helicopter that had landed on the street in front of our subdivision. I became more hysterical, begging the county personnel not to let Steven die.

I put on my tennis shoes and a jacket and turned to get my car to follow Steven. A female deputy stopped me, saying that she would take us to the hospital. She led me to believe that she was concerned for our safety because I was visibly distressed. Of the two of us, Kristina was unusually calm and was the level-headed one. The deputy told me that if we rode with her, we would arrive faster and would receive curbside service, not having to deal with the hospital's massive parking garage. Kristina kept insisting that she be allowed to drive me. I consented to the sheriff, wanting only to be with Steven and not caring how I got there.

When we pulled out of the driveway, I noticed Justin leaning on his car across the street from our private subdivision. There is no reasonable explanation as to how he could have arrived so quickly after Kristina's supposed phone call to him since his parents' house was miles away. When I questioned Kristina about his presence, she told me that she called him from the bar telephone in the house. I just dropped it and did not ask her or Justin again. I should have been more persistent; this has often bothered me. I question how he could have been outside the house and believe he must have been already in our neighborhood. I wonder why he would have been in the vicinity at 3:00 a.m. because it is highly unusual. I also wondered why he did not approach us to inquire or console us. Often, guilty people return to the scene of the crime; is this the explanation as to his curb side appearance? I later asked my attorney if phone records could indicate if Kristina did call him from the house. At the trial, numerous phone records were submitted into evidence, yet that call Kristina claimed to have made was not listed on the spreadsheet. It was not until later on that I learned Justin also had a key to Tracey's house, another odd piece of information.

When we arrived at Brackenridge Hospital, Kristina and I were escorted into a small private room off the entrance to the emergency room. It did not take long to realize that the police were not concerned about us. The first thing they asked us was for permission to take a gunpowder residue test. I complied and asked as to why we were being treated as suspects. When it was apparent they found no gunpowder residue, they started questioning us about who would want to hurt my husband. I could not answer their questions because I honestly did not know. I was not sure what happened to Steven yet and was looking for someone to tell me. My focus was on his well-being and told them that my only concern was for his survival. Kristina told them that Tracey was a possible suspect and explained how she retrieved a handgun from Tracey's house, yet leaving a shotgun in her closet. The other teenagers were questioned separately, and I do not recall what they said they told the police. Everything became a blur.

Kristina made calls to Ana, Philip, Bailey, Gus, and Dawn. Soon everyone descended upon Brackenridge to wait with us in the emergency waiting room. Ana gave me a couple of Valium to calm my nerves. I remember Philip talking to the police because he was not only our close family friend, but also an attorney. I recalled being cold and lying in the middle of the floor. Kristina had piled more than ten jackets on top of me, and I still could not lose the chill. I had asked Philip to deal with the police because they were not telling me anything. I lay quietly praying to God and making deals to spare his precious life.

After Steven's 14-hour surgery, one of the surgeons told me that he had about a 10% chance of survival. I was devastated and in shock. They allowed me to see my husband for a couple of minutes, as he lay unconscious and full of tubes. I just wept and kissed his forehead. I whispered in his ear how much I loved him.

Christopher made arrangements for us to stay at a hotel close to the hospital using my credit card. Steven's friends had long since gone home, and Dawn made arrangements with her family for her to stay with me. I begged to be allowed to stay at the hospital, in case Steven woke up. Dawn persuaded me to go to the hotel and at least take a shower and get out of the pajamas I had been wearing since the previous night. Jennifer and Christopher had gone back to the house and retrieved clothes for us, along with my Suburban from the hospital parking garage. I do not remember if Kristina or Dawn drove, but do recall being in the back seat.

Philip arrived at the hotel with a couple of attorneys from Minton, Burton, Foster, and Collins, a prestigious law firm in Austin. Philip said he felt that Steven and I needed this firm to look after our interests. My husband had always drilled into my head not to make any decisions without the advice of legal counsel so I agreed to retain them, no questions asked.

I recall remembering how Brackenridge Hospital had treated Steven when taken to their hospital by helicopter in 1996 after he split open his head. Arriving at the emergency room, I found him lying on a gurney, abandoned in the hallway, wearing only his stretched-out underwear, not even covered with a sheet, his family jewels exposed. They had stitched his head without any painkillers, claiming that his blood alcohol level was more than twice the legal limit. They had assumed he was nothing more than a derelict until I arrived and admonished them for their neglect. Dr. Dennison assured me that Brackenridge Hospital was the best trauma hospital in the county. I wanted Austin's finest to ensure Steven would receive the best treatment possible.

A few hours later Dawn, Kristina, and I returned to the hospital to check on Steven. Visiting hours were strict for ICU, with patients limited to ten minutes of visitation every few hours; I did not want to miss any windows of opportunity to see him. Walking to the back entrance of the hospital, one of the cell phones rang, it was Tracey. She told me that the police were questioning her about the shooting. I told her to call Philip. I had previously referred her to Philip after she received a DWI charge. Having no intention of discussing my husband's condition with her, I handed the phone to Kristina.

All future calls were handled through my daughters, no matter who was calling. I had tunnel vision and was not thinking clearly. I was consumed with worry for my husband's recovery. Any decisions, not directly affecting Steven's care, went through Jennifer or Kristina. It was Kristina who took care of most of our affairs, because Jennifer spent the majority of her time away from the situation, out of town with Christopher. I thought that was odd, but rationalized at the time, it was too much for her to deal with after her father's suicide, so I did not push the issue. I depended on Kristina and allowed her to play the role as my "parent" in all things except Steven's needs. A month before the shooting Steven had threatened to kick Kristina out of the house. Marilou and I heard him tell her that he could care less if she lived on the streets or ended up on welfare, that he had washed his hands of her. She became riddled with contempt for Steven. My only concern was for Steven's well-being. I could not even concentrate on my precious Nikki for the first time in her life. The girls took all the pets to the veterinary clinic to be boarded until some unknown future date when we would move back into the Toro Canyon home.

When we arrived back at the hospital for my first visit, after changing clothes, we were met by Travis County Sheriff's Detective, Rick Wines. Dawn, Kristina, and I were sitting in the ICU waiting room when Detective

Wines sat down and began asking questions. Kristina dominated the conversation by questioning the detective concerning the whereabouts of Steven's watch, ring, money clip, and wallet. With all the chaos at the house after the shooting, I was unaware of missing items and wondered how Kristina knew these things were missing. I became irritated with her because I was trying to find out if Steven's condition had improved, while her focus was on material things.

With his condition listed as guarded, Detective Wines said that Steven was able to answer his questions by blinking his eyes in response to "yes" or "no" answers. I did not agree with this form of nonverbal communication, and I was concerned because Steven was heavily medicated, was hooked up to a ventilator, and was intubated in various parts of his body. His arms and legs were restrained to stop him from pulling out the medical apparatuses that were keeping him alive. I was still feeling the effects of the Valium, coupled with the trauma of the unspeakable events that were unfolding. While Detective Wines was questioning us, I remained subdued and was unable to offer any opinions to him because I was trying to not fall apart when my husband needed me the most. The medical staff made it quite clear that Steven was not to see me cry. This could cause his condition to deteriorate.

After visiting Steven, it was apparent he was in emotional distress, not to mention the physical pain he was enduring from the gunshot wound. The pleading and terror in his eyes conveyed to me that he was frightened. I asked him if he wanted me to bring the police back. He violently shook his head "no," and not with any "yes/no" blinking. It broke my heart to see him in this condition. When I promised to make sure they left him alone, he calmed down. I held his hand and told him how much I loved him and that he was going to pull through this. The medical staff allowed me extended and more frequent visits because they noted I was the only one who had a calming effect on him. The nurses often called me at home after visiting hours were over to come back to calm Steven if he was having a difficult night. I rushed to the hospital at any hour of the night to comfort him.

Not letting Steven see me cry or look worried was the hardest battle I ever fought in my life. I had to tell the only person who ever really knew me, that all was well when I did not know if he was going to survive one night to the next. I went to see our attorney, Charles Burton, and told him that Steven did not want to talk to the police and what had transpired with Detective Wines questioning him when he was in obvious distress. A sign was posted on Steven's door. Anyone wanting to visit required clearance through our attorney Charles Burton. The police never tried to talk with Steven again, not even when he was released from Brackenridge and admitted to HealthSouth Rehabilitation Hospital. The sign did not follow him to HealthSouth, which leaves me to wonder why there were no follow-up discussions with my husband once his recovery stabilized. Under oath, Detective Wines testified at the trial that he only interviewed my husband one time, the occasion where he was blinking his yes/no answers. Those answers should not have been considered definitive; my husband was heavily sedated at the time. Considering the severity of the crime, Steven should have had the opportunity to speak and offer his input. The outcome of the trial might have turned out differently if the detectives were more thorough in their investigation.

While at Brackenridge, Steven again became agitated. It was during one of Kristina's first visits to the ICU. Even though he was ordered restrained for his safety, the nurses allowed me to untie his hands, while sitting with him. On this particular occasion, I had him hold a cup of ice chips in his right hand, while I took out the ice chips and rubbed them on his lips. The ventilator was still in so he could not have water. When Kristina came up beside him, he took the cup of ice and water and intentionally thrust it at her. The contents hit her in the face. She started crying and made a few strides towards the door. I became upset with Steven, because the anger, bitterness, and hatred that oozed from his eyes were directed at Kristina, and she saw it all.

Kristina probably wanted me to stop her from leaving, but I could not. Steven was not out of the woods yet, and she was healthy. She looked at me like I had just performed the ultimate act of betrayal. My staying with Steven caused a rift between Kristina and me, one that she was never able to forgive.

I made every visitation time available to be at my husband's side while he was recovering. Becky testified to this as true when she was deposed at the civil trial. I brought him special meals from his favorite restaurants, once he was able to eat solid food. His cardiologist was so concerned about the excessive amount of weight Steven was losing that he instructed me to bring him red wine to help thin his blood, and anything at all to eat, as long as I could get him to eat. No matter what class or variety of red wine I brought, Steven flat out refused to drink it. Once HealthSouth realized I was trying to get Steven to drink red wine, they curtailed it, despite the fact that his doctor recommended he drink it to help prevent blood platelets from sticking and clumping together and forming clots. Steven implored me to sneak in his beloved "Wolfshit," even trying to bribe me with expensive gifts and promises of future vacation destinations.

I stood firm and refused his request because his doctors said he was suffering from alcohol withdrawal and giving him vodka would be detrimental to his health. He pouted, cursed me, and gave me the silent treatment, but deep down he knew I was only looking after his best interests. Eventually, the hallucinations, shakes, and other side effects from the detoxing stopped, and he began looking forward to not having our evenings centered around cocktails when he came home. I, too, was looking forward to spending that time with Steven.

As my husband's health progressed, he began tending to his business affairs from his hospital bed. Unbeknownst to me, November 9, 1999, thirty-six days after the shooting, Steven signed contracts for the second phase of the shopping center to begin construction. These documents were brought to Steven by our attorney, David Kuperman. I knew Steven had our architect and builder working together to begin construction on the maids' quarters, an exercise studio, and an additional garage for our Toro Canyon home. We needed an additional four-car garage to accommodate the girl's vehicles along with those of the maids. He removed his daughter, Becky, from sharing the responsibilities with me regarding his Medical Power of Attorney and began meeting with our attorney to increase the size of my inheritance. My husband's actions and decisions were that of a man who was protective and believed I had nothing to do with his shooting.

On November 23, 1999, while Steven was still at Brackenridge, and without my knowledge, Mr. Kuperman, who was our attorney until after my husband passed away, amended the Marital Trust. He placed Phase I and Phase II of the upscale Davenport Village Shopping Centers into the Marital Trust. Mr. Kuperman brought the papers to the hospital and explained the amendment to Steven. By signing the documents, Steven changed his will and placed an additional $40 million of assets into the trust. Now, only about $230,000 was projected to go into the Children's Trust. This new change infuriated all five children when they found out after Steven's death.

I was unaware Steven had obligated himself more than $20 million dollars for the second phase of the shopping center and did not realize the increase in my inheritance until after he died. The only change he ever mentioned to me was about removing Becky from the Medical Power of Attorney. He said she was obstinate and uncooperative and he did not feel it fair that I should have to deal with her. For Christmas in 1999, he had an exquisite diamond and black opal ring, pendant, and matching earring set specially made for me. The set was made from the opals I had purchased in Australia. These details were shocking for me to learn after his death because I did not know that he had so much going on.

When he was moved to the rehab hospital, I was asked by the medical staff not to stay all day. He needed to work on his physical therapy and should not rely on me to do everything for him. I brought him breakfast, lunch, and dinner and spent every evening with him. I knew he was having visitors during the day and working on the first shopping center because he gave me the artist's rendering he had commissioned of "Celeste's Bronze." This was the name he came up with for the upscale sculpture business that I was planning to open in the shopping center. He was financing my business adventure, but giving me all the credit for coming up with the idea earlier in the year.

While Steven was hospitalized at Brackenridge, the Toro Canyon house was having the security system updated, which we seldom used unless we were vacationing. The house was being made handicapped-accessible for Steven. The lake house was also getting an upgrade of its security system. We anticipated that he would come home in a wheelchair and I wanted him to be able to move freely around the house. I had our carpenter, Doug, install wooden ramps over the stairs that could be removed when Steven was ambulatory. I had handrails installed at all three stair locations so he could steady himself while going up or down the short flights of stairs. Steven was pleased that I had given him so much thought.

During my trial, a huge issue was made by the prosecution because I spent more than $26,000 to have the handrails made of bronze. I knew that any handrails of lesser quality would have looked like an afterthought, and would destroy the continuity of our home. When he saw them, he was proud of the elegance they added to our home. Steven had always drilled into my head that appearance is everything.

During his hospitalization, I asked our attorney, Charles Burton, to talk to Steven about the shooting. Earlier that morning, Steven had asked me, "Why'd that man shoot me?" When I told him that Tracey had been arrested, he no longer wanted to talk about it. I asked

Charles to speak privately with Steven to give him a complete account of what had transpired, as we understood it.

Charles Burton interviewed Jennifer and Kristina in his office on October 5, 1999, making notes. He also typed memorandums; Kristina's was dated November 10, 1999, and Jennifer's was dated February 19, 2000. Neither of their interviews implicated me in Tarlton's plan. They profusely claimed my innocence. They dramatically changed their stories during the trial; they did a complete about face.

After the meeting, Steven asked me to never bring up the subject again. I told him about feeling responsible because I was the one who had brought Tracey into our lives. He assured me that he loved me and when I asked for his forgiveness, he said there was nothing to forgive. I told him the police probably still wanted to talk to him, but he responded that he did not want to talk to anyone. He just wanted to go on with our lives and forget about the entire incident. I never again brought the subject up. Had I persuaded Steven to discuss the attack further, I most likely would be a free woman today.

While at HealthSouth, my husband started planning our next trip and continued working on the details of my new business adventure. He had a ruby and diamond ring and earring set in platinum made for me as a surprise for my birthday in February. He had the jeweler find an 8+ carat diamond ring for me to celebrate our anniversary. I already knew about this search, because the jeweler had been working on it for some time before the shooting. Unbeknownst to me, Kristina retrieved the ruby set from the jewelers after Steven's death in April 2000. She did this shameful thing after I had revoked her use of my Power of Attorney a few days earlier. I still have not figured out why she never gave me the jewels. Another one of those unexplained peculiarities that deserves an answer.

Steven was on the telephone daily with everyone from his jeweler, to our attorney, architect, builder, and his business partner. The prosecution conveniently contorted the facts at my trial indicating that I was at his side 24/7 because of being afraid he would turn me in as an accomplice to the shooting. They took bits and pieces of information and put their twist on things. Had Steven wanted to talk to the police, he would have called them or had one of his minions call them. He spent hours alone in his room at the rehabilitation hospital. He would not have rewarded me by substantially increasing my inheritance, planning a business venture for me, nor entrusted me to make all his medical decisions, if he harbored any doubts that I wished him harm.

When Steven had his days at the rehab hospital without me, I did what I knew best, redecorated and remodeled. Gutters were added to the house and bronze "water lily" waterways were made for the downspouts. Some furniture was replaced to make it easier for Steven to get in and out of, and changes were made with the paintings in different areas of the house to better suit the new furniture. Renovations to Jennifer's bedroom were completed. Kristina changed her bedroom furniture within the first week after the shooting and without my knowledge. I thought her timing was odd, after discovering when she had done it. To be fair to Jennifer, I did the same for her. Steven had instructed our attorney to counsel me on my expenditures, so I reasoned that if anything else needed change, I had better do it before he was discharged. I was certain Steven would be delighted with the necessary accessibility renovations on his behalf, but at the same time, I was not ignorant to think he would not set a spending limit. I rationalized that all my work had kept me occupied while waiting for Steven to be released and allowed to come home.

I purchased a $36,000 Cadillac Catera for each of

the girls, telling Steven it was an additional graduation present. The girls became distant with me; I felt like they had stopped loving me since I had not spent much time with them. Steven did not care about the expense of the cars because he knew it made me happy and the girls needed reliable transportation back and forth to college. He was adamant that I not list the cars in the girls' names because we would pay cash and therefore, no lien would be put on them. He yelled at me and made me say, "Okay," because he said he would get them a used Ford Escort, if he had his way. I did the opposite of what my husband requested of me and have regretted it ever since. The twins insisted that if I loved them, I would trust them enough to list them as the registered owners of the cars. I did not know they had ulterior motives and were planning to replace the cars.

When the girls arrived home and received their cars, they arrogantly told me they would rather have a BMW or Mercedes. Kristina pitched a hissy-fit because it was not a BMW. This crushed me because I had gone behind Steven's back, only to be shown ingratitude and thanklessness. I heard through the grapevine that they both traded their cars for a BMW and a Mercedes. This was another of my extraneous offenses that was ignored in the trial.

When I was spending all of my time at the hospital, Kristina and Jennifer enjoyed their freedom and wanted me out of the picture. Kristina and Justin began acting like the Toro Canyon house was theirs. Kristina was furious when I stopped her from getting metal or plastic mini-blinds installed in the kitchen, breakfast area, formal dining room, and living rooms. The few windows with wooden plantation shutters were those in our bedrooms, bathrooms, and closets for privacy. We built floor-to-ceiling windows more than 15 feet high to admire our beautiful landscaping. All of the windows had sunscreens installed that blocked the harmful sun rays from coming in, but did not obscure our view outside. Our vast kitchen was built on a steel bridge so that our Koi pond in the backyard, with the antique bronze fountain, would flow under the kitchen into one of the waterfalls that cascaded into the main Koi pond out front. We had a walking bridge over this Koi pond, and we had several decorative bronze statues elegantly showcased around the pond and gardens.

In the box of papers the girls brought to the district attorney, I found a note in Kristina's handwriting regarding the installation of the mini-blinds. Her mother-in-law suggested the blinds, and it can be assumed they would have ended up being installed as soon as I was disposed of by the girls.

It was around this time that I became suspicious of my daughters and their friends. They were becoming tumultuous, acting secretive and sneaky, and were behaving outside their typical character. I caught them telling lies and covering for each other. Whispered conversations would abruptly end when I entered the room. I felt a storm brewing. Things were not adding up, and I could not put my finger on it. I did try to find out what they were up to on many occasions, to no avail. To this day, I think my daughters knew more about the shooting than they were leading us to believe. At the trial, this behavior continued with contradictive responses on the stand that did not match the questions previously asked.

When the time grew closer for Steven to be discharged, I began looking for private duty nurses. I thought he would want to have some input on the final selection, but was not prepared for his wrath when the conversation was approached. He told me that he unequivocally viewed this request as me abandoning him in his time of greatest need. He refused to have a private nurse, making it clear to me that if I loved him, I would take care of him. I agreed but was apprehensive about his

280

wound care because after he left Brackenridge Hospital, his wound looked worse instead of better. I discussed this with the staff and was shown how to change the ileostomy bag. The ileostomy is created by bringing a portion of the small intestine through an opening in the abdomen. The discharge is relatively constant, watery, and contains large amounts of salt and digestive enzymes. Water cannot enter, because of its outward shape, so it did not require covering it for a bath or shower. The ileostomy bag pushed the liquid waste out of his body, requiring it to be changed at least once a day. I was given hands-on instruction by nurses and felt competent with my ability to attend to changing the bag.

The gunshot wound, which still required daily care, concerned me. I told Steven that I did not feel adequately trained to attend to this type of care and asked again about a private duty nurse coming in to do just this particular treatment. The gunshot wound had been getting worse while he was at HealthSouth Rehabilitation Hospital. I had expressed my concerns about the progress of his care at HealthSouth with one of my husband's physicians, Dr. Handley. We were able to work it out with the rehab hospital for me to bring Steven in once a day for wound care. Steven told me he did not want me to leave him during the day after he came home, just as he had done when Elise was sick. My promise to him was to always take care of him.

When Steven left Brackenridge Hospital, he was able to walk for short distances, and go to the bathroom unassisted. He was starting to regress and began to depend on his wheelchair once at HealthSouth.

The gunshot wound was healed except about the size of a thumbnail. While at HealthSouth Rehabilitation Hospital, his walking ceased. When they were ready to send him home Steven complained that his legs hurt, it was a deep aching pain. After his first surgery, he was prescribed a blood thinner, Heparin, but HealthSouth discontinued giving it to him. I always thought there was a correlation between his legs hurting and the stoppage of the blood thinner. A simple test of the pain in his legs would have saved his life. Dr. Coscia knew my husband had suffered significant injury, and was a high risk patient for blood clots. He needed the Heparin to survive. I expressed my concerns with the doctors about his readiness to come home. When my husband heard about my concerns, he got upset and accused me of not wanting to take care of him. The hospital staff assured me that Steven was ready, but just lazy, and insisted once he returned home he would start doing more for himself. His testicles were red, swollen and resembled thick, cross grained-leather. When I complained to his doctor, I was told to put cornstarch on Steven's testicles. I felt as though everyone thought I was lazy and did not want to take care of him. Against my better judgment, I made preparations for him to come home.

I had a wheelchair delivered and a Hover-Round on order. A shower chair was not needed because all our showers had bench seats and detachable spray wands. Steven did not want me to order a hospital bed until he first tried our bed for comfort. On our way home, I scheduled a manicure and pedicure for him, his favorite indulgence. By the time we arrived home, he was happy but exhausted. Our carpenter, Doug, helped get him into his wheelchair and bed. Even though Steven had lost a tremendous amount of weight, he was still too heavy for me to move by myself. He just said he was too tired to be of any help. Providing care for him was fine with me, as I was happy to have him home.

As the evening progressed, I stayed with Steven in our master bedroom. He made me close off our wing of the house, not wanting the cats on the bed with us. We both worried they might walk on his stomach while he slept, they had done this often, prior to the shooting. I fed Steven dinner in bed; it was all of his favorites, finishing up with a bowl of ice cream. I had to improvise a urinal from a Tupperware pitcher, as it had become evident that he was too weak to get out of bed. I initially thought the trip to the salon was what had tired him out.

As the hours passed, Steven was becoming more combative and unruly. His testicles were hurting and looked frightening. He had a rough night and could not get comfortable. I told him that I would order a hospital bed to be delivered the next day. When morning came, I changed his ileostomy bag and prepared his sponge bath. He insisted on taking a shower. The entire process took hours. I had to keep rescheduling his wound care appointment as it was impossible for me to get him showered and dressed in a hurry. I was quietly frustrated and contemplating calling an ambulance to bring him to his appointment. He kept telling me he was sorry and asking, "Do you still love me?"

By mid-afternoon, with Doug's help, I got him in the car, and we were on our way to HealthSouth. When I told him that I planned on telling the hospital he was not ready to come home, he began crying like a small child and promised to "be good." I felt torn, knowing that he was not ready to come home and at the same time feeling as if I was betraying him because I had promised to take care of him and wanted only to do what was best for him. It was apparent that he needed immediate medical attention.

When we arrived at the hospital, I complained to the staff. They had me take him to Brackenridge Hospital where I explained the situation and told them the severe condition Steven was in and how inflamed and painful his testicles were. Considering his doctors were male, I expected compassion regarding his testicles. They continued to act as if it was merely a diaper rash. Steven kept promising to be good if I would take him home and his request broke my heart. Marilou had been an RN for nearly 50 years; she impressed upon me that Steven was in no condition to be home.

Finally, I got my way, and Steven was admitted into Brackenridge. Dr. Tram admonished me, letting me know that if anything happened to him, it would be entirely my fault. I called Marilou crying, and she assured me that Dr. Tram was wrong and had no right to speak to me that way. She fully understood how much I loved Steven. She convinced me to stand my ground for Steven's health.

On the second day, they had discovered Steven had a bloodstream infection, a severe condition called sepsis. They moved him to Intermediate ICU and told me he

Celeste

would need powerful antibiotics. One nurse went so far as to congratulate me for my persistence. At times, Steven seemed incoherent, but at least we knew that I was correct in believing Steven was in no condition to be at home. Once they got rid of the infection, all would be well.

286

Celeste

11

Steven Passes Away

The following day, day three, they told me Steven was
going to be transferred to the urgent care ICU. Regularly
drawn blood tests were ordered. The doctors diagnosed him
with sepsis. Immediate treatment was critical.

Antibiotics were prescribed, but after five hours, he
still had not received a dose. His condition had taken a turn
for the worse. How could the medical professionals forget
to give him his medication, considering his dire
circumstance? I did not know they forgot to administer the
antibiotics until my trial. It was noted in Steven's chart that
he did not receive the antibiotic and it was underlined three
times. Someone was fully aware of the negligence. They
assured me that he would be all right, he just needed the
care of the ICU staff. I was told to go to lunch, and by the
time I returned he would be transferred to the unit. "I love
you," I said as I left to go to the restaurant.

Celeste

I walked around the corner to the Brick Oven
Restaurant for lunch with Justin and Kristina. Steven
wanted me to bring him back a meatball sandwich. I tried
to eat, but could not shake an ominous feeling in the pit of
my stomach. When we returned to the hospital ICU, I knew
something was wrong. The look on the nurses' faces
confirmed my greatest fear. There had been a
"complication." They told us Steven was dead. Those
words still echo in my ears.

I did not stop to talk to anyone but ran into his
room. He was still lying on a gurney and was still warm. I
pleaded with him to wake up. In hysterics, I kissed him,
then shook him. My entire world had just stopped. When
Steven's life ended, I did not know where my life would
begin. All I could focus on was Dr. Tram's blaming me for
bringing him back to the hospital. To calm me down, they
injected 40 mgs of Halodol, into my thigh, through my
jeans. I was put in a bed with high rails resembling a crib. I
was in a private room with a security officer standing guard
at my door.

Dr. Coopwood signed the death certificate as death
caused by septic shock, Beta Hemolytic Streptococcus,
Group A. At the trial, Dr. Coopwood, Dr. Satterwhite, and
Dr. Petty testified to the severe infection as being the cause

288

of death; their conclusion, Steven died of natural causes. The proof to support their conclusion was the results of the multiple blood tests they ran. The infection was believed to have entered his system from the rash on the infected testicles and through the anus, it was not anywhere near the gunshot wound and did not enter his bloodstream until a few days before he died. It took weeks for Steven's testicles to become so inflamed. Marilou was convinced that HealthSouth sent him home, knowing that he was dying but did not wish his death to be listed in their records.

When I came to, Dr. Michele Hauser, and Kristina's therapist, Peggy Farley, were standing beside my bed. Dr. Hauser had the hospital release me and Kristina drove me home. I was inconsolable and still in shock. I took several sleeping pills when I got home and prayed that God would have mercy on me and just let me die in my sleep. I just wanted my suffering to end. I woke in the middle of the night and recalled that I had never felt so alone in my life. The house felt like a mausoleum; depressing, lonely, and lifeless.

Like instant replay, I could not stop thinking about my husband; he was not in a healthy condition when he left the HealthSouth Rehabilitation Hospital. Something happened to Steven after he went out the Brackenridge Hospital's door. He was having difficulty walking at HealthSouth and he complained to me about his legs continuously hurting. It was written in his medical records that he was walking at the beginning of his rehab, but then toward the end, he refused to walk because it was too painful. Medicare would not pay because he was progressing in the therapy, so HealthSouth sent him home. We insisted he stay because we were paying for his care, not the insurance company. Many times I questioned the personnel regarding his ability to walk once he arrived home. They said Steven was lazy and once home, he would have no choice but to move around. Blood clots slow the circulation and the person's legs and feet feel laden with lead and that was why my husband was complaining.

It was Dr. Petty, the Forensic Pathologist for the defense, who explained to the jury that blood clots could pass to a safe spot when vital passageways are not obstructed; Steven would have lived. If the clots stuck, because it was too large or sticky, it would cause death. It was a realistic chain of events for Steven's body to die of blood clots, especially since his Heparin medication, prescribed to treat the clots, was discontinued. It is a common occurrence in the elderly to have thick and sticky blood, doctors treat the blood with oral thinners and diet. Heparin is an injection and is strong. Steven's consumption of red meat was a contributing factor, eating four pounds of steak at one meal was over the top! Drinking in moderation, alcohol can act like a natural blood thinner, but Steven drank to excess. Once hospitalized for the second time, and not having alcohol, contributed to his blood becoming thicker and stickier. It was the natural condition of Steven's body and had nothing to do with the shooting; it was proven to be two completely separate situations. Dr. Bayardo was charged by the prosecution to support their case of Capital Murder and intentionally skipped over this important part of the medical record testimony because it did not prove their case for Capital Murder.

Had we taken the extended European trip, he may have died while we were overseas from blood clots. It was the jury's mistake that they did not correctly apply these facts. The juror's just wanted to go home. One juror, who should have been dismissed over this statement, said it all, "Oh God, let's just get this damned thing over with."

I wandered through the house and saw Steven everywhere, making the pain of his death unbearable. I went to his closet and smelled all of his sweaters and laid out one of his outfits on the leather chair. I collapsed in tears on top of the clothes grieving the loss of my husband. In a hypnotic state, I sprang to my feet and began to gather his clothing for his son, Steven III, because they shared the same monogram. His shoes and personal effects that did not seem appropriate for his son were boxed and given to the Salvation Army.

I kept Steven's light-blue cardigan sweater and wore it with everything. I could still smell his scent on it and wearing it, gave me the tenacity to have his bigger-than-Texas ideas. A few days later the maid washed it, and I went crazy. Not only did she clean one of the only items that had Steven's scent, but she put it in the dryer and shrunk it. She quit working for me, either because she thought I was psychotic, or felt so guilty about the sweater being Steven's, or most likely both. I just never understood her thinking about washing it. We always took everything, including our sheets, to the dry cleaners. Thank goodness I still had the handkerchief he had in his pocket on October 1st.

I retrieved all of Steven's jewelry from the safe and thoughtfully divided it amongst his three grown children, my two daughters, and his two grandchildren. I ran out of jewelry and wanted to give something to his great-granddaughter. Not wanting her to feel left out when she grew older, I gave her a pair of diamond earrings in the shape of a flower that Steven had given me for our first Valentine's Day together. I gathered his antique bank collection and put them aside for his grandson. I decided to send his son, Paul, the antique blanket chest and dry sink in the foyer. I wanted Becky to have the paintings in the hallway by the office, as at one time they hung in her bedroom on Terrace Mountain. I loved all of these pieces. Steven had told me years ago that his children wanted these particular pieces. I had wanted him to give the pieces to them when we moved into Toro Canyon. I told Steven that I did not want to become attached to them. He told me to keep them, because, as he said, "You deserved them more than they do." I gave the furnishings to his natural children after he died, knowing in my heart that it was the right thing to do.

I amassed piles of Steven's personal effects and labeled each collection with the names of his close friends or family members. I chose each item as if Steven himself had personally hand-picked it. I gave personal consideration to each recipient's likes, wanting to share Steven with everyone. I was not trying to get rid of Steven's memory. I just wanted to do what was right. I proudly kept all of our photos displayed as always, even after I remarried. The two houses were filled with memories of Steven. What everyone forgot was that our art and furnishings held special and intimate memories of our unique love affair. I could walk through any part of either home, look at anything and experience a private moment with Steven; I did not share this with anyone except Marilou. After losing her husband, she had moved to Texas. She knew exactly how I felt about losing my husband and the escalating estrangement from my daughters. Now every physical memory I shared with Steven was sold to pay almost $2 million in legal fees.

The girls were furious with me. I was amazed at how quickly the girls forgot all we had done to have them end up with nothing more than their father's clothing, after his suicide. Their father's storage room held nothing but junk. Everything that we purchased for Craig and Jennifer was nowhere to be found. I remember so well, as we stood in the storage space, that all Steven did was shake his head and tell me that he was right. Those people were trash. No matter what my personal feelings were concerning Steven's friends and family, I was determined to do right by the memory of my husband.

The entire time I spent dividing his personal effects, Jennifer and Kristina followed me around the house, arguing with me and urging me to stop. Not because they felt they were losing him, but because of greed. They made it clear how they felt by all of the hateful things they said about his relatives and friends while trying to convince me that I was giving away valuable property to undeserving people. This was the first time I saw pure greed in my daughter's eyes, and it was not pretty by any means. Marilou stood beside me, urging me to follow my heart.

I stood my ground. The more the twins tried to fight me, the more alone I felt. I remembered wrongly thinking that Jimmy's mother did not like me. Even though I had left her son and remarried, when she died, she left instructions for Jimmy to give me a specific momento. I remember how good that gift made me feel and how proud Steven was of me. When I told him how I felt, he insisted it should be prominently displayed in our office. I was hurting because my husband was gone and all I wanted was for the pain to stop. There were no ulterior motives for my giving. During my trial, they implied that I was uncaring and evil. Had this been the case, then Steven's belongings would have ended up being sold or donated instead of meticulously dispersed to those he cared about.

Marilou reminded me that the next task was to focus on Steven's obituary. I wrote the following and had it available for our attorney, David Kuperman, to review at the funeral home before releasing it for publication:

STEVEN F. BEARD. JR.

Steven F. Beard, Jr. 75, died Saturday, January 22, 2000. Steven boasted an illustrious career in advertising. He attended Texas Christian University, Southern Methodist University, and the University of Georgia majoring in Advertising and Marketing. Steven's education was also influenced by the onslaught of World War II. In the Navy Air Corps, he was trained as a pilot and later as an engineer at the United States Maritime Academy in Kingspoint, Long Island, New York.

After the war, he returned to his university studies, and soon to his career. In 1947, as a salesman with KRLD in Dallas, he handled the development and sales of the first FM commercial radio operation at KRLD. He proceeded with his media career as an assistant to the president of the largest advertising agency in the south, Tracy Locke Advertising.

After another two-year period, he helped establish southwest regional sales operations for John Blair & Co.

In 1981, he became a partner and the general manager in KBVO TV, the first independent station in Austin, then acquiring the Fox Network Affiliation in 1985. Throughout his illustrious career, Steven exhibited great progress and innovation in the broadcast industry.

Upon the sale of KBVO in 1995, Steven became active in real estate investments. He established Broadcast Representatives of Dallas (B.R.A.D.), and he organized "The Texas Showdown" as a Media Client function, while President of B.R.A.D. He was a developer and director of the Town North YMCA in Dallas, as well as the Director of the Red Cross in Austin.

He leaves behind his wife, Celeste, and their twin daughters, Jennifer and Kristina Beard. His first wife, Elise, preceded him in death. Steven is also survived by his children, Steven III, Becky and Paul; his grandchildren, Steven IV and Kelly; and his great-granddaughter, Allison.

You were truly a gifted, generous and strong man. Your family and friends will sorely miss you. These words cannot begin to touch every aspect of your life. You were my darling husband, and you brought nothing but joy to my life, and I will love you and miss you forever.

Informal visitation will be held for friends and family on Tuesday, January 25, 2000. Calling hours will be between 2:00 and 9:00 p.m. at Cook-Walden, 6100 North Lamar in Austin. Funeral services will be held at Cook-Walden/Capital Parks Funeral Home, 14501 North IH 35, Pfugerville with Pastor John Gilbert presiding on Wednesday, January 26, 2000, at 11:00 a.m. Immediately following the funeral service, the family will be receiving friends at Austin Country Club.

David made a couple of minor changes and seemed surprised that I had written it. I never did figure out if he meant because I took the time to think it through or if he was surprised that I even had the intelligence to write it, or perhaps a little of both.

12

Meeting Donna Goodson

Not long after Steven's funeral, Jennifer and Kristina were feeling burdened by my presence and lack of motivation to get dressed or leave the house. They embarked on a quest to find me a friend, companion, or anyone that would spend time with me so they would not have that task. In hindsight, I realize they wanted me occupied, but not by anyone who already knew the inner workings of our family. At the time they made me believe that Marilou, Dana, and even my mother and sister wanted nothing to do with me.

I had never felt more alone in my life. The twins convinced me that no one wanted to be around me because I was too clingy and too needy. At Jennifer's urging and introduction, I latched on to the receptionist, Donna Goodson, at the hair salon in our new shopping center and made her my new best friend after the girls formally introduced us. Jennifer and Kristina insisted I hire her to be my assistant. Soon, my days revolved around drinking, and going to the nightclubs with Donna.

At the time I did anything the girls asked of me, in hopes of easing my pain. I felt vacant; I desperately wanted that feeling of emptiness to go away. The twins' sought independence. Their need for freedom coincided with Steven's death. Losing Steven and being pushed away by my daughters was more than I could bare.

I knew absolutely nothing about Donna Goodson. I was told she was transgender, and did notice some masculine qualities about her appearance. I told anyone who made sure I knew she was once a man, "Who cares. It did not matter to me." The girls liked her, so it never occurred to me to ask her for references. I hired her and paid her to babysit me, as there was nothing for her to do. Within a matter of days, Donna began hand-feeding me a combination of tranquilizers, mood elevators, and anti-anxiety medications. I obediently swallowed the pills, using vodka as the chaser. We slept all day and filled our nights with carousing the bars in downtown Austin. I was drowning my sorrow.

It was during one of our party nights that Donna bragged, in detail, about how she beat her ex-husband with his billy club. I grew to become afraid of her and realized she was a loose cannon, capable of anything.

A Greek man, Nick, managed one of the nightclubs we frequented. Although he was a few years older than me, I became attached to him. I was happy to listen to him talk for hours, his thick accent being melodious and comforting to me.

Nick took an instant dislike to Donna and tried to persuade me to "get rid of her." I should have taken heed to his advice. She was stealing from me, and when Detective Schuessler served a search warrant on her mother's house, they found pawn tickets from a shop in Louisiana and were able to retrieve the items stolen from me. She was arrested and charged for the thefts, but the charges were dropped in exchange for her perjured testimony against me.

Nick listened to my regrets, self-blame, and self-pity as a trusted confidant and friend. He understood my grief and loneliness. He had left his wife and son in Greece while saving enough money to pay the attorney fees for them to join him in the United States. We shared many stories of our loved ones. He rescued me in the midst of my deep despair. Caring about me as a friend, he taught me to begin to look at life as an opportunity rather than a burden, struggle, or a headache. When he told me that if I

301

continued to let loss and regret rule myself, my life would be ruined, I began to feel stronger.

I met my current husband, Spencer Johnson, bartending at the 311 Club on 6th Street in downtown Austin. Donna introduced me to him and gave me the impression that she and Spencer were old friends. I later found out that she was trying to get out of paying a former bar tab that she owed the club owner. Like a fool, I paid her overdue bill. It was nearly 2:00 a.m. and I was drunk and I wanted to go home. I had been chatting with Spencer while he was serving customers, I told him, "My driver will be back at 3:00 a.m. to pick you up and take you to my house."

I remember arguing with my limo driver, Al, because he thought that it was a terrible idea to invite Spencer home because I had just met him. Spencer asked his friend, John, to join him when he came to my house. Al did as I requested and went back to pick up Spencer, after dropping me off at my home.

By the time Spencer arrived, I was wearing a set of my pink pajamas and already in bed. Spencer came into my room and woke me while John stayed in the living room with Donna. I told Spencer I did not want sex, just wanted to fall asleep with him and he complied. A few hours later, he woke up and met my daughters in the kitchen. Kristina woke me and berated me for bringing two strange men into "their" house.

The twins did not want me "hanging out" with these men, solely based on how they dressed. I tried to reason with the girls and reminded them how they felt when Steven refused to allow them to befriend a teenage boy because he was black.

I was drawn to Spencer because he did not try to pressure me into having sex with him. He asked, I declined, and that was it. I felt safe and comfortable in his arms and wanted to spend all my time with him. This behavior agitated Donna and my daughters.

I wanted to go to New Orleans since that was where Steven and I had spent our anniversaries. Donna liked the idea and decided we should drive rather than fly. I packed and left without even having a hotel reservation for the first time in my life. While on the road, I contacted the OnStar concierge with the simple press of a button on the dashboard and reserved a room for us at the St. Charles Hotel. I was comforted because this was not the same hotel as Steven and I shared on our last visit to New Orleans. I do not think I could ever stay at the Loews again. This hotel reservation was quite a feat as Mardi Gras was in full swing. Donna was delighted since I paid all of her expenses in addition to her salary. I found out at my trial that Donna returned to New Orleans when I was in Timberlawn and pawned items she stole from my house.

When we got there, we stopped at a local costume shop and bought several colorful wigs to wear to the the Mardi Gras festivities. I took a large vodka drink with me while walking around and observing the floats. I learned that the cheap, plastic beaded necklaces were highly sought after by the tourists. I could have bought them, but wanted to earn them the same way everyone else did, by exposing my breasts. I left New Orleans with my car trunk filled with those cheap souvenirs. The twins were appalled.

By nightfall, I was missing Spencer. I contacted the hotel concierge and asked him to book a first-class flight to New Orleans for him. I called Spencer after the reservations were confirmed, and he agreed to join me, he told me that he could only miss three days of work at his day job. That was fine because I needed to get back to Austin, as the twins were having a fit because I failed to tell, nor invited them to join us.

Spencer arrived the next day, and I was there to greet him. If he thought I was crazy, because I was the only person wearing a neon-colored wig, he never mentioned it.

Celeste

Donna had been spending her time with a man visiting
from India who was in New Orleans for business. She met
him while we were bar-hopping. Spencer and I spent every
minute together. The three days he stayed with me were a
blur. We partied all night, and slept all day. When it was
time for him to return to Austin, I told him that I planned to
drive home the following day, because Donna wanted to
say goodbye to her new friend. Every day for the next
eleven days I called Spencer, telling him, "It'll be
tomorrow." I was avoiding returning home to face the
twins rejection.

After Spencer left, Donna and her date would
allow me to accompany them only at the beginning of the
evening. After I had consumed a few drinks for courage, I
ventured off by myself. One night, the last thing I
remember was drinking and dancing with a group of
college baseball players. I told them that I was only going
to dance since I was old enough to be their mother. I
remember one young man was persistent and kept trying to
kiss me. I was getting aggravated and excused myself to
use the restroom, but instead made a bee-line towards the
door.

The next morning I woke up fully dressed in my
bed at the hotel. Donna had not returned from the night

305

before. I was relieved that she was not there. I was beginning to have a panic attack. I could not remember what I had done after I left the baseball players.

I went to find my purse to see if I still had my credit cards and cash. I had about $600 in cash and all of my credit cards. I also had several "Get Out of Jail Free" cards that were given to me by some of the local police officers for earning strings of beads from them. I suspected I must have passed out after arriving at the hotel, but was not sure.

My heavy drinking was a phase that began after Steven's death. I decided to not dwell on it. I made up my mind, it was time to get my act together and go home. Party time was over. I did not like my irresponsible ways and needed to get back to basics. I did not realize it at the time, but did come to understand that I expressed my grieving in a reckless manner.

When Donna returned to the hotel later that afternoon, she was not pleased to find our suitcases packed and ready to return to Austin. Donna was upset at my bold stance, insisting it was time to go. She had no choice but to accompany me since I was paying all her expenses.

I found out during my trial, while I was in New Orleans with Donna, Kristina was going through my computer and printing some of my personal information.

She admitted she did this just one time but was caught lying on the witness stand about going on my computer more than once. Unbeknownst to Kristina, Jennifer, and their cohorts Justin and Christopher, it is possible to review log files to see when the computer was accessed and what areas were being viewed. My attorney asked Dana Whatley to run a query on my computer, and she was able to identify dates, times, and what files were downloaded to the CD drive. The computer was accessed only during times when I was away traveling or at Timberlawn. If it were true that I allowed the twins to use my computer, as they testified, then why act sneaky and do it while I am away? They testified at the trial that everyone knew the password to my computer, but they failed to be forthright and admit they were the ones freely giving my password out, which they stole from a folder in my filing cabinet. As for my trip to Mardi Gras, the girls were having as much fun rifling through my affairs as I was collecting beads.

When we arrived back in Austin, I took Donna to her mother's house and told her not to let the twins know we had returned. I told her that I would continue to pay her salary, but needed a few days alone. Instead of going home, I drove straight to Spencer's house. One of the roommates let me in, I went into Spencer's room and fell fast asleep in his arms.

Spencer was a carpenter and left early on weekdays for work. During my trial, they made a big deal about Spencer being a carpenter, as if this was a bad thing. He had a Bachelors degree; he just chose not to use it. If I had testified, I would have reminded them that Jesus was also a carpenter. Spencer moonlighted at the 311 Club as a bartender, mostly on the weekends. We affectionately referred to his room as "The Cave." It was my sanctuary. I stayed there for three days before returning home.

I was not truthful and told the twins I had just returned from New Orleans. My relationship with my daughters was strained. I was no longer allowing them to tell me how to live my life. They did not want me around them, but they now did not want me around Donna or Spencer, either. I did not let them know Spencer came to New Orleans. They ranted about him; he wore a motorcycle jacket, worked as a laborer and was not up to their "high standards." They grew to forget their humble roots.

Celeste

13

My Life Unravels

One afternoon, when I was still in bed, I was approached
Kristina and Jennifer; they wanted me to give Kristina my
Power of Attorney because I had decided to return to
Timberlawn Hospital to further treat my depression. Kristina
pleaded, "Mom, I would never do anything to hurt you. You
can trust me." I signed over my Power of Attorney to
Kristina, against my better judgment, and Spencer drove me
to Timberlawn Hospital, where I was admitted on March 22,
2000.

By April 1, 2000, things were so stressful between the
three of us that I revoked my POA in front of Dr. Gotway on
April 4, 2000 because my check bounced for the Timberlawn
Hospital bill. Furious that I would not allow her hands in the
proverbial cookie jar any more, Kristina told my friend,
Dawn, I was a "fucking bitch for revoking the POA." In May,
weeks after the POA had been revoked, my daughters and
Justin were forging checks on my account. It was not too

difficult for them to dupe me, as I was desperate for any contact with them. The girls left home, leaving no explanation or a forwarding address. Justin was the "intermediary" and relayed "supposed" messages from the twins. I was consumed with worry. I thought that perhaps they were hiding from me because I yelled at them, giving them a scolding they deserved.

One morning I opened the newspaper and saw the front page headlines, *"Victim's daughters get legal protection."* I could not believe what my daughters were telling everyone. Not long after the newspaper story broke, they had me served with an Order of Protection in June of 2000. This was only done after I reported to Bank of America in May of 2000 that the kids were forging checks for tens of thousands of dollars from my checking account. Their attorney was paid for with funds stolen from my bank account. He quit representing the girls once he discovered the lies they told him.

When the Order of Protection was signed into effect, the lawyer sent to represent me claimed to have authority to enter the order and findings. I did not give him the authority. The Order of Protection expired by its own terms due to the inaction of the twins. So much for them fearing for their lives, it was just a farce; just so they could get media attention.

I received an anonymous letter encouraging me to

commit suicide; it was a hateful message calling me a dyke and to join my dead husband. What a coincidence that other anonymous letters showed up in my criminal trial three years later. Letters, supposedly typed by me, because the girls said so, were introduced into evidence at my trial. Much of what they said was taken as fact, and that bothered me because no research went into proving things they said. Without proof, their account of things should have been stricken from the record.

While the girls were convincing a family court Judge that they were in fear for their lives because of me, they were busy stealing the two Waverunners that we owned. Also stolen was Steven's birthday dog, jewelry my husband bought for me, and tens of thousands of dollars were withdrawn from my checking account. They stole the house keys, forcing me to have all the locks replaced. They took the car keys, all my photographs, yearbooks, and personal files. Kristina was not authorized to do so, yet accessed Steven's and my PO Box to collect mail to give to ADA Mange. The girls were never charged in those thefts, even though it was conclusive the thefts occurred at their hands. They did not deny the thefts. It took over 90 days to receive a bank statement because Kristina changed the address for the statements to go to a private mailbox in Dripping Springs. They ransacked every room of my house and locked me out of both my safes by changing the master code. They tried to steal the Suburban that Steven had custom-ordered for me when we returned from Washington in the fall of 1999. They turned off the video surveillance equipment at both homes so that they could freely come and go to remove property without leaving a video record. They purchased a Jeep with money stolen from my checking account so they could tow the Waverunners. Claiming to be afraid, they did some pretty bold acts and committed felonies along the way. All charges they faced were dropped and they received immunity in exchange for their testimony in my criminal trial.

I was fragile after Steven's death, and the twins played on my emotions. I was distraught and entertained thoughts of suicide again. They sent messages to me through Justin, telling me that if I agreed to remain in Timberlawn Hospital, they would come home. They completely duped me.

After leaving Timberlawn and returning home, I visited my psychiatrist, Dr. Michele Hauser, weekly. I was unaware that her partner and my daughters' psychologist, Peggy Farley, allowed the girls to move into her home in Dripping Springs with Peggy and her husband. Dr. Hauser knew that I was consumed with anguish as I did not know where the twins were. She never told me their whereabouts and allowed me to continue being concerned. It seems like a conflict of interest and a violation of ethics having the girls live with Ms. Farley, especially since I was paying for all their sessions with her. During the trial, Ms. Farley said she stopped treating the girls the moment they moved into her house because it was unethical.

Without my consent, the twins loaned Peggy's husband $20,000 of my money so that he could purchase some land. When she found out her husband did this behind her back, she made him return the money immediately. As all of these crimes were playing out, I told Dr. Hauser what was going on. She never let on that she knew where the twins were hiding. I only learned of this trickery at my trial in 2003. I felt betrayed by Dr. Hauser. She knew about all of the crazy messages I left for the girls on their cell phones, begging and pleading for them to come home. Dick DeGuerin should have asked her to explain her actions to the jury.

During preparation for my trial, Dr. Hauser was issued a subpoena for the psychiatric records for the twins by my attorney. She refused to comply and provide the records. The purpose of the subpoena was to show interest, bias, and matters that would affect the credibility of the twins. The Judge had signed a second order that was served to Dr. Hauser. Even then, she was protecting her best interests and not those of the court.

Unrelated to the charges I was facing, and shoring up a weak case of guilt, the State embellished every ridiculous, eccentric, or sexual thing I did before the jury like the plot of a cheap romance novel. Portraying our marriage as disrespectful, which it was not, was a misdirection tactic to cause the jury to lose sight of the real case at hand.

From hearsay or otherwise, I believe the conclusion of guilt had been formed in the jurors' minds due to the character assassination through the extensive media coverage. The media was so anxious to report anything and everything because they were making money. They reported what I wore to court every day as if the trial was a fashion show. During Voir Dire, potential jurors had preconceived conclusions and did admit their opinions were influenced and impartial because of the considerable media coverage. One juror admitted to Judge Kocurek that he read the newspaper, in violation of the court order. She allowed him to remain on the jury when he should have been excused.

The State sought to corroborate Tarlton's accomplice witness testimony with mobile phone records. The phone records produced could not prove what particular people were communicating at specific times. The State was allowed to submit these records as fact, even with Tarlton's testimony and several other witnesses that no one person could be attached to any particular cell phone. ADA Allison Wetzel succeeded in confusing the jury because the Judge allowed the prosecution to manipulate the facts.

Celeste

I was in daily contact with my attorney when Steven's children and the twins filed the civil lawsuit against me for Steven's estate. I gave a deposition on August 25, 2000. My lawyers reserved the right to examine me until the trial of that case. Judge Herman ruled that there was no evidence indicating that I intentionally and willfully participated in Steven's shooting. My highly qualified civil trial attorneys, A. Boone Almanza, Bo Blackburn, and David Duggins, were skilled, expert attorneys. Boone judged it unnecessary to put on a defense after hearing David Duggins' summary and rebuttal of the plaintiff's case. He considered it stirring and brilliant, one for the record books. Judge Herman said it was obvious the girls were not telling the truth. The case never went to trial, because the petitioners dropped the lawsuit the day before the teenagers were scheduled to give their depositions, beginning with that of Justin Grimm. The teenagers knew their videotaped deposition was going to incriminate them. Their attorneys quit after that trial; they wanted nothing further to do with the girls, their dishonesty was apparent. It took over two years of meeting with the ADA, on a daily basis, to polish the twins' testimony enough to be able to sway the jury into believing their lies and convict me.

The Judge gave this instruction at my criminal trial, "These questions by Mr. Powell (the attorney for the adult

315

children of Steven Beard) are hearsay, but they are not being admitted for the truth of the matter stated. They are being admitted to provide context, if they do, for the answers and statements of Celeste Beard Johnson."

I was full of anxiety, and Dr. Michele Hauser suggested I take two Xanax before arriving to give the deposition; she said it would calm my nerves. The jurors were never informed that I was sedated during the deposition, which was definitely the reason for my lack of emotions. I suspect Dr. Hauser wanted me sedated because she, along with her partner Ms. Farley, were concerned that their unethical behaviors would be discovered and could jeopardize their careers.

Marilou and Dawn convinced me to fight the twins regarding their "perjured testimony" given at the Protective Order hearing. Charles Burton, my attorney before the hiring of Dick DeGuerin, instructed Spencer and me to leave Austin, and preferably the state, until after the hearing. Angry, Marilou called Mr. Burton to tell him it was a grave mistake for me to not be at the hearing. Marilou and Dawn promised to testify on my behalf and begged me to return to Austin.

Spencer and I decided to comply with the attorney's directive. I was paying the firm to look after my interests, and I tried to explain this to Marilou. Mr. Burton said I was to never tell anyone about his urging me to leave to avoid a summons. I thought it was a tactic, looking for more time. I never agreed to have my new "family lawyer," Mr. Mueller, testify on my behalf; I hardly knew him, and he knew nothing about the inner workings of our family. Charles Burton insisted that I retain Mueller. I only learned about him testifying on the witness stand all these years later, after the statute of limitations ran out. To this day, I cannot fathom what kind of lawyer would do this. I have noticed most lawyers will protect their own, just as the police and prosecutors protect their own. I began to realize they are all incestuous in Austin, especially when it appeared they were in bed with the Bank of America. Our attorney, David Kuperman, now works for Bank of America along with Donna Goodson's attorney and our accountant.

Mueller happens to also be the last name of Emily Basham's attorney; I am uncertain if the last name is a coincidence or if it is the same man. Emily worked for Tracey and attended the "Book People" party at the lake house. On February 12, 2003, she had a DUI pending with a blood alcohol level of .17, almost twice the legal limit. For her deal with the State, she fabricated a story of seeing Tracey and me kissing.

The amount of money stolen and the combined value of the items stolen was staggering. The girls were ruthless in their pursuit. Bank of America returned all of my money after

I filed a police report. Had the checks been legally written, they would not have returned the missing money. To reimburse the bank, the twins had money taken from their trust fund. This was unethical.

Donna Goodson, the twins, Justin, and Christopher were never prosecuted. Each of their thefts totaled in excess of tens of thousands of dollars. They all had perjured themselves on the witness stand with evidence supporting what the truth was; their lies were confronted by my defense team. Once cornered for telling lies, they suddenly "could not remember."

14

My Arrest

I sold the lake house and the Toro Canyon home because my life, as I had known it, in those two homes, was over. I was, and still am, estranged from my daughters – like Israel and Palestine. I will always be remembered by them since they look just like me. They may not be in contact with me, but they do see me every time they look in the mirror. To be closer to Spencer's family, I purchased the home in Southlake, it was five hours outside Austin, far away from the girls.

I was arrested on March 28, 2002, when I was on my way to pick up my dogs from their groomer. After spending three days in Tarrant County jail, I was transported to the Travis County jail and remained in custody until this day.

Wife is indicted in 1999 slaying. This article in the Austin-American Statesman newspaper, Saturday, March

30, 2002, stated, "District Attorney Ronnie Earle on Friday attributed the arrest to hard work by prosecutor Bill Mange and Travis County Sheriff's detectives."

"It has taken two years to unravel the mystery surrounding the death of Steve Beard," Earle said in a written statement. "This indictment is the result of dogged persistence by Bill Mange and the Sheriff's office. They never gave up."

My first appearance in court was to ask for reasonable bail on June 14, 2002. The grand jury requested $20 million, but Judge Julie Kocurek said, "I considered that, but after I have looked at all the case, the briefs by the attorney, the court cannot set it at $20 million. I will set it at $8 million."

Assistant district attorney Allison Wetzel's husband, Rick, worked for the Appellate Court that was considering a decision to reduce the $8 million bail to $500,000. A defendant released on bail has a greater probability of being found not guilty and can offer more assistance to the defense. Dick filed an appeal to have the bail lowered to $500,000 and won. That amount was a reasonable figure to obtain bail; I would be free while awaiting my trial. Rick Wetzel notified his wife, Allison, of this before my defense team was notified. The DA's office returned to court that evening with another indictment for $15 million dollars for the trumped up charge of Conspiracy to Commit Capital Murder.

ADA Mange had given the court his two months' notice, left the district attorney's office and went into private practice as a Board Certified Criminal defense attorney. After the new indictment, Mange solicited me, offering to represent me on the new Conspiracy to Commit Capital Murder charge. This was unethical.

Another appeal was filed, but this time the Appellate Court could make no ruling before the start of the murder trial. Judge Kocurek would not approve any extensions for starting the trial at a later date.

Mr. DeGuerin: "The State has complicated that matter, Judge, choosing to bring the second indictment. Frankly, I think the bringing of a second indictment was because the State was fearful that the Court of Appeals would set a reasonable bail in the case that originally was before your Honor. And the timing of the bringing of that indictment, based as it is on facts that had been known before that, long before that, suggests to me that the State simply files this new case in order to prevent Ms. Beard from receiving a reasonable bond from the Court of Appeals, and from posting a bond. Nonetheless, that is my

321

opinion." It greatly complicated the investigation and preparation of the main case. Dick had less than five months to prepare for my trial.

"The new indictment, although I still haven't seen it, even though it was returned Monday and we have requested it, deals with an alleged murder-for-hire plot, alleging that Ms. Beard Johnson asked a friend, named Donna Goodson, to find a hit man to kill Tracey Tarlton. It's ludicrous, but nonetheless, they have filed that pleading."

Steven Beard's murder trial would have been the high point of Bill Mange's career. It would have been the trial of a lifetime. I believe he was forced to leave the district attorney's office because he had knowledge that my daughters and their boyfriends were lying and had tampered with the "so-called" evidence. There were no evidence logs documenting all the information brought to Mr. Mange. I believe he was responsible for orchestrating the cover-up and tampering with the evidence. The Judge sealed all of Mange's files as "work product." The DA was not playing straight with me. I never had a chance. The entire trial was built on a foundation of lies.

15

Collecting Evidence

The teenagers testified that most of the so-called evidence they gave to Bill Mange was retrieved from my trash. They said I told them to throw out plastic bags filled with files and documents. I never authorized any "throw away" of personal papers, bank statements, pictures, or journals. It was a ritual that Steven and I shredded any papers that were trash and any papers we thought needed to be saved for tax purposes were organized in file boxes, by year, and kept in a storage area in the garage attic. When the police searched the garage attic, they found a shotgun, which Jennifer secretly purchased, in a box that was the same gauge as the one Tracey used to shoot my husband.

Jennifer said she bought it for Christopher's birthday. It was revealed she bought the shotgun with money she stole from me. Jennifer testified that I was unaware that this gun was hidden in the attic. Why had she secretly purchased a weapon that was similar to the one her father used to commit suicide? Years later, Jennifer posted pictures on her Facebook page of at least a dozen guns, the caption read, "Can you ever have too many guns?" Why weren't these items retrieved by the police during their extensive search of our home, grounds, and vehicles? The answer is because when I signed off on the search warrant, the police found nothing to take that amounted to evidence.

A reenactment was done using an identical shotgun and scenario to test the theory that the shotgun blast could not be heard in the twin's wing of the house. Someone was in the master bedroom and another person was in Kristina's bedroom when they fired the test shot. Their conclusion backed what I had told them all along: the blast could not be heard that far away. This proved I did not know Steven was shot until the blinding lights and screeching sirens woke us the night of the shooting. Even Nikki, with such keen hearing, did not hear the shot and wake us.

I never gave the teenagers permission to rifle through my papers and computer. The evidence submitted to Bill Mange was illegally obtained and should not have been allowed. The kids told the attorneys during the trial that they took it upon themselves to decide what to throw away and what to keep, per my instructions. This was a total fabrication. Jennifer's boyfriend, Christopher Doose, admitted removing items from my home and hiding them in his parent's house. They pilfered on the sly while I was a patient at Timberlawn. Rather conveniently, and appearing to be schooled on how to respond to questions, Kristina, Jennifer, Justin, and Christopher could not remember facts and details of what was taken, and who took what and when, during their testimony. Many times "I don't remember" and "I don't know" appear in the trial transcripts. Between the shooting and the death of my husband, this was a significant and stressful time in our lives. One does not quickly forget details of such importance. I find it convenient that all four teens suffered from massive bouts of forgetfulness, yet they never lost sight of the fact that if I were convicted, they would become very wealthy young ladies.

The twins said it was "the family" computer, but it was not. That was another fabrication. The computer was located in Steven's and my office in our wing of the home. The girls were repeatedly told to keep their hands off of my computer and to stay out of our wing. Why didn't they copy the files or take the computer to the DA's office to prove their claims? The evidence they supposedly retrieved from my computer was an anonymous letter. My daughters each had their own laptops and PC's in their bedrooms to keep them off my computer. They even had their own satellite dish in their wing to keep them from coming to our area uninvited.

During the Motion to Suppress Evidence hearing, I testified that Steven and I never threw papers in the trash; they were shredded. The "trash story" was important, because law enforcement may examine discarded garbage without a warrant. They say the owner has given up any ownership rights. The Judge ruled against me in favor of the State even though our handyman, Doug Byers, testified that Justin Grimm was illegally inside the third storage room in our garage hiding while sorting through our papers. Bills and statements illegally taken from my home became evidence in the murder trial.

Dick DeGuerin, with 38 years of practice and a law instructor, was hired to be my defense attorney with less than five months to prepare for a drawn-out, high-profile Capital Murder charge. It was a seven week trial, with over 200 witnesses, and forty-eight volumes of testimony. Judge Julie Kocurek denied all requests by Attorney DeGuerin for more time to prepare. I did ask Dick for a change in venue, but that did not happen.

There was a lot of antagonism between Bank of America and me following my husband's death. I admit I was bold and said some vulgar things to the bank employees. I could not get past their rudeness and abruptness towards me. Bank of America routinely dragged their feet when subpoenaed for bank records. An Order of Enforcement from the court was necessary to get them to cooperate. Such obstacles made it difficult for my attorney to be prepared on time for the trial. A truck had to be rented by the bank to deliver all our financial records.

Another delay tactic was the twins avoiding subpoenas. I believe the girls expected to receive subpoenas and that is why they had the trumped-up Order of Protection drawn against me so that they could hide. Dick was particularly interested in their tax records to show motive. A court order was presented to the IRS to get certified copies of the requested records. The twins were witnesses for the State, and they may have been instructed as to how to make things difficult for the defense, although nobody would ever admit to such underhandedness.

The Austin-American Statesman newspaper had an 8" x 5" color picture of me wearing a full-leg cast stating, "Celeste Beard Johnson returned to court Tuesday to ask for a reduction in her $15 million bail on a charge of Solicitation of Capital Murder. Her assets totaled $7,289 her accountant testified. Johnson also faces a Capital Murder charge in the death of her husband, Steven Beard Jr., a TV executive; Johnson's leg was in a cast because she broke it after passing out in jail. The bail hearing will continue today." The news reported that I purposely broke my leg to attempt an escape. The media circus was in full motion.

I was startled awake after taking 400 mg. of Trazadone to help me sleep; I jumped up and felt dizzy. The officer told me to sit on the stool and place my head between my legs. My last memory was complying with her direct order. I woke up and was splayed out on the floor with intense pain in my right leg. I had broken my leg. The officer said that the sole of my shoe must have stuck to the painted concrete when I passed out. My leg twisted in the fall. The x-ray showed that it was a spiral fracture in my tibia and two displaced fractures in my fibula at the knee and ankle. The media accused me of breaking my leg on purpose.

Donna Goodson was arrested, but she was never tried in court for stealing my jewelry and other things because she agreed to testify against me while she perjured herself under oath. Donna Goodson lied so that she would not face prison time for stealing. If Donna had been found guilty of the theft of my jewelry, she risked being sentenced under the very harsh Three Strikes Law. In 2000, she filed for unemployment benefits against me. I fought the unemployment compensation claim because I viewed Donna Goodson as a contractor and not an employee.

Celeste

Donna won and received the unemployment compensation
payments because the State agreed that all the checks I
wrote to Donna were for her wages, as an employee, not a
contractor. In my trial, Donna testified that those same
checks were now payment so she could retain a hit man.
The defense was not allowed to tell the jury about the
unemployment ruling regarding those same checks paid.

After the revocation of Kristina's Power of
Attorney on April 4, 2000, I discovered forged checks
where tens of thousands of dollars were transferred out of
my account. Valuable items were removed from the house,
resulting in charges being filed against the young adults
involved in the thefts. This ignited their desire to move
forward in their plan to have me convicted. Around April
7th through 9th, illegally recorded audio tapes were brought
to ADA Mange by the four teens. Jennifer and Kristina
appeared with their lawyer, Wayne Meissner; he soon
resigned from representing them and told my lawyers the
twins were deceitful. Justin Grimm, Kristina's boyfriend at
the time, though they later married and divorced, appeared
with his lawyer, Alan Bennet. Bennet also represented Donna
Goodson and Bank of America, which does cause a conflict
of interest. Jennifer's boyfriend at the time, Christopher
Doose, appeared with his lawyer, Ron Tonkin.

329

The teens continued to bring items to Mange after this date, unaccompanied by any attorneys. Dick had questioned Justin Grimm, "Was there some reason why you took these things to Mr. Mange on several different occasions rather than all at once?" Justin Grimm testified, "We couldn't remember the different places we stashed things." Both boyfriends of Jennifer and Kristina feigned hiding the documents in their houses.

Sgt. Bergman and ADA Bill Mange did not have an evidence log of any of these items. Sgt. Bergman, a 31 year law enforcement officer, testified he did not take custody of the items the kids gave to ADA Mange, yet an evidence envelope shows his signature and date of December 18, 2000. Judge Kocurek allowed every questionable piece entered into evidence against me. The teens were never convicted for the forged checks or thefts because they agreed to testify against me.

At the pretrial hearing, Dick DeGuerin stated his concerns before the court that Detective Mange had not preserved evidence and made no record of when, how, and by whom items were received. With no inventory record of the items, my attorney wanted the evidence suppressed because the State could not prove the mandatory chain of custody with any of the material the teens stole and gave to the prosecution. Regardless of the shoddy police work, the evidence was admitted for use during the trial.

The conspirators, Kristina and Justin, testified that the unsigned letters they gave the prosecution were printed from my computer. The Judge allowed them to be admitted as evidence.

Kristina and Justin made audio tapes that were misleading since they did not contain the entire conversations. The recordings were blatantly edited. Scientific testimony by Doug Morrison, director of the premier U.S. recording school, Dallas Sound Lab School for the Recording Arts, had 30 years experience in the industry. He gave an impressive testimony on the electronic editing and splicing of these tapes. He demonstrated to the court, using computerized sound waves and graphs, and utilized both audio and visual techniques, to confirm his findings. The results proved words were alternately added and eliminated throughout the tape and that the original conversation was not as it appeared.

The Judge allowed the altered tapes to be admitted into evidence and said, "She's (Kristina) familiar with all of the voices that are on this tape. This is the original tape (because Kristina says it is) and the court is satisfied that this tape has been properly authenticated and that it is what the proponent claims it to be. It will be overruled."

The tape was entered into evidence, even with Kristina's testimony that she cut pertinent parts of the conversation out of the tape.

The police investigators and prosecutors ended up seeking out circumstantial evidence that confirmed their prior beliefs rather than the hard evidence that challenged these beliefs. They ended up interpreting the ambiguous evidence in ways that agreed with their preconceptions.

The prosecutor's case was based on character assassination, innuendo, anonymous letters, debatable forensic science evidence, and the unreliable and non-credible testimony of informants with criminal charges pending against them that were later dropped in exchange for their false testimonies. The media convicted me before the trial commenced; they did not look for anything to dispute or discredit the testimony of the informants. The State listed 200 witnesses to further complicate matters and confuse the jurors. This case proves that their "facts" did not prove anything, but were lumped together with suspicious and dubious theories.

The Judge did not allow the civil trial transcripts to be introduced during the trial. This would have exposed the teenager's lies and dubious acts. That was a blow the defense.

Tracey Tarlton was the State's primary witness. The credibility, believability, and her state of mind outlined a pattern of untrustworthy conduct and propensity for violence.

16

The Indictment

Assistant district attorney Wetzel read the Indictment on March 28th of 2002. A Travis County Grand Jury returned a three-count indictment against me for the offenses of Capital Murder, Murder, and Injury to an Elderly Individual. I was convicted on two of those counts and sentenced twice. Capital Murder means the prosecution has to prove that the principal actor (Tarlton) did intentionally, and knowingly, cause the death of an individual (Steven Beard) by shooting him with a firearm, a deadly weapon; that it was done for remuneration or the promise of remuneration, and that is, namely, money or the estate of Steven Beard or the assets of the Trust created by Steven Beard."

The Solicitation of Murder charge, based on Donna Goodson's claim of being hired to find a hitman to kill Tracey, was heard before Judge Julie Kocurek on September 2004, I pled no contender and received a preagreed five-year sentence to run concurrently with the other sentence. The time-served started the first day I was arrested in 2002.

I originally paid $250,000 to go to trial for this Solicitation charge because it was completely false. After being in prison for a year and a half, I knew I could not endure being housed in Segregation again, alone for 23 hours a day, at the county jail for possibly over a year while awaiting trial.

Dick told me it would be at least five years for all my appellate work so I asked him to make a plea deal for five years time served. I thought I would get a refund of most of the $250,000 paid, since we did not go to trial. I did not realize the contract I signed to pay the fee of $250,000 was for a trial or a plea deal. I would have gone to trial had I realized this.

Hans Sherrer, of *Justice Denied*, wrote, "A universal tactic used by prosecutors, who have little actual evidence, is to expose the jury to as much extraneous testimony and character assassination (bad character evidence) as possible. Many defendants today are not convicted by a jury based on evidence of their guilt. Prosecutors are taught that they need minimal (if any) actual evidence of guilt if they can smear a person."

17

Criminal Trial

Trial Court Cause Number 9020236

The State of Texas in the District Court, Travis County,

Texas

390th Judicial District

VS.

Celeste Beard Johnson

Assistant District Attorneys for the State

Ms. Allison Wetzel

Mr. Gary Cobb

Attorneys for the Defendant

Mr. Dick DeGuerin

Ms. Catherine Baen

Mr. Matt Hennessy

Honorable Julie Kocurek, Judge presiding

Celeste

"We're seeing a lot of craziness in this trial all around"

-Judge Kocurek

I believe Judge Kocurek knew there were serious problems with this case and secretly desired to assist the State in this high-profile trial. In her first trial of this magnitude, she would be on television often.

She became personally enmeshed in the proceedings and had assumed the role of prosecutor. My best friend, BJ, noticed the cozy relationship between the Judge and Allison Wetzel while they shared a meal together on more than one occasion.

Judge Kocurek excluded much of my evidence, and treated my witnesses unfairly in comparison to how she treated the State's witnesses. She improperly limited my evidence, cross-examinations, and rebuttals. The record is permeated with favoritism. We did not expect a perfect score, we just wanted fairness and a level playing field.

Kristina Beard

It was difficult for me to listen to the testimony of my daughter, Kristina. She was not forthright, under oath, most of the time. At other times she was telling the truth, making it difficult for the jury to distinguish fact from fiction. I was admonished by the Judge for rolling my eyes during part of her testimony. That is how hard it was for me to sit and listen to some of the lies. I always felt the Judge favored the twins. Perhaps it is because she also has twins. Both my daughters became estranged from me in the months that followed my husband's death. They preyed on my vulnerabilities. My world came crashing down, and I was left alone, frantic with worry. I felt helpless. I loved my daughters more than anything in this world, despite their raucous behavior. They began acting out by stealing from me and forging checks from my bank account. They left home and went into hiding, claiming they were afraid of me. I would never hurt my daughters, and they knew that to be the truth. I never spanked or even disciplined them. The real reason they disappeared was that they did not want to be located after I discovered the forged checks, thefts of expensive jewelry and the Waverunners. After being kicked out of Farley's house, they raided the Toro Canyon house to set up their new apartment with my property. My friend BJ was house sitting and was frightened by the twin's behavior, she threatened to call the police. They waited until I was admitted back into Timberlawn then ransacked the house and stole some of my belongings to give to the district attorney to use as evidence against me. They were also in hiding to avoid the process servers, something an innocent person would not do. I accept complete blame for their behavior. Had I given them a more solid foundation, been more strict in their upbringing, and raised them as my children and not my best friends, then they may have grown to have decent moral characters. Instead, they were proven dishonest, and their testimonies to the defense attorney's questions indicated that they knew more about what happened than they let us believe. In answering defense questions under oath, Kristina replied "I don't remember" and " I don't know" a whopping 298 times. When the prosecutors questioned them, they knew exactly what to say, without any "I don't know" replies. Considering the seriousness of the crime and the damaging effect it had on our family, it is difficult to believe anyone could forget important details surrounding the shooting and death of my husband and the twins' adoptive father, Steven

Beard. The girls stood to gain millions of dollars if I was convicted. Otherwise, they would not inherit until I died.

Not presented in any particular order and to the best of my recollection are highlights of Kristina Beard's testimony:

- Admitted to continue writing thousands upon thousands of dollars in checks from my account after I had her Power of Attorney revoked. When asked about when the Power of Attorney was revoked, Kristina did not remember that happening. She pitched a fit and called me a "bitch" when she no longer was my POA. How could she have forgotten it was revoked? A lie.

- Stated that Charles Burton was not her attorney until she was shown a signed contract with Burton and acknowledged her signature. Caught in a lie.

- Admitted she hated Steven and called him a fat slob, a fat fuck and other derogatory names. She said she hated sitting down to have dinner with him, even though he prepared gourmet meals daily. She did agree that she mocked him behind his back.

- When questioned if I threw my husband's prescriptions out the car window, during one of our

339

trips, and replaced them with sleeping pills, she redacted her previous statement that claimed I did do that, and said, "It was not true."

- I told my attorney that I drove to the lake house the night of the shooting. I had both dogs, Megan and Nikki, with me. I left Megan at the lake house with the kids because Amy Cozart, the consummate dog lover, asked if I would leave her. When Kristina was asked if I ever took Megan to the lake house, she told the jury that Megan never went to the lake house. When she was asked the question later in the testimony, she forgot she lied and said Megan went to the lake house often.

- Kristina testified that she never heard me call Steven a "fat fuck", but does remember Tracey Tarlton calling him that all the time.

- For a high school graduation gift, I gave the twins a gracious gift of matching Cadillacs. When questioned on the stand about receiving the car, she lied and said she was not mad that it was a Cadillac. The truth was, the day I gave the girls their cars, she said she wanted a BMW and pitched a fit that I did not give her the car she wanted.

- Kristina stole a journal from Tracey Tarlton's house and gave it to our attorney, Mr. Burton. He produced that journal for evidence. When Kristina saw the journal, she denied stealing it and giving it to Burton. When caught in the lie, she suddenly did not remember.

- During a trip to Australia, Kristina told the jury that I never left the hotel room. She said I did not participate in the day tours we had planned and that I spent the day sleeping and talking on the phone with Tracey. When the photos of the trip were displayed for the jury, showing me in numerous pictures with the girls, she realized she was caught in another lie and changed her answer, saying I did leave the hotel room.

- Being caught telling inconsistent statements between the probate court and the criminal trial, Dick DeGuerin had to show her direct testimony, which did indicate she said different things to both courts. He told Kristina that she had changed her tune of the accuracy of events because she turned against me and was fighting the answers all the way.

- During the probate testimony, Kristina said I gave her signed, blank checks for her use. At the criminal trial, she said she forged the checks. She lied in the probate court. Dick was not allowed to impress upon the jury about her check forging lies during the civil trial in the criminal trial.

- Kristina told the prosecution I gave Tracey Tarlton a ring for Christmas. They were inferring the ring was a wedding band. When the defense cross examined Kristina, she continued to stick to the story that I bought the ring. Jennifer appeared in court wearing that exact same ring, including size, that was listed on the receipt. Dick DeGuerin presented the receipt into evidence that bore Kristina's jewelry selections and signature. The receipt listed all the items purchased. Those gifts of jewelry were gifts Kristina bought for Christmas to give to her friends. There was a $100 gift certificate for Amy Cozart listed amongst the purchases. When shown the receipt, Kristina said the signature could be hers, but could not remember.

- Kristina had a friend, Kim Griffs, who lived in Newburgh, New York. In late 1999 to early 2000, Kim sent Kristina an invitation to her wedding.

When Dick DeGuerin asked her if she received the invitation, she said she did not get any mail from Kim. Kristina did testify that she attended the wedding. When asked how she knew about the wedding if she did not get the invitation, her reply was, "I do not remember." When asked if Kristina spoke with Kim Griffs on the phone, she did not remember. When shown the cell phone records of a 26 minute call to Newburgh, New York, Kristina said, "I don't remember, the three of us traded phones all the time." The relevance of this line of questioning was to show the jury, one, that Kristina was a liar, and two, that the cell phones were traded routinely between my daughters and me. This line of questioning was also setting a precedent to debunk the voluminous phone records presented in evidence by the prosecution to show who called whom, and when.

- Dr. Hauser presented notes about Kristina requesting guardianship over me when I was in Timberlawn, after my downward spiral since Steven died. She denied asking for guardianship, despite proof she did request it.

- Kristina denied contacting an attorney, David

Botsford, when I was at Timberlawn following Steven's death. Kristina tried to hire him to have me committed to a state mental institution. He told her "no."

- Checks were presented to the court showing Kristina wrote and signed checks to Donna Goodson while Donna was in my employ. Kristina denied writing checks for Donna Goodson even though she eventually did admit the checks bore her signature. Donna claimed these checks were payment for hiring a hit man. I am the one who is paying the price being sentenced for that lie.

- I had loose diamonds locked in my safe that went missing. Kristina said she saw Donna Goodson with the stones, and then amended her statement claiming she did not remember.

- I received an anonymous letter in the mail. The letter called me a dyke and told me to die and join my dead husband. A handwriting expert was called to testify and verified it was Kristina's handwriting. She denied writing the letter

- In probate court and the criminal trial, Kristina's testimony confirmed that Tracey Tarlton was very angry with Steven because he called her, "South Austin trash," and told her she was no longer welcome in our house. This outburst from my husband happened when Tracey tried to kiss me on our front porch when she got drunk after the graduation ceremony.

- At the probate court in August of 2000, Kristina testified that she only saw me with Tracey two times and that she thought we might be more than friends. During the criminal trial, she changed her answer from two times to multiple times. When asked which answer was accurate, she did not know.

- Kristina spoke with our attorney, Mr. Burton, several days after Steven was shot. His notes were evidence in the trial. Such answers included:
  - Steven would get angry when the twins would not be home for dinner.
  - She swore she was home by 11 p.m. and I was home before midnight the night of the shooting.
  - She said we talked for a few minutes before going to sleep and that I slept in her room.
  - She verified I went to the lake house to see

Jennifer and her friends and that I took both dogs with me, but left Megan there.

- ○ She said I woke her up in the middle of the night when I heard someone pounding on the front door. (The door was too far away for this to be true.)

- Another meeting with Mr. Burton included Kristina giving him a recorded message she received from Tracey Tarlton. The tape was authenticated and played for the jury. Kristina denied providing the tape to Mr. Burton. She told the court she had no contact with Tracey after Steven died. That recorded message was Tracey calling Kristina, she was not calling me. Admitted into evidence was a picture of Kristina's caller ID showing Tracey calling Kristina directly on her newly changed phone number. That new number was given to Tracey by Kristina.

- Kristina told the jury about a phone call she recorded from Donna Goodson and gave to Mr. Burton. On the tape, Goodson said she was going to tell the police there was a contract out on Tracey Tarlton. Goodson said she was going to incriminate me unless I dropped the theft charges against her.

Goodson was facing the "Three Strikes Law" due to previous convictions and would have been incarcerated. She stole precious stones, jewelry and other items from me while in my employ and was planning to blackmail me so I would drop the charges against her. I never dropped the charges. The DA dropped them in exchange for her testimony against me.

- When questioned why she dropped the civil suit, Kristina answered," I felt there was no need to pursue." The civil suit was brought against me because Steven's three adult children and the twins wanted the court to control the money in the estate that was now in the marital trust. I was given $7,500 a month from the Trust. They were all angry that they did not receive their expected share of the money. The real reason the suit was dropped was that Kristina and Jennifer realized the day before they were to testify, they were going to have to do so under oath while being video recorded. Telling the truth was the motive for dropping the suit.

- After Steven passed away, Kristina helped me pay bills and run errands. She felt HealthSouth was responsible for his death. She admitted she wrote on a bill we received from HealthSouth " Don't pay. Find out what for. The neglect caused my father's death."

- Kristina told the jury about my struggles after Steven died. She told the court how I fell apart and was doing crazy things. She told them I would not get out of bed for several weeks. This was the truth, and I was seeing my therapist regularly at that time to try to regain my composure.

- Kristina was required to submit handwriting samples for an expert to analyze. The purpose was to prove, beyond doubt, that she wrote an anonymous letter to me calling me a dyke and telling me I should die and join my husband. She denied writing the letter. The court ordered her to write her signature twenty-four times. In defiance, she printed her name and had to return to court to write her name in cursive. The results: Kristina did write that letter.

- Kristina testified that I put Ambien in Steven's food. Medical records and pharmacy records produced showed the only prescribed sleeping pill was Temazepam. All the pills in the bottle were accounted for at the time of the shooting. Another lie.

Completely improper, Kristina and Jennifer bonded with the

prosecution during the two years of daily coaching and preparation for the criminal trial. Had the jury been able to see their testimony during the civil trial in comparison to their testimony during the criminal trial, they would have not recognized them. Their performance was stoic and rehearsed, as were the hugs from Kristina and Jennifer to the shooter, Tracey Tarlton, after Tarlton was excused from the witness stand.

Justin Grimm

Justin methodically inserted himself into our family when he began dating Kristina. He was at our home nearly every day. At first, I did not mind having him around. He seemed like a nice young man. He appeared intelligent, honest and trustworthy. He was useful and asked me if there was anything he could do for me. In the beginning, he lent a helping hand, contrary to his lazy behavior at Peggy Farley's ranch later on. He earned my trust. Over time, I could see his true colors come through; he was a wolf in sheep's clothing. I saw how he slowly began to manipulate my daughter and control all aspects of her life. I grew cautious about their relationship and blew a gasket when I found out they were having sex. Justin's mother took Kristina to get birth control pills behind my back. He was somewhat of a computer geek and loved to tinker with electronics. During the trial, he loved being in the limelight. I recall someone describing Justin, "If you asked Justin what time it was, he would tell you how to build a clock." In the end, my instincts about Justin were correct. He became sneaky and did things I would have never thought he would do to me:

- He changed the combination on both of my safes and would not give me the new codes.
- He was caught stealing documents from boxes in my private storage area to give to ADA Mange.
- He was involved with the theft of jewelry and the Waverunners.
- He admitted to forging and endorsing checks.
- He was caught, red-handed, adjusting the newly installed security system cameras so they were not in focus and not aimed in the direction as they were supposed to be.

The list was endless.

After Steven was shot, Justin started to behave suspiciously and became a seasoned liar. His testimony was riddled with contradictions.

Not presented in any particular order and to the best

of my recollection, highlights of Justin Grimm's testimony:

- Confirmed on the witness stand: The night Steven was shot, Justin and Kristina went to dinner and a movie with his parents. He testified he dropped my daughter off at home around 11 p.m. and then went home. He lived with his parents and was home for the weekend from Baylor University, where he was a freshman.

- When the ambulance arrived, and Star Flight was preparing to fly my husband to Brackenridge Hospital, it was around 3 a.m. The police said they would drive Kristina and me to the hospital. As we were getting into the police car, I saw Justin standing beside his car watching everything. Justin's parents live about 15 minutes from our house. When questioned why and how he could have been there at that time, he said Kristina called him. No phone records introduced into evidence could corroborate the claim.

- Justin was told the meaning of hearsay when he took the stand. He was instructed to answer questions as asked, to not use hearsay, and not to elaborate on questions, just answer as asked. Throughout the trial, he continually filled his testimony opposite of the instructions he was given. It was difficult to get an answer out of him and, as often as possible, his answers were, " I don't remember," and "I don't know."

- He went to great strides to squeeze in bad things about me when the prosecution was questioning him. At one point, he felt the need to get the last word in and told the jury I peed on Jimmy Martinez's lawn. When my attorney objected to his answer and asked the Judge how does going to the bathroom on someone's lawn make them a killer, the Judge agreed and told the State to move along. Justin sat on the witness stand with a smug grin.

- When asked where the girls were staying when they left home while I was in Timberlawn, Justin testified he did not know where they were. He was caught lying, because he did know the girls were staying with their therapist, Peggy Farley. During her testimony, Peggy Farley said Justin was at her house every day hanging out.

- Justin said he helped Steven pack and get ready for our vacation to Europe. When shown crime scene photos, the suitcases were still sitting empty on the shelf in the closet. Several empty duffle bags were sitting on the bedroom floor. We had not packed yet and Justin had no explanation to his answer saying he helped pack.

- Justin was questioned about the theft of the Waverunners. He did admit he was in on the theft, but he justified taking them because I did not ride them anyways. He was shown pictures of different outings when I was riding them, and he was present and visible in the background. He was caught in a lie.

- After the book store party at the lake house, Justin and Kristina came the following morning saying they showed up to help clean up. They brought a disposable camera that day and photographed the aftermath of the party. When asked why he was taking pictures, he said it was for fun. He went on to say he saw me in bed with Tracey Tarlton. When asked why he did not take a picture of us in bed, he said he did not know why he did not take a picture. He went on to say he saw us in bed from the bathroom doorway. When shown an architectural rendering of the house, you cannot see a view of the bed from where he said he was standing. The real reason he did not photograph us in bed was that he did not see us in bed. He was caught in a lie.

- The night of the shooting, Justin told Detective Knight that he heard Tracey Tarlton say she was going to bring her shotgun to our house on Toro Canyon. At the trial, he denied saying he told the detective this. His testimony was refuted when Detective Knight took the stand later in the trial. Justin told Jimmy Martinez the same story and then claimed he never told Jimmy about Tracey bringing the shotgun to the house. When Jimmy took the stand, he testified being told about the shotgun by Justin. More lies.

- After the shooting, Justin talked about High Fidelity, the security system company hired to install the alarm system our house. Justin testified that he did a walk-through several times with the workers and the supervisor to show areas he noticed were not functioning correctly. It was noted that the security system was malfunctioning and that some of the sliding and hinged doors and the panic button by our bed were not working properly. It was on the crime report that the security system was off the night of the shooting, but the truth is, the system was not correctly installed from the beginning. We rarely used the security system and were unaware of the malfunction.

- Justin told the jury he signed my name to some of the home repair receipts. His signature was authenticated with the signatures on checks he forged from my checking account. He continued to deny forging the checks.

- To verify that I took our dog, Megan, to the lake house from time to time, Justin said he would help me get her in the SUV. Later in his testimony, he contradicted himself and said he could not remember doing that.

- Justin admitted he had a financial stake in the outcome of the case, should I get convicted. He knew if he married Kristina, and I was arrested, that he would become very wealthy.

- When questioned about changing the code for my safe, he admitted to doing it and said he refused to give me the new code. The reason he did not want me to have the new code was that he knew I would discover many pieces of jewelry missing.

- Our handyman, Doug Byers, caught Justin going through my files in the storage area. According to

Doug's testimony, Justin was sitting on the floor in the center of the room with stacks of files spread around. Justin was startled when he was caught, but went on to say I gave him permission to go through the boxes. I never gave him permission to sort through my information. Justin testified that he took volumes of files, journals, cards, and photographs to the DA's office.

- Justin was questioned about recording my phone calls and messages. He testified that he turned the tapes over to the prosecution. During the pretrial court hearings, the tapes were analyzed by an expert. It was determined the tapes were spliced and edited with information deleted and added. In doing so, the context of the messages were not original. Justin denied altering the tapes.

- A forensic analysis was done on my computer to identify when my computer was illegally accessed and what files were downloaded. I was in Timberlawn during the theft of personal information from my computer. The home security system, now repaired, indicated what code was used to turn the alarm off during the times of the computer being accessed. The number entered into the security system was the number issued to Justin by Kristina. Files were printed and turned over ADA Mange. Justin was questioned on how the information ended up with the ADA. He could not remember.

Jennifer Beard

Kristina's identical twin sister, Jennifer, testified at the criminal trial. She was more truthful than her sister and was not as evasive with her testimony. Jennifer has never been very close to me, but was still a caring, loving daughter. She quickly began to enjoy the wealth that came with being adopted by Steven. Slowly, over time, she grew to depend on the money and the expectation that she could have whatever she wanted, whenever she wanted. In 1999, Jennifer requested I leave a note in my will that would state who would buy all my possessions. This led her to slack off on her studies and plans for her future after graduation. Kristina, Justin Grimm, Jennifer, and her boyfriend, Christopher Doose were close and spent a great deal of time with each other. I have suspected that the relationship between the four of them was the catalyst for all the terrible things they did to me. Jennifer participated in the stealing and knew about everything that was going on. Her silence qualified her as an accomplice. Jennifer, as it turns out, is a lesbian. It is not her sexual preference that is my concern, but rather the book found under her bed. It was a book about homosexuality. The girls testified the book was mine and claimed I was becoming a lesbian because of Tracey Tarlton. I always denied knowing about that book, but believe Jennifer was questioning her sexual preference and was reading up on the subject. In an ironic turn of events, Jennifer survived being shot twice in the stomach by her tenant in 2017. As of the time of this book publication, she underwent ten surgeries while the shooter was sentenced to 40 years in prison for murder and attempted murder. I question the fairness of his punishment. I am innocent and am sentenced for life and this person killed one man, tried to kill my daughter and others, and only gets a 40 year sentence.

Not presented in any particular order and to the best of my recollection, highlights of Jennifer's testimony:

- On the night Steven was shot, the prosecution attempted to manipulate the events of the evening to fit one of their many theories on my involvement in the crime. They were trying to establish a time line of my whereabouts. The prosecution made it appear as though I forced Jennifer, Christopher Doose, and Amy Cozart to spend the night at the lake house so they would not be home while the shooting took place. Jennifer corrected that line of thinking when she testified that they asked a week prior if they could spend the night at the lake house. The kids loved going there because it was fun, so I permitted them. The kids went grocery shopping in advance, packed their overnight bags, and made plans for other friends to come out the following day.

- The prosecution questioned Jennifer about telling the truth, trying to get her to say that I never went to the lake house. Jennifer testified that I would come out to the lake house often to check in and to visit for a while. She mentioned that I usually brought Nikki and Megan with me so they could run around and play. Even the dogs loved going to the lake house.

- Several days after the shooting, Kristina and Jennifer met with our attorney, Mr. Burton. During that interview and the trial, Jennifer said I arrived around 10 p.m. and left around 11:30 p.m. the night of the shooting. The prosecution was trying to place me at a different location at the same time I was at the lake house; Jennifer corrected them.

- Jennifer told the jury that I loved Steven, even when he was a pain when he was drunk, just as I had stated. She said I was looking forward to our extended vacation to Europe even though the prosecution tried to make it sound like I did not want to take the seven week holiday with Steven.

- Questions about Tracey Tarlton calling all our phones non-stop was verified during Jennifer's testimony.

- When asked about one specific call where Tarlton said she was going to come to the house with her shotgun, Jennifer confirmed the call and said we turned off the lights and watched out the windows to see if Tracey was lurking out there.

- Jennifer verified that Tarlton was obsessed with me. She said Tracey was a crazy, mean drunk.

- Jennifer verified that it was common for me to sleep in their rooms and said we would talk late at night and have fun visiting. She said the CPAP machine Steven used at night was loud and I could sleep more soundly in their room. She mentioned that I kept clothes in the closets and toiletries in their bathrooms.

- In the days that followed the shooting, Jennifer told the court she was "absolutely supportive of me." She mentioned how I fell apart and began doing crazy things, including self-mutilation.

- Until reminded, Jennifer said she forgot it was Steven who bought the family plot a year before he died, not me as initially thought. The day we went to pick out his casket, she did admit feeling threatened that I suggested we pick our pink caskets out at the same time. Bonita Thompson was employed by the funeral home. She testified that she wanted me to change the caskets because regulations had changed.

- After the twins moved out of the house, they went to live with their therapist, Peggy Farley. Jennifer said this was true and did say that Farley stopped being their therapist the day they moved in. As if this made everything ethical.

- Bank of America allowed the girls to draw from their trust account after they were charged with check forgery. Jennifer admitted this as true.

- Jennifer verified that everyone traded cell phones with regularity.

Donna Goodson

Donna Goodson worked as a receptionist at the hair salon in our shopping center. I did not know her well, other than to say hello and to share small talk. At my daughter's insistence, I hired her to be my assistant. What I found out later is that Donna Goodson is nothing but a scam artist, a thief and a liar.

- Donna Goodson testified to pawning some of my jewelry in Austin and Louisiana. She claimed I gave her the jewelry so she could pawn it to pay for a $600 car repair bill. Then she said she accidentally took the jewelry and other items. I did not give her my jewelry, and it certainly was no accident. A search warrant was issued for her mother's house, where Donna lived. The pawn tickets verified the sale of my items. The police discovered she pawned a Sony camera, a 2" color television, gold, a 7.5 carat diamond ring, a quartz watch, rings, bracelets, chains, necklaces, and purses. It was not until later that I discovered she

362

stole loose gemstones from me.

- Donna Goodson was arrested for the thefts and was facing a Motion to Revoke Probation, due to a previous felony conviction. She knew the Three Strikes Law would apply and that she would serve time for her crimes. Goodson testified that the prosecution made a deal with her and she received an Immunity Agreement and her probation was reinstated. The deal: she would not get prosecuted for stealing and pawning my jewelry and other belongings as long as she testified against me.

- Goodson's attorney was also the attorney for Bank of America and was a participant during the financial testimony part of my trial. Another conflict of interest ignored by the Judge.

- The prosecution was relentless in trying to prove I became a lesbian. They kept pounding away saying Tracey Tarlton recruited me. You just don't become a lesbian, and I had a difficult time understanding their reasoning. A picture of me with Donna Goodson was presented at the trial; the prosecution began the lesbian rhetoric all over again. The picture was taken at Mardi Gras when Donna and I went there together. Donna testified the picture was

of her and me. The picture shows Donna touching
my breasts. What the picture does not show is the
context in which the picture was taken. It is said a
picture is worth a thousand words. Who is it that
gets to determine which thousand words accurately
depict the content of a picture?

- Donna Goodson testified she never told anyone that
  I asked her to hire a hit man to kill Tracey Tarlton
  until ADA Wetzel approached her. The reason she
  never mentioned this to anyone is that I never asked
  her to hire a hit man, so there was nothing to tell.
  Goodson had a motive to make up the hit man
  story: to keep herself out of jail.

- I was trying to distance myself from Donna
  Goodson, once I realized she was a rotten apple.
  She kept calling and I would not take her calls. She
  tried to blackmail me because I was no longer
  befriending her. She verified this under oath.

- By the time her testimony was done, Donna
  Goodson had admitted befriending me to swindle
  me out of money.

Celeste

Annetta Black

Travis County District Attorney's Office,
Associate Forensic Analysist

- Annetta Black testified she analyzed voluminous
  phone records supplied to her by the prosecution;
  several hundred pages containing over 8,000 calls
  from the Beard family phones and those of Tracey
  Tarlton were submitted into evidence.

- She verified she did not analyze land line calls, just
  cell calls, as requested by the prosecution.

- The defense argued that the facts are misleading
  and that the calls were cherry-picked by the
  prosecution.

- The State claims the spreadsheets of cell calls
  relates to who was using what phones, even though
  other testimony said everyone traded phones all the
  time.

- Names and numbers on the spreadsheets indicated
  who supposedly owned which phones. These were
  provided by Jennifer and Kristina as the District
  Attorney took it as fact. When the defense asked

Black who the account holder was for each phone, her answer was Steven Beard. She went on to say all subscriber information was in the name of Steven Beard and that she is not certain who owned which phone. She went on to admit she did not know who used which phones, based on the spreadsheets.

- Annetta Black testified that she only analyzed records provided to her by the prosecution.

- When the defense questioned the spreadsheets, she said she did not have all the phone entries to support who she identified and the owner of the phone.

- Dick DeGuerin states to the court, "The defense sufficiently preserved their objections and memorandum to the States phone call spreadsheet. He tells the Judge that the probative value is far outweighed by its prejudicial effect. It is not a proper summary." The Judge overruled and allowed the phone records to be submitted as evidence.

Celeste

Dr. Bernard Gotway

My Clinical Psychologist

- Dr. Gotway told the jury he began seeing me initially for PTSD trauma. He described my background to the court as a sexual abuse victim. His notes stated I refused to deal with the abuse. He mentioned my long-standing problems with depression and my numerous hospitalizations for suicide attempts.

- He told the court that I was ripe for treatment by the time I came to him.

- In relationship to my overspending, he said that whenever I felt bad, I would buy something as if to run away from my depression.

- He said I displayed characteristics of Obsessive-Compulsive Disorder.

- He diagnosed the trigger of my repressed feelings as starting when my mother came to Austin and stayed at the lake house.

- He said Steven was very concerned that I get the help I needed and emphasized that my husband really wanted me to be happy. He told the court that Steven would attend my sessions often and would participate in the meeting or wait outside the office for me to be done. He said we had a good relationship. He stated that my husband and I exhibited sincerity in wanting to work out our problems.

- Dr. Gotway saw me daily, for weeks at a time and noted progress in my treatment.

- He stated that when I talked about the sexual abuse, he could see it caused anxiety.

- He said I needed to focus on myself first and then focus on Steven next.

- When Dr. Gotway would bring up Steven's drinking during a session, I would tell him my husband would not mince words, and verbal battles would ensue. He said he genuinely liked Steven, but did notice he had set opinions and that he was not shy to let anyone know what they were.

- Dr. Gotway told the jury I felt responsible for Craig's suicide and I held a deep sense of guilt.

- Written in his notes, he mentioned Tracey Tarlton is possessive and I need to set boundaries. He said

Tracey was trying to get all my attention, was trying to control me, and was acting pushy, and possessive.

- To try to control my over spending, knowing I was helplessly out of control, Dr. Gotway said I need to have my own money to spend, have my own credit cards and live within a budget.

- Dr. Gotway was telling the jury that he thought I was managing well and perhaps it was time to go home. He said I disagreed with him at that time because I felt I was not ready to leave.

- My problem, Dr. Gotway mentioned, was that I am not able to say no to people and that I loved pleasing people.

- During a session, Kristina and Jennifer joined me. Dr. Gotway said we seemed to have a good rapport. He evaluated Kristina that day and recognized she was clinically depressed. It was during that session, he recommended Kristina to see Dr. Hauser.

- Dr. Gotway recalled a time for the jury when I was discharged and placed in the day out-patient treatment. He said my anxiety level and depression worsened. I was readmitted for in-patient treatment because I could not stop crying, I was tired, and not feeling well. I stayed for another twelve days.

- During a session when Steven joined me, I told Dr. Gotway that he was discussing divorce and I said I did not want a divorce. Steven's response, told to the jury was, " I was only doing this because I thought it is what she wanted."

- Several times during his testimony, the doctor said Steven was willing to do whatever I needed.

- Dr. Gotway told the jury that I made a lot of progress. He said I worked hard and I was a good patient. Once I could get my ups and downs under control, he wanted me to transition to Dr. Hauser for further treatment.

- When questioned about my being readmitted on March 22, 2000, Dr. Gotway told the court I was distraught. He mentioned I told him that I wanted to join my dead husband. He said I was not suicidal at that time, just that I wanted to die. He described how the conflict with Kristina and Jennifer was pulling me apart and how they wanted me declared incompetent. Dr. Gotway said I was not incompetent and told the girls it made no sense.

- As the questioning continued, Dr. Gotway discussed a time when Kristina and Jennifer met with him. They told him I was depressed and was not doing anything. The bills were not getting paid, and things were being let go. Kristina recommended becoming my guardian. Knowing Kristina was trying to control me, Dr. Gotway called our attorney and said this is a very bad idea to make Kristina a parenticized child and reverse roles with her mother.

- I gave in, and Kristina did become my Power of Attorney. Once I became more assertive, Kristina and I met with Dr. Gotway. At that meeting, I told Dr. Gotway I no longer wanted Kristina as my POA because she was abusing the authority. He noted this in my chart and recounted the meeting with the jury. Kristina knew she no longer had POA that day, but continued not to acknowledge this during her testimony.

- Another hospital admission was questioned. The date was April 17, 2000. Dr. Gotway told how I checked back in because I was very depressed from conflicts with my daughters not coming back home to live, and not returning any of my calls. His notes indicate that I felt hopeless. By the end of that month, I became very angry and wanted to disinherit them.

- Dr. Gotway explained to the court that during the course of my treatment, he saw me for approximately 90 hours. He said I was complex. I tended to be histrionic and impulsive. I am not a strategic thinker or planner. My PTSD was his underlying concern.

- He was asked about my ability to develop long-term goals, and strategic thinking. When asked if I was capable of developing a long campaign to convince Tracey Tarlton to kill my husband, his reply was, "It is highly unlikely. It does not fit with the way she operates."

Melissa Caldwell

Clinical Director at Timberlawn

Melissa Caldwell was called as a witness to discuss a request I made when I was an in-patient at Timberlawn. She verified I came to her and told her I did not want

Tracey Tarlton as a roommate. Concerned about her reaction, I asked for a staff member to be present when I told her I did not want to share a room with her. I only wanted Tracey as a friend, but it was evident she was looking for more than friendship. Melissa Caldwell told the jury that, once I left the room, Tracey became very angry and began pacing back and forth saying, "Why does this always happen to me? I am tired of this happening." The testimony concluded with Caldwell telling the court that Tarlton was relocated to an adult psychiatric unit to get stabilized and to be closely watched.

Dr. Howard Miller

Medical Director of the Trauma Program at Timberlawn

Dr. Miller testified about my psychological evaluation in 1999. He was asked if it was possible that I faked the psychological test. His reply, "It is almost impossible to fake a psychological testing report." His report was read to the court:

- Symptoms of depression and suicidality.
- Completely overwhelmed.

373

- Shuts down feelings and distances herself from things she finds overwhelming.
- Defensive.
- Likely to become volatile, unpredictable and self harmful at moments when she is unable to escape the provoking and distressful circumstance.
- Severe recurrent PTSD; acute.
- Cyclothymia: a bipolar disorder characterized by instability with mood and a tendency to swing between euphoria and depression.
- Personality structure is dependent with a need to please people to a fault.
- Would become irate and demanding and would rapidly become regretful and apologetic.
- Displays considerable obsessive-compulsive symptoms, sufficient enough to require medication.
- Phobic about germs and concerned about cleanliness.
- Her nature is not even and she tends to keep the focus shifting.
- Has difficulty being close to people and jumps from person to person.
- Celeste lacks the mental capacity for long range

planning and manipulation of Tracey Tarlton to kill
Steven Beard. It is evidenced that the things she did
were ad hoc, short term, on impulse. Her attempts
to manipulate people were uniformly ineffective.
She lacks skills to make a plan and carry it out.

- It appeared Steven and Celeste care for each other,
  and she genuinely wants to improve her
  relationships with her husband and daughters.

Doctor Miller was questioned about his observations of
Tracey Tarlton. He relayed his findings to the jury.

- Bipolar.
- Delusional.
- Hallucinations.
- Paranoid.
- Distorted perception of reality.
- At times, functions at a psychotic level.
- At times, mental functioning was such that speech
  was disordered and did not make sense. Did not
  speak in coherent sentences.
- Severely misinterprets meanings of things.
- Contradicts herself about the character of
  relationships.
- Has a desperate need to be loved to help her heal

emotional pain.

- Abusive voices in her head told her she was worthless and deserved to die.
- She knows she engineers failure in relationships and that she ultimately sabotages them.
- She believed Celeste loved her and that Steven Beard was the bad guy in her life by pushing them apart.
- At times, she cannot organize or collect her thoughts.
- At times would make up words and create a language out of a distorted thought process.
- She comes up with a distorted thought process.
- Has swells of anger at herself and others.
- Her life was filled with a pattern of violence, which helped us arrive at her diagnosis.
- She is prone to violence.
- She gets overwhelmed with anger.
- Shows evidence of self-loathing and worthlessness.
- I agree that she is capable of murder.
- When Tracey was released from the hospital, she was still quite disturbed.
- She thought her survival depended on Celeste.

Celeste

- In regards to Tracey Tarlton playing Russian Roulette: this is a very violent person.

Susan Mulholland

Intern at Timberlawn with Master of Arts in Counseling

Susan Mulholland was Tracey Tarlton's psychotherapist and her evaluation was presented to the court:

- Tracey Tarlton came to me because she was suicidal, diagnosed with PTSD, bipolar, and alcoholism. The first session was to try and stabilize her.

- In regards to the back rubbing incident between Celeste and Tracey in their room at Timberlawn, I noted Tracey would not focus on herself. She did a lot of caretaking for Celeste and needed to learn to set boundaries. Patient was very upset when she was relocated to another room.

- Tracey was beginning to show signs of being less suicidal. She recognized the relationship with Celeste as just friends. She did say she had dreams of having an affair with Celeste.

377

- We discussed Tracey's pattern of forming relationships with married women. Her response, "I fall in love with married, heterosexual women. We would have a relationship for one or two years. Then I leave or act out, forcing them to leave me."

- During one session, she said, "I want to drink and break the bottle and cut myself."

- I noted she had delusional thinking that Steven Beard had her moved to the psychiatric unit. When I told her that was not true, she became upset and could not understand it.

- Tarlton's identity is to be involved with someone, to give herself purpose. She anchors herself to a person for stability because she feels she cannot stand alone.

- Patient told me she goes from one extreme to another. When I questioned her about a time when she was on the day program, I asked if she drank, did drugs, or had sex with a peer. She said she did all those things. The following session, she said that was all a lie. She has a pattern of lying and I advised her to be honest.

- During a session, Tracey told me, "This would all

be solved if certain people met with untimely deaths." I was concerned because I knew Celeste was trying to set boundaries with Tracey. It seemed that she had a one-sided attraction with Celeste. I asked her about the statement and Tracey acted like it was a joke and said, "Just speculation." I have noticed that she makes up stories to fit a situation and then infers it as a joke.

- I did report the death threat incident to supervisors with therapy team members present. Tracey would not confirm the meaning of the statement and since it was so vague, nothing further happened.
- Sessions were getting very tense and becoming more difficult due to her lies.

At the conclusion of Susan Mulholland's testimony, she told the jury that she told another therapist, "Tracey Tarlton is suicidal, homicidal, and delusional. She cannot be fixed."

Dr. Michele Hauser

Private Practice of Psychiatry

I sought treatment with Dr. Hauser for depression and medical management, per the referral of Dr. Gotway. She discussed my sessions with the court:

- "Celeste was voicing suicidal ideations."
- "I ordered an EEG to rule out seizure disorder because of the erratic behavior with over spending and other things."
- "I had to remind Celeste about boundary issues. While at St. David's Pavilion, she bought everyone pizza. Another time she bought clothes for a patient that had no clothes."
- "There was a session where Celeste and Kristina came together. Celeste was very upset because she discovered Kristina had lied to her about sexual relations she was having with her boyfriend, Justin Grimm. I recommended both mother and daughter go to Kristina's therapist, Peggy Farley, to work on trust issues. Farley worked in the same office as

me."

- "During another session, Kristina was present with her mother. Kristina was very angry with Celeste because Celeste divulged to her daughter and Justin, that the twins were conceived out of rape by their dead father."

- "There was a session where I advised Celeste to end the relationship with Tracey Tarlton. I told her Tarlton was mentally unstable and I was fearful that Tracey would influence her in a negative way."

- "Celeste did exhibit a focus on her marriage to Steven. She never mentioned sexual relations with Tracey."

- "Celeste came for her appointment another day and was depressed. We discussed that Steven was drinking heavily and was getting verbally abusive; she began overspending again."

- "Steven Beard spoke with me once. He was concerned about his wife. He questioned her medication because Celeste was tired all the time. He said she was seeing a number of doctors. She was worried that he was mad at her and she was acting guilty. He said Celeste would get violently upset and throw screaming tantrums. He said she was making plans without consulting anyone. He discovered she had different charge card accounts using aliases."

- "Celeste did not make any appointments for a while. The next time I saw her was after Steven was shot. When Steven died, she came to the office and had an upper respiratory infection. She had difficulty sleeping and could not stop thinking about her deceased husband. She was filled with anger towards the hospital and the poor medical care Steven received. She was angry that his children did not spend much time with their father after their mother died five years before. She was angry that they were all in her business and wanting things. She was angry that one son went to the country club and stole Steven's golf clubs."

- "After Steven died, I received a call from Timberlawn that a strange looking woman was there looking for Celeste when she was not there."

- "Celeste expressed guilt and anxiety over her husband's death. She blamed herself because she brought Tracey Tarlton into the picture and befriended her."

- "Celeste often cried after Steven died."

- "I concurred with Dr. Gotway; Celeste was not incompetent, and it was not a good idea for Kristina to become her guardian. I found out days later, that Kristina was in hiding, yet was pursuing guardianship of her mother."

- "Celeste spoke of how angry she was at a session when we were discussing her daughters. They left home and were hiding out; they would not return phone calls. This was very upsetting to Celeste. She was angry at herself for poor parenting. The twins were stealing from her, they were forging checks, and they were lying. Celeste said she did not want to press charges against her daughters because she did not want them to get into trouble. Kristina sent her a threatening letter, further fueling her anger. She spoke of Donna Goodson stealing from her. She felt betrayed. I encouraged Celeste to go to Timberlawn because she did not appear to be stable."

Dr. Hauser failed to mention she knew my daughter's were staying with her partner, Peggy Farley. In keeping this a secret, she added to my instability. Instead of doing what was in my best interest, Dr. Hauser prescribed Xanex for me, in addition to my depression medications. How unethical is that?

Dr. Hauser read notes in her file from Austin psychiatrist, Dr. Kreisle:

- Major recurrent depression.

- Borderline personality disorder: is a combination of nine personality disorders and it is a constellation of symptoms expressed over time where a person has trouble being alone. They alternately idealize and devalue people, have difficulty with anger management, have flashes of anger and rage, and other symptoms.

- Celeste shows manic episodes which are associated with overspending.

I stopped seeing Dr. Kreisle because his daughter was on the same softball team as Kristina and I was embarrassed to see him at the games.

Tracey Tarlton

I have harbored tremendous guilt over the death of my husband and the estrangement of my twin daughters, Kristina and Jennifer. I blame myself for everything that has happened. If I had not befriended Tracey Tarlton, my husband would still be alive, my daughters would not be strangers and they would still love me. It has taken me a long time to let go of the anger and hatred. I have learned to compartmentalize my resentment because it is not healthy for me to hold onto the pain and suffering. Tracey Tarlton is a complex and deeply troubled individual. She spent a substantial length of time on the witness stand. My attorney, Dick DeGuerin, requested that the court move forward for an instructed verdict on the basis that the State has failed to corroborate her testimony. The request was denied. The testimony was filled with many contradictions. At one point, Dick DeGuerin says "It's all lies!" The Judge responded, "I know. It is a matter of who is telling the truth."

In no particular order, and to my best recollection, is the testimony of Tracey Tarlton.

- Tracey Tarlton pled guilty to the murder of Steven

Beard on April 1, 2002.

- She understood her psychological assessment: the patient is bright, but manipulative and has delusional misinterpretations of other people and has distorted thinking.

- She testified that she was told in recovery that she needs to quit obsessing about me and focus on her own recovery.

- She confirmed telling her therapist that she wanted to kill Steven Beard.

- A police report was introduced into evidence concerning Reginald Breaux, a stranger she picked up in a parking lot. The charge against Tracey was aggravated assault with a motor vehicle. The night of the incident an altercation ensued. She tried to run Breaux down with her car after the two were driving around drinking beer. Her testimony and account of the details varied from the police report.

- Tarlton told of how she played Russian Roulette for five days in a row. When she backed off playing the deadly game, she admitted to hearing voices telling her to kill herself. The voices told her she "was being a chicken," and the voices grew louder at night.

- When discussing hallucinations, she admitted that once when she was driving, a rabbit was running alongside her car.

- She spoke of times where she wanted to take a razor to her wrists.

- She verified writing in her journal, "I think I am ready." The meaning was to kill herself.

- She acknowledged in therapy that her relationships fall into patterns that are doomed for failure from the beginning.

- Hospital records state Tracey said she and her brothers had once discussed hiring a hit man to kill their mother. She verified this under oath.

- The subject of Tracey being transferred to the adult psychiatric unit at Timberlawn was brought up. She admitted she believed Steven was responsible for her relocation to the suicide floor. She did not believe I told the staff I did not want to be roommates with her. She told her therapist that "Steven is coming between us using his money and influence." The therapist told Tracey she was delusional. That same day, she wrote in her therapeutic journal, "Celeste has decided to leave me. She will not look at me. She says I am too pushy."

- The testimony included many questions regarding Tarlton's mental stability. Her psychiatric and psychological history dates back many years. Tracey acknowledged her diagnosis's from various doctors:
    - When involved in interpersonal relationships, her thinking is overcome by severe psychotic disruptions.
    - She has a sexual addiction problem.
    - Severe vulnerabilities in her capacity to manage feelings.
    - Bounces from one therapist to another because she would not follow through with the treatment.
    - Is often flat and without emotion.
- Questions arose about a claim that Tracey made, saying we arrived at Timberlawn on the same day. Admission records indicate I arrived three days later. She believed her version even though admission records verified my arrival date.
- Tracey spoke of a time when she was meddling in

our marriage, and I told her, "Mind your own fucking business." Tracey became enraged.

- Tracey admitted to telling her therapist her dream was to have an affair with a peer, meaning me.

- Tracey admitted telling her therapist, "I want to drink a bottle of beer, break the bottle, and kill myself with the glass. I don't want to live."

- She testified that she could not help falling in love with married, heterosexual women. Prior to admittance to St. David's Pavilion, she had an affair with a married woman. When the husband learned of the affair, he committed suicide. The woman broke up with Tracey, adding to her instability. The Judge did not allow the woman to testify, but Tracey did confirm the relationship and the particulars.

- This is how Tracey thinks she can run to the rescue of a grieving widow and this is why she shot my husband. She wanted me to love her.

- When asked about whether I spent the night at her house, Tracey told the court, yes. Further into the testimony, she said just the opposite and claimed I never spent the night.

- The testimony turned to the making of botulism. Tracey said she made it when the girls and I were in Australia. She said she planned to make chili dogs and add botulism to the sauce. She claimed Steven ate the poison hot dog and did not get sick. Jennifer testified that Steven was a gourmet cook and never ate a chili dog in his life. Tracey could not provide any details as to how it came to be, as she claimed, that Steven ate the hot dog.

- Tracey admitted she and Kristina bought Everclear together as Kristina was not old enough to purchase alcohol. She said they mixed Stolis vodka with Everclear at her house and Kristina took it home. Steven only drank Wolfschmidt, why she mentioned a different vodka is unclear. Kristina denied the entire incident.

- Tracey told the jury she was very jealous of Steven. She said she would get so jealous and nervous about our upcoming trip that she would become short of breath and feel suicidal.

- Tracey, Kristina, Justin, Jennifer, and Christopher would make fun of Steven behind his back and call him derogatory names. Tracey said they did that all the time.

- The questioning turned to the relationship between Tracey and Kristina. She told the court the two were close and that Kristina would often come over to visit. She had a key to Tracey's house.

- Tracey testified she bought Ecstasy, crushed it up, and put it in Steven's drink.

- She talked about a fantasy she had to put a bag over Steven's head and suffocate him. She said she could not go through with it though.

- Tracey was convinced if she killed Steven, she would be saving my life. She admitted this was her rational thinking and the reason she went into the bedroom and pulled the trigger.

- When questioned about which type of door she entered the night of the shooting, she said she went through a door on hinges. Crime scene photos show the doors were sliders. She said she did not lock the door when she left, yet the EMS had to break the glass to get inside.

- Tracey was telling the jury she knew where to go in the house and where the bedroom was because she had been in the bedroom before. She said she went

391

up a small set of stairs, but no stairs lead to the bedroom.

- Several days after the shooting, she admitted trying to overdose with pills and alcohol because she was feeling terrible about what she had done. She admitted feeling tremendous remorse for the crime.

- A dispute arose during Tarlton's testimony. Tracey said I was at her house at 11 p.m. the night of the shooting. Jennifer and Amy Cozart testified I was at the lake house at 11 p.m.

- Appointment records for Tramps Salon were logged into evidence. They show Tracey's date and time of a hair and nail appointment. This contradicted her testimony that she made saying she was at my house at that same date and time. Teri Meyer, a manicurist at Tramps Salon, testified that Tracey was quite serious when she talked about killing Steven.

- Beauticians at the salon said they heard Tracey say, "If Steve hurts Celeste, I will kill him." She admitted to saying this.

- She claimed we were in constant communication after Steven was shot. Evidence shows all our phone numbers were changed because she was calling non-stop. The only phone number not changed was the fax machine. Tracey admits she was desperate to talk to me, so she went to Office Depot and sent me a fax to call her. That fax was entered into evidence. I had immediately given that fax to my attorney, Charles Burton.

- Tracey told a fellow inmate how she got a sweet deal because she was having a sexual relationship with Rosemary Lehmberg from the DA's office. When questioned about this, she told the jury it was a lie. Yet, Tracey did double-date with the Travis County DA.

- The plea agreement was questioned. The prosecution offered a deal to Tracey that said she would get only 20 years for killing Steven Beard. Her role in the agreement was to give, "A believable testimony to incriminate me." She would be sentenced after my trial was over. She admitted to saying, "I would lie to protect myself." When the mail was being intercepted by the guards at the jail, correspondence between Tracey, and her jail house wife, Felicia Hicks, was copied. In that letter, Tracey bragged that she would be out in as few as ten years. My attorney showed prison records indicating she was reading up on parole in preparation for the trial and her reduced sentence. She said the DA's office groomed her for testimony for hours and hours, sometimes three to five hours at a time, two to three times a month. Prison visitation records verified this to be true.

- The jail was copying mail and sending it the DA's office. Once my attorney became aware of this underhanded practice, he subpoenaed the mail. He told the Judge it showed bias and interest, a reason and a motive for Tracey Tarlton's testimony.

A 2004 Northwest University study found that snitches are the leading cause of wrongful convictions in this country, particularly in Capital cases. Loyola Law School professor, Alexandra Natapoff, conducted a study on *"How Snitches Contribute to Wrongful Convictions."* She determined that prosecutors are so invested in their informants stories, that they lack the objectivity needed to step back and identify when their sources are lying. They begin to believe the lies themselves.

Tracey and the others were able to manipulate their

version of the "facts" precisely because they knew which facts were verifiable from those that were not. The jury inferred from the details provided by them and took what was told as true.

The State dropped all criminal charges pending against all four teens and Donna Goodson in exchange for their testimonies. Tracey faced a life-sentence and instead was given just 20 years with parole guaranteed at 10 years.

The prosecutor provided a powerful incentive for all of them to lie.

Laylan Copeland

A reporter for the Austin-American Statesman newspaper

The reporter verified an anonymous letter he received. The letter, read to the jury, was written to sway public opinion about my innocence. Based on the contents, only a person with in-depth knowledge could have been the author of the letter. This letter was supposedly taken off my computer by the kids when they were stealing from me while I was in Timberlawn. There was no proof as to who wrote the letter. I was not aware of the existence of this letter until I read it in the paper. It was never revealed who penned the letter, but I suspect the kids might know something about that.

I would have had no reason to send an anonymous letter. At my request, Charles Burton and I met with Laylan Copeland and the Austin-American Statesman editor, Rich Oppel, to discuss the shooting. The teenagers never know about this meeting so an anonymous letter would have been superfluous.

Dr. Teresa Valls

Psychiatrist at St. David's Pavilion

Dr. Valls testified she was on call for Dr. Hauser at St. David's when she received a call from a nurse on the unit. The nurse said a strange looking woman walked onto the unit looking for me. That person was identified as Tracey Tarlton. I was not a patient during this time. Dr. Valls thought I was in imminent danger and called me. She suggested I step up security at home and have security with me at all times. The notes from that meeting were presented to the court:

- "The patient shows quite a bit of distress."
- "She is tearful, upset, emotional, crying, and has sadness."

- "She expressed a tremendous amount of feelings because her husband just passed away."
- "She has feelings of guilt that she brought him home from the hospital too soon. He was not medically ready to be released."
- "She expressed anguish at not having done enough for her husband. She feels she should have hired a nurse."

Jimmy Martinez

Jimmy Martinez and I were married in 1991, our marriage lasted about three years. We had an amicable divorce and remained friends. I admired that he loved Kristina and Jennifer as though they were his own daughters. He was always kind and generous with us after we went our separate ways. We had mutual friends and would see each other socially from time to time. The girls were friends with members of his family and we would see each other at gatherings. Jimmy owned a security system company and did contract work for other companies. He is a hard worker and is well respected in his line of work. Everyone liked him because he was fun and outgoing. Jimmy was an integral part of our life and was called to testify. On the witness stand, he answered with honesty which was more than I could say about some of the family and friends that were subpoenaed to testify.

His testimony is presented to the best of my recollection and in no particular order:

- Jimmy told the court he loved Kristina and Jennifer like his own. He would call and check on them at least once a week. He took them to dinner from time to time and surprised them with gifts.

- He disliked when Kristina and Jennifer bad mouthed Steven. He told them, "give the guy a hug." He said Jennifer told him, "he is too big, we don't know if we can get our arms around him."

- Jimmy talked of a time when he and the girls came to visit me when I was at Timberlawn. It was Easter, and we made baskets for all the patients.

- He testified that I never spent the entire night at his house, but that I would visit occasionally. The twins lied when they said I spent the entire night with him. After I was married to Steven, he admitted we did have sex a few times but did not consider it an affair.

- When asked if he met Tracey, he replied, "I met her

once and thought she was weird."

- When my daughters graduated from high school,
  Jimmy hosted a party for them. I got a bit tipsy that
  night and went to sleep it off. He was questioned
  about the events of that evening. His reply,
  "Kristina came to get me and said, 'Jimmy, will you
  come get Tracey off my mom?' I went to the room
  to find Celeste sleeping, fully clothed and under the
  covers. I saw Tracey on top of Celeste trying to kiss
  her ear and fooling with her hair. I told her to get
  up, and she ignored me. I grabbed Tracey by her
  shoulder and told her she needed to get out. At that
  point, Kristina was trying to lead Tracey out of the
  room. I remember Celeste saying, 'tell her I am not
  a lesbian, tell her to leave me alone.' Suddenly,
  Tracey was back in the room. Kristina and I had to
  force her down the stairs and out the door. We
  knew Tracey was drunk, Justin offered to give her a
  ride home. She insisted on driving herself home and
  shouted into the house, 'You tell Celeste to be at
  my house in one hour'. The following day, I was
  told 'that weird looking girl got pulled over last
  night.' That was when the collect calls began
  coming from Travis County. I hung up on her and

took the phone off the hook."

- He testified that Kristina came over the next morning and said Tracey would not stop calling the house and that Steven finally answered. Tracey told Steven that I was in bed with Jimmy.

- Jimmy verified that Kristina called him, saying Tracey called and threatened suicide and that she had a shotgun. He told the court he advised Kristina to call 911.

- Jimmy was asked how he found out Steven was shot. He said he returned a missed call from Kristina. Justin answered and told him Steven was shot with a shotgun. His first thought was that Tracey did it and told Justin to tell the investigators about Tracey Tarlton.

- Jimmy testified after Steven was shot that Kristina asked him to come to the house and check their security system. Justin showed him some doors that were not tripping the system and Jimmy took notes about the doors in question. It was discovered that one sliding door of a set would trip the alarm, and the other door of that same set would not trip the alarm. The sliding doors in the master bedroom did not trip the alarm at all. He claimed some of the switches on the doors did not set off the alarm because they were cheaply made and not of good quality. He advised Kristina to get their company out to the house immediately to rectify the situation.

- In the coming weeks, Jimmy testified that he installed video cameras in all the key locations around the outside of the properties and a monitoring system with recorders at both Toro Canyon and at the lake house. He installed video phones on the front doors so visitors could identify themselves before we opened the door. He worked on the weekends and in between other accounts to get the system up and running to his satisfaction. Once the installation was completed, he came back the following weekend to check everything one final time. He noticed a ladder that extended up to a camera and asked Justin what was going on. Justin told Jimmy he was trying to get a better view. Jimmy told the jury there was no valid explanation why Justin was repositioning the cameras and putting them out of focus as they were perfect as they were.

- Jimmy told the jury he asked if the security system

was on or off the night of the shooting. Nobody knew. Crime scene photos showed the keypad in the master bedroom. It had blood on it. I wanted to know how that could be? Whose blood was it and how did it get there? Why was that not part of the investigation?

- When it was time to get paid for the work, Jimmy told the court I wrote a check for $74,000. He did tell me this was not the amount on the invoice. He signed the check over to me. A new check was written to Jimmy, plus a tip, to cover the cost of the installation. Sometime later, Jimmy told the court, he was called to the DA's office for an interview. He was shown an invoice for $74,000. He told the prosecutors the invoice they showed him was not the invoice he had prepared. He was steadfast in his declaration. He never found out who faked that invoice.

- The prosecution tried to manipulate Jimmy's testimony to make me look bad. During the trial, they presented a total of 287 things they considered bad acts to confuse the jury and to shore up their weak case. This thinly veiled ploy was done throughout the trial with anyone which they could curry favor. One such example: They seem to have forgotten that Jimmy and I were married at the time the nickname was thought up, when they questioned him about the term I called his penis. This line of questioning had no bearing on the charges I was facing. To the objection of the defense, he was made to tell the jury I called his penis a BMW. Embarrassed that he had to interpret one of our most private secrets aloud, he said, "Not a car, a big Mexican wiener."

- Jimmy was asked about the fact that I took my dogs everywhere. I would bring Megan and Nikki to his house to play with his German shepherd, Alice. He said they especially loved running through the Blue Bonnets when they were in bloom. This line of questioning refuted Kristina and Jennifer's statement that I never took Megan anywhere.

Katina Lofton

Katina Lofton, a ten-time convicted felon and an inmate serving six years in the Texas Department of Corrections was called as a witness. She was convicted of tampering with government records, theft, and forgery. Before the testimony of Lofton began, the Judge reminded the witness that she did not have the right to plead the 5th. She was warned to tell the truth, and not say what she thinks each side wants to hear. The Judge said she told two completely different stories to the prosecution and the defense. Katina denied that and never wavered in her testimony for the defense. The Judge told her that if she did not tell the truth, she would be charged with aggravated perjury. Both sides argued about the scolding Lofton received. The Judge insisted she had to read her the riot act because Lofton is not a truthful person. Lofton was the only witness called to testify who had to swear on the Bible.

Katina Lofton was called by the defense to testify about conversations she had with Tarlton in the county jail. Tarlton told Lofton that I had nothing to do with Steven's shooting and that she (Tarlton) intended to lie to implicate me. My attorney addressed the court, following a collect call he received from Lofton. In that call, Lofton said the DA's office threatened her and would retaliate against her for being a witness. Lofton received an anonymous letter threatening that if she testified for me, her parole would not be granted. She told DeGuerin that ADA Wetzel had visited her in jail three days after the parole hearing and told her the parole was denied. Lofton mentioned Wetzel took her papers from the jail. Lofton goes on to say a lover of Tarlton's, Kathy Roberts, threatened her during a prison van transport. After informing the Judge of this call, for her safety, Lofton was ordered to be moved to protective custody. She was placed in the cell directly across from Tarlton.

- Katina Lofton testified she was a cell mate with Tracey Tarlton from March through April 2002.

- Lofton said she had nothing to gain for testifying, she felt threatened because she had received an anonymous letter saying if she took the stand, she would not get parole. She did take the stand and did not get parole.

- She told the jury the incriminating things Tracey Tarlton told her:
  - Tracey said she shot Steven Beard. She said she was going to falsely claim I was involved because she was not going to rot in jail while I lived happily ever after.
  - Tracey said after she shot Steven Beard, she called the house to tell me to get the shotgun shell. She said I hung up on her. There was no call and no record of a call. A blatant lie.

o Tracey said she continued to talk with Kristina after the shooting, as verified by recorded messages submitted into evidence.

o Tracey said she wanted me to be her girlfriend because she loved me and I did not love her back the same way.

o Tracey said she had influence in the courthouse. DA Rosemary Lehmberg used to be her girlfriend and they were seen at the Dart Bowl together. The DA was going to get her sentence reduced, get her free world food, and cigarettes. This would explain how Tracey was made a Trustee – unheard of with a capital murder charge hanging over her head.

o At the bench, it was confirmed with the prosecution that the double date did occur. It would be impossible for Katina Lofton to know this had Tracey not told her.

o Tracey said she made bacteria, then she said it was not true. Tracey said she told the prosecutors she made bacteria, even though it was not true.

o Tracey said she told prosecutors and the

court that I coerced her to kill Steven Beard. Then she said she made that up; it was not true.

- o Tracey said if she "said things," she would get 20 years; she would get a deal.
- o To promote her version of the facts, Tracey said they were making a book about the case, titled *Pink Coffins*. Lofton confirmed she saw the manuscript in the cell. She said the court got hold of a copy of the manuscript and now she could not write it.
- o Tracey said she shot Steven Beard because she did not like him.

- Lofton said she met with DA Wetzel and an investigator, Debra Smith. She said Wetzel told her to not talk to the defense, and if you testify, you will get torn apart on the stand.

- Lofton testified that she placed a collect call to Dick DeGuerin's office to tell him about the threats of retaliation from Wetzel. She told Dick that Wetzel took her papers from the jail and that she was threatened by Tarlton's jail house girlfriend, Kathy Roberts, during a prison van transport to court. Because of the threats, Lofton was placed in protective custody and was locked up directly across from Tracey Tarlton.

- She testified that the prosecution did not record their jail interviews. The defense brought a court reporter to record their interview.

- When asked about how she met me, she said we met in jail and knew each other for several weeks. She told the jury we corresponded occasionally. She mentioned a time when she needed money, and I put $200 in her commissary account; another time she needed stationary and I gave her some. Lofton told the jury I gave things to other people too, and that she is not testifying because I gave her things.

- Lofton said there was a time when Tracey Tarlton gave her a message to pass to me. In prison, this unauthorized message is called a "kite." Lofton wanted nothing to do with Tracey and did not pass the kite along.

- When the prosecution cross examined Lofton, she became angry that her past came into question and her credibility ruined. Things that had no regard for the case at hand were brought up to discredit her testimony. Lofton said Wetzel was twisting the meanings of what she was saying. She testified to telling the truth.

Charles Burton

The attorney that once represented the twins and me

Our family friend and attorney, Philip Presse, asked Mr. Burton to represent us in the days that followed the shooting.

Mr. Burton wanted to get all the details written down, as told by the girls, in the days that followed the shooting, while the information was relatively fresh in their minds.

In no particular order, the interview notes and his testimony:

Jennifer's interview:

- Jennifer testified that she, her boyfriend, Chris, and friend, Amy, shopped for groceries and supplies days before the shooting because they had made plans to spend the weekend at the lake house with friends. They were not forced to go to the lake house by me, as the prosecution was indicating.

- Jennifer testified that I showed up at the lake house at 10 p.m. and stayed until around 11:30 p.m. the night of the shooting. The prosecution was trying to put me in a different place at that same time.

- When Jennifer heard Steven was shot, she assumed Tracey did it.

- She talked about how Tracey always wanted my attention.

- Jennifer testified that I loved my husband, even when he was a pain in the ass when he was drinking.

- Jennifer confirmed I was looking forward to the seven week trip to Europe with Steven.

- Jennifer mentioned the night Tracey said she was coming over to our house on Toro Canyon with a shotgun. She mentioned how frightened we were; we were not sure if we were the intended target or if she was going to kill herself. We turned out all the lights and watched out the window for hours to see if Tracey was out there.

- Jennifer told Mr. Burton that I told the detectives about that incident after Steven was shot.

- Jennifer said Tracey was a bad person. She was mean and crazy when drunk. She saw Tracey with a book on how to kill someone.

- On the day of the shooting, Jennifer confirmed we spent the day together until 2 p.m. This contradicts Tracey's testimony that we were together at the same time.

Kristina's interview:

Burton said Kristina came in often, more so than her sister, to discuss the case.

- Kristina said Steven was demanding about the family having dinner together. He was not a physically violent person.
- She talked about my molestation when I was a child.
- She said I had a short fuse.
- Kristina confirmed I came home a little before midnight and went to bed at midnight the night of the shooting and that I slept in her bedroom, just as I had been saying all along.
- She recalled waking up just after the shooting. She remembered me waking her up because someone was at the door.
- Kristina said Justin dropped her off around 11 p.m. She mentioned going to check on Steven, who was in bed sleeping.

411

- She emphasized that Tracey was obsessed with me and tried to kiss me.

- When questioned about me being friends with Tracey, she repeated what I said from time to time, "I felt sorry for her because she is pathetic."

- Kristina said it was getting quite tiresome that every time the phone rang, we would cringe. Tracey would call every five minutes sometimes.

- Kristina testified, "We were supportive, protective and totally on my mom's side after the shooting."

Other notes of interest during Mr. Burton's testimony include:

- After my husband was shot, it was Mr. Burton who noticed I was not doing well. He told me to go back to Timberlawn as a necessity for my mental health issues.

- When he found out Donna Goodson took items from the house, he had her return the items. Goodson told him she was going to sue me for $500,000.

- I took his advice and did get admitted into Timberlawn. During that time, the girls rummaged through my belongings and took some things. Mr.

Burton got the girls to return some of the items.

- Mr. Burton testified that he came to the hospital when Steven was shot. He saw the critical condition my husband was in, and he saw many people congregating in the waiting rooms on Steven's behalf. It was total chaos, and I was scared he was going to die and was not thinking clearly. It was Mr. Burton who recommended I put a note on the hospital room door that nobody could enter without him being present. His name and number was written on the note. The detectives and the prosecution were trying to make it seem like I was impeding the investigation when we were looking out for Steven's best interest. His life was hanging in the balance. Mr. Burton confirmed these facts.

- Burton told the jury about a call he received from Jennifer, sometime later, after the shooting. She told him she got a call from a neighbor at the lake house. There was a rumor going around that the girls shot Steven.

Philip Presse

Criminal defense attorney and Beard family friend

Philip and his wife, Ana, were long time friends of my husband. Ana was my Matron of Honor at our wedding. We went to dinner and traveled together. They were considered our best friends, and we enjoyed their company immensely. Philip was our advising counsel after my husband was shot and helped guide us through the process. Whatever he recommended, we considered in our best interest.

This is his testimony to the best of my recollection, and written in no particular order:

- Philip confirmed that he spoke with me at the hospital after my husband was shot. He interviewed us and gave us advice. Philip said he recommended that we reach out to Mr. Burton for legal representation.

- Kristina told Philip, and he then told the jury, about a time when Tracey Tarlton called the house, before the shooting. Tarlton told Kristina and Jennifer to come to her house, which they did. When they arrived at her house, Tracey was throwing a fit and

414

was talking about shooting Steven. The girls took a handgun from her and took it out of the house; they turned it over to the Austin police department.

- Philip said when he was doing the interviews, Justin was present and spent the entire time taking notes.

- He told the jury that I brightened Steven's life considerably. He said we loved each other and we were fun to be around.

- Philip said Steven drank all the time, often to excess. Philip was asked if he could tell the difference between Everclear and vodka. He told the court about a time he dropped Everclear on his floor and it burned the floor. He said Steven would most definitely know the difference between vodka and Everclear because Everclear tastes like gasoline. He said he often saw me helping Steven when he was drunk.

- He could not recall any incidents where we displayed bad feelings towards each other. After my husband was shot, Philip mentioned how attentive and concerned I was about his welfare. He said Steven's reaction towards me was loving and Philip noticed my husband held my hand when laying in the hospital bed.

- Philip recounted a time when Tracey Tarlton called his office after the shooting. The gist of the phone call was she was looking for an attorney because she knew she was going to be charged with the shooting. He gave her the number of an attorney to contact.

- Jennifer was interviewed by Philip. During the interview, Jennifer complained to him that Tracey would not stop calling all their phones. He was specific when he told them to not speak with Tarlton. Jennifer also told him that she heard Tracey threaten to take Steven's life.

- Concern was expressed by the note placed on Steven's hospital room door. Philip said Steven was near death. People were coming and going from the room without permission. Once word got out that Steven was shot, people converged on the hospital.

Ana Presse

Wife of Philip Presse and family friend

Ana was briefly questioned because she was a close friend.

She said she thought we were a happy couple. She said Steven was crazy about me and I was proud of him. With the amount of time we spent together, she said she never heard me bad mouth my husband. She said I had a great sense of humor and that I always made Steven laugh. She told the jury how she spent the day at the hospital with me and I was crying, very upset, and red-eyed. She said she did not think Kristina cared for Steven. My daughter told her that she hated him. She could not explain her observation, but thought Kristina was acting very unusual with the police when they were conducting interviews at the hospital. She told the jury how I fell apart and how she consoled me the day of the funeral.

Dr. Terry Satterwhite

Member of the University of Texas in Infectious Diseases

Dr. Satterwhite was called as an expert witness to testify to his findings as the cause of death for Steven Beard. He reiterated several key factors in his conclusions: Steven's EKG showed an abnormality happening in the heart; the blood clots did not come from the gunshot wound because it was healed and it more than likely came from the heart when he entered the rehab hospital; going off the Heparin thickened his blood and made it more sticky. Pneumonia, thick blood, and heart attack were the natural chain of events to cause death by the blood clots. Adding sepsis to his condition: Steven had no chance of surviving.

His conclusions and testimony are recorded to the best of my recollection and are written in no particular order:

- Dr. Satterwhite reviewed the final four days of medical records for Steven. His findings: death was caused by Group A Streptococcal Septicmeia. This is a bacteria blood infection.

- His conclusion: the infection was not related to the gunshot wound.

- In analyzing what happened to Steven, the skin rash was present at his discharge from HealthSouth on January 18th. Dr. Satterwhite said that having been readmitted to Brackenridge on January 19, 2000 for treatment, Steven's fever spiked on the afternoon of January 21st. That was an indication something else was going on.

- He said Steven's chart contained no notes on Group A Streptococcal Septicemia during the previous three months of hospitalization.

- During the testimony, Dr. Satterwhite reiterated several times that this infection did not come from the gunshot wound.
- Steven's chart listed his temperature as normal on January 19th and 20th. Brackenridge was planning to discharge him.
- On January 21st, Steven's fever spiked to 102.5. Dr. Satterwhite outlined the chain of events for the jury:
  - Steven was seen by a cardiologist at 5 p.m. that same day; he was worried about an infection in the breastbone. Autopsy records later indicated no infection was present in the breastbone.
  - White blood count increased which implied infection. Slightly elevated creatinine, which affects kidney function, was noted.
  - At 8 p.m. more blood was drawn to find an infection in the blood stream. Dr. Satterwhite elaborated on the seriousness of the finding because it can lead to death. This was called sepsis, and it is noted in the chart. The infection is a highly aggressive organism with a significant mortality rate,

especially in the elderly. For the court to understand more about the infection, the doctor explained that Steven was a high risk factor to acquire sepsis. For the infection to occur, Steven had the following contributions: alcohol abuse, diabetes, myelitis (abnormal proliferation of bone marrow tissue), chronic obstructive pulmonary disease (COPD), heart disease (autopsy showed an enlarged heart), and an abnormal EKG. He still had the rash in the scrotal and groin area.

o Steven's temperature and pulse rate remained elevated; no shortness of breath was noted. His pulse and blood pressure were getting low, indicating Steven was getting worse. More blood work was drawn. The creatinine level increased, which indicated decreased blood flow to the kidneys and organ damage. Steven was diagnosed with severe sepsis.

o At midnight, Steven still had a fever and an elevated heart rate.

o January 22nd at 8:00 a.m., Steven's

temperature was 99.8. His heart rate was faster, respiratory rate up, blood pressure up, white blood count up, and blood was low on oxygen and was alkaline. Steven was becoming delirious and was wheezing. A strong antibiotic was ordered at that time, but for some unexplained reason, was not administered until 1:00 p.m., five hours later.

o At 11:30 a.m., his heart rate, blood pressure, and pulse had continued to rise.

o A note in his chart, underlined three times, states patient had not received antibiotics yet; it is 1:00 p.m. Patient was receiving oxygen, and his oxygen saturation level was improving.

o By 2:00 p.m., blood work shows the creatinine level was worse, causing kidney failure.

o January 22, 2000, at 2:35 p.m., Steven goes into cardiac arrest. Resuscitation was unsuccessful and Steven Beard is pronounced dead.

• Dr. Satterwhite made sure the court understood his

opinion and conclusion by reiterating that Steven's death was not related to the gunshot wound. Sepsis was sufficient enough to cause death.

- When asked if the infection could have been introduced into Steven's bloodstream by changing the colostomy bag with dirty hands, the doctor's reply was no. When asked how the infection entered the bloodstream, Dr. Satterwhite said it was likely through the rash and <u>definitely not</u> through the gunshot wound or ilestomy bag. No infection was noted where the shotgun pellets caused damage.

- Questions about the autopsy were asked. The report said Steven had pulmonary emboli, which is an acute respiratory insufficiency. Dr. Satterwhite said this was the conclusion of Dr. Bayardo, who performed the autopsy. Dr. Satterwhite said sepsis and pulmonary embolism share the same symptoms, however, Steven's symptoms were inconsistent with pulmonary emboli. He said, when reviewing the autopsy report, he did not have microscopic findings to examine.

- When asked, "Was it determined in the autopsy how old the pulmonary embolisms (blood clots) were?" The answer by Dr. Satterwhite was "no."

- Dr. Satterwhite's opinion on the cause of death was Group A Streptococcal Septicemia.

Dr. Coscia

Trauma Medical Director of Brackenridge Hospital

On October 2, 1999, Dr. Coscia and his team were waiting in the emergency room for Star Flight to arrive with Steven. They prepped my husband for emergency surgery. Dr. Coscia was called to testify about the care Steven received while at Brackenridge during his final days, and to offer his professional opinion as to the cause of death.

To the best of my recollection and in no particular order, the testimony of Dr. Coscia:

- On January 19, 2000 I brought Steven back to the hospital when the rash in his perineal had worsened. I had to fight and argue with the admissions department because they said Medicare would not pay; I argued that we would pay and to admit him. The hospital staff did not see this as an emergency. Dr. Coscia testified Steven was admitted and that a resident intern, Dr. Haas, advised putting cornstarch in the area and to discharge the patient. An ointment was prescribed and by 9:30 the following morning, it still had not been administered. Dr. Haas noted in the chart that my husband needed a dermatology consult on out-patient care; Dr. Coscia interpreted this for us and said it means "to get him out." By now, my husband was experiencing chest pain, had a rapid pulse, and no fever was noted. Tests were run to determine his condition.

- January 22, 2000, 8:00 a.m., medical records state:
  - Steven was having a hard time talking, seemed to have delirium, and had a fever of 102.5. He began wheezing and his blood pressure went down. A surgical resident states, "now appears septic, start IV antibiotic, Zosyn."
  - A blood test revealed a positive blood culture. Gram positive cocci, with a change, was written in the chart. Strep or staph, rapidly progressing infection or contaminant. "It is now five hours that has passed, and the patient still has not received Zosyn." This is underlined three times on

the chart. Steven was ordered to ICU.

- o January 22, 1:30 p.m., septic shock was rapidly occurring. Steven suffered respiratory failure. Attending physician, Dr. Tom Coopwood, wrote the cause of death as septic shock.

- Dr. Coscia, under cross examination, stated his opinion: Steven died of pulmonary embolism, blood clots in the lungs, possibly septic. The blood clot was not considered a complication of the gunshot wound.

Dr. Roberto Bayardo

Chief Medical Examiner for Travis County, Austin, Texas

During his career, veteran testifier, Dr. Bayardo, received more money on the witness stand than he earned performing autopsies. It is estimated he collected more than $3 million dollars as he was called to testify as a self-proclaimed expert. The job of the Medical Examiner is to search the autopsy and medical records to make his decision about the cause of death. Dr. Bayardo only looked at the autopsy, he did not read the hospital records nor HealthSouth records. The autopsy showed Steven's gunshot healed and he entered the hospital with pneumonia. The autopsy report did not mention sepsis, gram positive cocci, or the opinion of the doctor who pronounced the death as gram positive septic shock.

David Fisher became an expert at investigating the Texas Medical Examiners. As a result of findings, Bayardo stepped down and the facility was completely revamped.

During the investigation of Bayardo, Fisher discovered that Bayardo lied about his credentials. To obtain the Chief Medical Examiner position for Travis County, Bayardo said he was the Deputy Chief Medical Examiner for Harris County. Bayardo was never hired in that position, or any other similar position in Texas or any other state.

My attorney, Dick DeGuerin, questioned Bayardo on the witness stand regarding his credentials, dating back to his schooling and first employment as a medical examiner. Under oath, Bayardo testified that he was Deputy Chief Medical Examiner for Harris County, Texas. This position immediately preceded his placement as the Chief Medical Examiner in Travis County, Texas. Roberto Bayardo committed perjury, leading to recanting his testimony in other cases. My case should be overturned based on his perjured testimony.

In a recent turn of events, and due to mounting, ongoing pressure from individuals, including Rodney Reed and Cathy Lynn Henderson, that he served injustices to by presenting inaccurate testimonies, he retracted statements he made under oath. Nearly two dozen inmates have been released from prison, including one inmate on death row for almost three decades.

Rodney Reed has been on death row for 22 years and is still on death row even though Dr. Bayardo recanted his testimony. Cathy Lynn Henderson's case was overturned because Dr. Bayardo withdrew his testimony in her case. In his recanting statement, he said he used "junk science" to charge her with murder. After spending over two decades on death row, she was sent back to Travis County jail while they were trying to make a case to retry her. She spent over two and a half years in the Travis County jail only to die of pneumonia.

An excerpt from the website innocenceproject.org: *Former Travis County Medical Examiner Roberto Bayardo, M.D., has also recanted much of his testimony that was used to implicate Reed at his 1998 trial. Although Bayardo testified that Reed's semen was left "quite recently," he has now changed his opinion. In a sworn declaration, Bayardo states that his finding "very few" sperm indicated that Reed and Stites had sex "not less than 24 hours before Ms. Stites's death."*

The death of the victim in Reed's case was caused by an object, most likely a police baton. Yet, Rodney Reed remains on death row as an innocent man. Ironically, both of Rodney Reed's parents were employed by Steven.

I am seeking retractions regarding the cause of death of my husband, Steven Beard, so that I may join the free world as an innocent woman. It was not a homicide, as Dr. Bayardo said. My husband died of natural causes, sepsis. My life is held in the balance of Dr. Bayardo's controversial opinion. I am hoping someone reading this information can step forward with legal representation to fight for my release. I have spent over 18 years, and counting, behind bars for a crime I did not commit. I want my life back which Dr. Bayardo helped take from me.

During pretrial hearings, the State told the court that the medical examiner, Dr. Bayardo, did not have blood and tissue samples from my husband to support his testimony.

Dr. Bayadro should be punished for committing crimes for remuneration; he testified in court on behalf of the deceased, without examining their bodies, and jeopardizing the freedom of defendants, including me.

- Dr. Bayardo testified he performed the autopsy of Steven Beard on January 23, 2000.

- He listed the cause of death as a blood clot going into the lungs, a common complication in gunshot victims. The blood clots formed in the lower extremities due to being bedridden. When being questioned about his autopsy procedure, Dr. Bayardo said he did not read the progress notes before preparing the Examiner's Report.

- He only read the last two or three pages of progress notes out of the eleven pages total. He said he only read those notes on the day of the trial.

- He did not read the Brackenridge or HealthSouth progress notes before writing his opinion.

- He did not review the medical records from previous hospitalizations or examinations. He said he did not know Steven had been diagnosed with chronic pneumonia and he said, "I do not care about that. Whatever happened before death does not matter to me."

- He became combative, angry and very hot-headed on the stand. He did not like being challenged with questions and dared anyone to contradict him. He was admonished by the Judge for being non-responsive and argumentative. His testimony was not objective.

- He testified that the new micro-organism invaded Steven's body around the third day before his death as a result of the gunshot wound from October 1999. Dick DeGuerin provided evidence that contradicted the doctor. Blood tests showed no prior infection, so it could not be gunshot related thus making his claims without merit.

- Dr. Bayardo said the blood clots formed because Steven was bedridden. He disregarded the fact that Steven was showing signs of progress after getting regular therapy in HealthSouth. He also disregarded the fact that Steven was pronounced fit to be discharged and ready to go home.

- He said, "The doctor who saw Steven during his lifetime was ignorant as to the cause of death."

- He said the areas that were surgically repaired showed no signs of infection.

- He said the streptococcus came from the lungs. He admitted he did not take cultures from the lungs to make this determination and that it was his unverified opinion.

- When he was told that Steven had a severe infection and was not given his antibiotics, Dr. Bayardo said he would still be alive today if the antibiotics were properly administered. The hospital's negligence should not have become my responsibility.

- Dick DeGuerin said the cause of death was malpractice. Dr. Bayardo insisted it was a pulmonary embolism, regardless.

- Dr. Bayardo's diagnosis:
  - Pulmonary embolism.
  - Bilateral bronchopneumonia.
  - Evidence of healing gunshot wound to the abdomen.
  - Repair of gunshot wound – right colon resection, removal of gall bladder, ileostomy.
  - Engorgement of internal organs.
  - Presence of dermatitis on external genitalia.

- Dick DeGuerin asked, "So would you have said that this was – his death was caused by the gunshot wound if he had gotten out of the hospital, gone to

– gone and gotten in an airplane, sat in a chair for a long time and got a blood clot as a result of that? Would that be secondary to the gunshot wound?"

Dr. Bayardo said, "Not under that scenario, no."

- Dr. Bayardo's opinion: Cause of death is the result of a gunshot wound to the abdomen. The immediate cause of death is pulmonary embolism, bronchopneumonia, and sepsis. This is an intentional death – homicide.

I cannot stipulate enough that the corruption of the Medical Examier and the prosecution sealed my ill-fated incarceration. It must be noted, and repeated: The autopsy showed Steven entered the hospital with pneumonia and his gunshot wound was healed. The clots did not come from the gunshot wound but from his heart. A heart attack was recorded by an EKG. Once the Heparin was discontinued, it made Steven's blood thick and sticky. The medical examiner is supposed to examine all the evidence before making a determination, but Dr. Bayardo only looked at the autopsy before declaring the wrong conclusion.

He was charged by the prosecution to support their case of Capital Murder and needed to find a way to connect me to the shooting. They needed the charge of Capital Murder and Dr. Bayardo gave the prosecution what they wanted by doing it through tunnel vision. Dr. Bayardo purposely did not read the hospital and HealthSouth records, so he would not know about the heart attack, when Steven was taken off Heparin, or the acute sepsis. I want to know if the autopsy records can be reviewed again by an independent examiner. Tracey was charged with Injury to an Elderly Person and that charge connected only Tracey Tarlton to Steven's shooting.

These undisputed facts were presented to the jury, yet disregarded during deliberations:

Fact 1. Dr. Petty showed slides of old and new clots in Steven's lungs. New clots had no timeline, so they could have passed right after the shooting and surgery 4 months earlier.

Fact 2. Steven was weaned off Heparin before leaving HealthSouth on January 18, 2000. Heparin is a strong blood thinner that has to be monitored by a physician. Steven's blood was thicker and stickier at that time. Broccoli in his evening meal could have further thickened his blood because it has vitamin K in it. He was served other foods that were also enriched with vitamin K. Steven was not being prescribed a proper diet, considering the severity of his condition.

Fact 3. Autopsy showed pneumonia in Steven's lungs - congestion for any clot sliding through.

Fact 4. Steven's hospital record annotated a heart attack. Irregular beating of the heart can throw off blood clots.

Fact 5. Sepsis was in the blood. It is a fast growing infection hindering the blood flow.

It took three days of no medical intervention, while he was hospitalized, for Steven's coagulated blood to stop moving, causing his death.

All these facts have nothing to do with the shooting. Unfair to me, one man's lies and poor medical practices became the basis for my lifelong incarceration.

Dr. Charles Petty

Dallas County Chief Medical Examiner/Crime Lab Chief

During his esteemed career, Dr. Petty performed and supervised over 40,000 autopsies. He has testified as a witness for the prosecution over 1200 times. Dr. Petty said he is usually called by the prosecution, but in this case, he was called by the defense to discuss his findings and to present his opinion about the cause of death for Steven Beard. Ironically, Dr. Petty was Dr. Bayardo's mentor.

- Dick DeGuerin asked Dr. Petty his opinion on the cause of death. His reply was, " He reviewed all of Steven Beard's medical records, not just the last four days as Dr. Bayardo testified doing." Dr. Petty reviewed the autopsy report and the microscopic slides. His professional opinion: Steven Beard died of an overwhelming infection, and it was proven by the blood cultures.

- He went on to explain that under Texas law, the medical examiner is to determine both manner and cause of death. In Steven's case, the cause of death was the infection. The manner of death was a natural disease process.

- He indicated the rash was not related to the gunshot wound. The rash was not related to the ilestomy.

- The infection, Dr. Petty was certain, entered the body through the rash.

- When asked about the significance of reviewing all

of Steven Beard's medical records, as opposed to not reviewing them as Dr. Bayardo did, Dr. Petty said it gave him an idea as to what actually happened and what the circumstances of his death were. Dr. Petty said, "I was in possession of a lot more information than Dr. Bayardo."

- Based on several pictures taken during the autopsy, Dr. Petty said it was not possible to tell if the blood clots were fresh, or post-mortem. He said he was able to determine that some of the blood clots had been there for a prolonged period of time because there was an area of the lung that was infarcted; an area of the lung was dead. The circulation had been shut off to that portion of the lung that's supplied by the artery that is cut off. It could have developed when COPD was diagnosed in the 1980's.

- Dr. Petty said Dr. Bayardo did not accurately record the size of the buckshot. This leads to questions about the accuracy of other findings by Dr. Bayardo.

- Dr. Petty said the gunshot wound was healing well and no infection was present.

- Dr. Petty consulted Dr. Satterwhite, and both concurred that strep infection, not the gunshot wound, was the cause of death.

Peggy Farley

Advanced Clinical Practitioner

Peggy Farley was Kristina's therapist for about a year. When my daughters pretended to be scared of me and went into hiding, Peggy Farley took them into her home. With all the money the twins stole from me, they could have stayed at a luxury hotel. Farley's testimony primarily focused around the time the girls spent with her.

- In April of 2000, while I was at Timberlawn, the girls left home. Peggy Farley invited the girls to stay at their ranch, much to the disappointment of her husband. To remain ethical, she terminated the therapeutic relationship immediately.

- Peggy said the twins stayed at her home for about three months. At first, they only brought a few items of clothing. Then they began making themselves at home and brought more clothes, a Jeep they purchased with the money stolen from my bank account, the Waverunners, their Cadillac's, and Steven's birthday dog, Kaci.

- Peggy told the jury that during the course of therapy,

437

Kristina said many derogatory things about Steven. She claimed he was disappointed in her, he picked on her, and he pushed her too hard to accomplish things she did not want to do. Once Kristina was living at her house, Peggy noticed Kristina contradicting many things she said in therapy. She overheard her calling Steven names like "fat fuck, stupid, drunk, and old."

- Peggy said Justin was at her house every day, all day long. He acted as though he lived there too. She said Justin talked non-stop about the shooting, ad nauseam. He tried to get Kristina to discuss it all the time with him. He wrote lengthy documents about everything, leaving no stone unturned. She said he left some writings in her printer and she read them. She said it could have been a manuscript because it was repeatedly edited and revised. The writings were very detailed. Farley said, "Finally, it got to be too much, and the girls and I told him this had to stop. We were sick of hearing and talking about everything, everyday."

- The questions turned to what it was like with the girls living at her house. Peggy said her husband was fed up with them being there and their presence did eventually lead to their divorce. She said the girls did not pay their share to stay with her, but they did help

438

around the ranch. They partied a lot. Justin was there every day and did nothing to help. He would invite himself to dinner and refused to eat leftovers; he was a difficult person. Peggy said she would ask the girls and Justin to help prepare dinner and clean up. The girls pitched in, but Justin never did.

- Farley said she encouraged the kids to contact me, but they refused.
- Secretly, the girls loaned Peggy's husband $20,000 that they stole from my bank account. Peggy told the jury when she found out he had taken money from the girls, she made him return it immediately.

Peggy terminated the therapeutic relationship because she knew she could not send me a bill because the girls were staying with her. If she knew or cared about being ethical, she would have never invited them to stay at her house.

Janet Masson

Forensic Document Examiner

I received an anonymous letter which the writer called me a dyke and told me to join my dead husband. Janet Masson was hired to examine indentations on the letter and to examine the partial signature. The conclusion: Kristina sent me the letter.

During the trial, I received two books in the mail, *An Hour to Kill* and *Killing for Company*. It was never determined who the sender was, but it does fit with the actions of Kristina.

During the trial the prosecutors asked each witness if I read true crime books, anyone who was considered a close friend was especially grilled about my preferred reading material. Each person responded with "no."

I believe the State was trying to relate the books sent to me to the case by implicating that I read true crime books to get ideas on how to commit a crime. This far-fetched idea gained no traction, but does show how the prosecution attempted to twist information to fit their theories because they knew their case was weak.

Douglas Morrison

Director/Instructor of Audio Engineering at Dallas Sound Lab

After my husband died, some of my phone calls and

messages left on answering machines were secretly
recorded by Justin and Kristina. The prosecution entered
the tapes into evidence. My attorney, Dick DeGuerin, hired
Douglas Morrison to analyze the tapes because they did not
appear authentic. After his in-depth demonstration before
the court to show the alterations on the tapes, the Judge
allowed the tapes to remain in evidence, despite the harsh
objections of my defense team. His conclusions and
testimony:

- Douglas Morrison prepared visual and audio
  displays for the court and the jury to see and
  understand where edits were made on the tapes that
  had been submitted into evidence.

- He said the tapes were altered. The calls were
  transferred to a microcassette and the conversations
  were altered. He identified edits and alterations and
  showed hidden splice points that were not
  effectively done.

- He said conversations were cut off on the tape
  before the actual conversation ended, changing the
  context of the conversation.

- He identified time differences in the recordings and
  noted background noise differences.

- He said the tape contained multiple, verified edits that were obvious.

- One section of the tape looks like I said, "I hired someone to kill Tracey," Morrison said parts of that conversation were altered and deleted.

- The opinion of Douglas Morrison was an analog recording with a microcassette was transferred to a computer, then to digital sound. Edits were made, and the revised tapes were replayed into a microcassette recorder. He said anyone with a computer and some basic skills has the ability to edit tapes.

Even Kristina testified that the tapes were not complete conversations, yet the Judge allowed them to be entered into evidence and for the jury to hear them.

Dawn Madigan

Dawn Madigan is the wife of the builder of our lake house. We became close over time and I considered Dawn to be my best friend. She was called to testify as a character witness.

- Dawn was questioned about her opinion of the relationship between my husband and me. She told the court we were loving to each other, and she never heard us calling each other names.
- She said I was witty, charming, generous, and kind. She mentioned the time I established a scholarship for her son.
- She said Steven drank too much and that I always took care of him when he was drunk.
- She recalled a time being at our house when I was feeling emotional because I recently spent too much money. She said my husband consoled me by saying, "It is not that important, I just want you to be happy."
- Dawn was questioned about Tracey. She said she met Tracey at St. David's and she thought she was very imposing. She said she was only there to visit me and Tracey would not leave so we could talk privately. She described Tracy as having a gruff demeanor. As time went along, she noticed Tracey being clingy with me. She sensed Tracey was very jealous of the relationship she and I shared.
- Dawn talked about the day Steven was shot. She

was at the hospital and could hear the police interviews. She said she heard Kristina ask if they found out who took Steven's wallet and ring. The police response was they had not yet discovered those items missing. I question how Kristina knew about the missing wallet and ring when it had not yet been discovered.

- Dawn said she spent the day with us at the hospital. She was questioned about something the girls said in their testimony about all of us leaving the hospital together and me stopping at a dumpster to throw out an empty Everclear bottle. Dawn set the record straight: she said we never stopped at a dumpster to throw a bottle out. She did say she saw me throw out a psychology book about self-mutilation; she clearly saw the cover of the book. The girls said the book I threw out was a poison making book.

- To continue breaking down some testimonies of the twins, Dawn was questioned about me traveling with the dogs. She said she often saw Megan and Nikki at the lake house with me.

- When asked about my demeanor the day my husband died, Dawn described me as being

444

distraught and very emotional. When the girls were questioned by the prosecution, they made it appear that the limo ride to the funeral was all fun and filled with laughter. Dawn told the jury it was a tense and sad time for us. She did say that she thought it was inappropriate that the girls were asking how much money they would be getting in the will, but the Judge struck that from the record because it was hearsay.

- Dawn described being with me the day I was dividing Steven's belongings up to give to his family and friends. She said I was being generous and she thought Kristina was more concerned about money, not things.

Marilou Gibbs

My husband and I met Marilou when we lived in the lake house while the Toro Canyon house was under construction. Her house was nearby, and we saw each other in the neighborhood; eventually, we became very good friends. She was like a second mother to me and loved me unconditionally. There is not a day that goes by that I do not miss her. We had great times together and she was the light of my life and a beacon of hope. I am a better person because of her. Like Dawn Madigan, she was called to testify as a character witness.

- Marilou opened the testimony describing Steven; she said he reminded her of Jackie Gleason.

- She told the jury that my husband loved me. She said he told me how to dress, how to fix my hair, how he wanted my nails done, and so on. She said I went along with his wishes because it made him happy.

- She talked about how I would stand up to Steven and how he loved that about me.

- Marilou told the jury Steven was overindulgent with me. She heard him tell me that I was free to spend as much money as I wanted, and she did also say there were a few times he was upset at my overspending.

- Marilou was questioned about the relationship between Kristina and Steven. She said Kristina would often call him names. Marilou said she objected to her behavior and would always tell her to stop. She told Kristina, Steven was kind and generous and to show respect. She said Kristina hated to be admonished.

- She said my husband was worried about me riding the Waverunners because of my osteoporosis.

- She said Steven drank every day until he passed out. She said she had seen me water down his vodka so he would not get so drunk.

- The questions turned to Tracey Tarlton. Marilou met her for the first time at a house party. She said Tracey kept trying to interrupt the conversation I was having with Marilou. She said Tracey would stomp away and slam doors; she acted jealous and rude.

- She said I was emotional and very upset for a long time after my husband was shot, and then after he died.

- She described how upset I was that Steven's condition was going downhill after he went to HealthSouth. When he was admitted there, he could go to the bathroom. Eventually, he could not get out of bed and had bedsores.

- She said I changed after Steven died. She said I was unreachable by phone. She said a lady, later to be identified as Donna Goodson, was screening the calls and hanging up on her. After several weeks of trying to reach me, she said I finally answered the phone, and she was very worried about me because my speech was slurry. Before we could have a conversation, she tells the court that someone jerked the phone away from me, told me not to call anymore, and hung up.

- When asked about my state of mind when the girls left home and went into hiding, Marilou described me as out of my mind with worry for the girls.

18

My Civil Deposition Testimony

August 25, 2000

My deposition was played for the jury in its entirety. Steven's three adult children, Steven III, Becky, and Paul, and my daughters, Kristina and Jennifer, filed a civil lawsuit against me. They were seeking a temporary injunction to hold the property of the estate until the criminal trial concluded. They claimed I had intentionally caused the death of my husband and should not inherit property.

The lawsuit had no merit because I was not charged in the death of Steven at that time. The suit was dismissed before the claimants were deposed; the burden of proof was less than a reasonable doubt.

Final ruling: "There is no evidence before you that Celeste Beard intentionally and willfully participated in the shooting of Steven Beard."

"We are trying to introduce too many things."

-Judge Kocurek

This statement was told in a scolding manner to the defense, yet the prosecution was allowed to submit volumes of boxes of "evidence" without reprimand.

*Should there be a limit of evidence when the defense is trying to save an innocent person from spending life in prison?

It should have never been allowed for the teenagers to meet with the prosecutors daily for almost two years "to rehearse their lines" like actors in a play. I am sure their tears were staged, the girls were easy to crying when it fit their agenda. The truth NEVER needs to be rehearsed. They were not able to rehearse in the Civil Trial and the judge noticed, as did their defense attorneys. That is the reason the hearing was ruled in my favor and their attorneys withdrew immediately after the hearing ended.

On May 12, 2013, *The Michael Morton Act* came into effect. This act makes evidence discoverable, regardless of whether it is a work product. It compels prosecutors to make their files available to the defense attorney's. Unfortunately, it is too late to help me. Or, is it?

Well known author of *Behind the Staircase,* Michael Peterson, chronicled his unjust 13-year confinement after his wife Kathleen's death. His incarceration mirrored mine; he was imprisoned due to the inaccurate testimony of Medical Examiner Agent Deaver; he lied under oath. Agent Deaver's perjured testimony included falsehoods about his credentials and training, leaving all else said under oath to be untrustworthy. Those lies led to robbing Michael Peterson, and others he testified against, of their just freedom. This account is told in detail in *Behind the Staircase.* A digital copy book is available for free online and can verify Peterson's injustice.

Judge Hudson overturned Peterson's murder conviction and ruled, "Deaver deliberately misrepresented and intentionally misled the court and the jury."

Medical Examiner Roberto Bayardo manipulated evidence during my trial, slanting his answers towards the prosecution. My case should be overturned, citing case law in Michael Peterson's overturned conviction.

19

Closing Arguments

Lacking decorum at times, the trial lasted seven weeks. Over 200 witnesses were called to testify. Over 500 exhibits were admitted into evidence. Hundreds of objections were made. Nearly all the evidence was circumstantial.

A juror approached the court with concerns over comments some jurors were heard saying, "Let's hurry this up and get this over with." And, "Oh, God. Let's get this damn thing over with." Another juror comment, "I am going to lose my job over this." The jury referred to themselves as, "The Jolly Jury." Some jurors fell asleep during testimony. The Judge individually called each juror into chambers to discuss their conduct. The foreman of the jury said some jurors were getting impatient and another was frustrated because she had problems with her children.

To prove their case of Capital Murder, an abundance of irrelevant information, including bank records, phone records, pharmacy records, and accompanying testimonies, were presented by the prosecution to confuse the jury.

Celeste

During the trial, Dick DeGuerin said, "The defense
has to defend every bad thing Celeste did because the State is
trying to shore up their weak case on Tracey Tarlton by
trashing Celeste."

The prosecution addressed the jury:
ADA Gary Cobb, one of the prosecutors, said in his closing
arguments, "It is said in the Bible, in the book of Timothy,
that those who desire to be rich fall into temptation, and that
they fall into many snares and many senseless and hurtful
desires. They fall into ruin and perdition. And what follows
that is one of the most famous phrases in the Bible that money
is the root of all evil. But that's not the phrase. The phrase
that follows that is that the love of money is the root of all
evil because that is what this case is about. People loved her,
but all she loved was money."

I interrupt to address Mr. Cobb at this juncture: Our
forefathers protected us from a situation like this by
separating church and state. The Bible verse was used in my
trial to impress a receptive jury. Permitting different doctrines
in trials is subjective and unfair. No, Mr. Cobb, what the
Bible says in (New American Standard):

Celeste

Isaiah 10-1&2:
"Woe to those who enact evil statutes,

And to those who constantly record unjust decisions,

So as to deprive the needy of justice,

And rob the poor of My people of their rights,

In order that widows may be their spoil,

And that they may plunder the orphans.

and

(New American Standard)

Isaiah 54:17

"No weapon that is formed against you shall prosper,

And every tongue that accuses you in Judgment you will

condemn. This is the heritage of the servants of the Lord,

And their vindication is from Me," declares the Lord.

Continuation of Mr. Cobb's address to the jury:

- Was the defendant involved in this murder, but did not do it for money? Then you should find the defendant not guilty of Capital Murder; it would be a murder offense.
- Did Tracey Tarlton do it on her own? If not, the defendant is considered guilty of Capital Murder.
- You still must consider the charge of Injury to an Elderly Person.
- The Law of Parties means that if you get someone to

454

do a crime, you are guilty as if you pulled the trigger yourself.

- You are instructed to consider all the relevant facts and circumstances surrounding the killing.

The defense addressed the jury:

- Tracey Tarlton pled guilty to shooting Steven Beard. The law says she is an accomplice, and automatically, she is a discredited witness. The conviction cannot be held upon the testimony of an accomplice.
- Tracey Tarlton is recognized to be a discredited witness because she had something to gain.
- In order to find Celeste Beard Johnson guilty, you have to find other evidence that does not depend on Tracey Tarlton to prove Celeste is guilty.
- No evidence connected Celeste to the crime. You must return a verdict of not guilty.
- The prosecution brought forth a lot of other outside evidence to prove their weak case. None of that evidence connected Celeste to the killing.
- The State's evidence did not corroborate Tracey Tarlton's testimony.
- Not one single witness testified Celeste did this for money, which discredits remuneration as a motive.

- The State took to smearing Celeste by bringing up bad things because they knew they had a weak case. You cannot consider that evidence of guilt.

- Don't forget about the ME, Dr. Bayardo – when questioned if he reviewed Steven Beard's medical records, he had the nerve to say, "So what."

- The State tried to shift focus from the major facts.

- Do not forget the twins turning on their mother: stealing, forging checks, and acting afraid. They stand to get millions of dollars by lying.

- During Kristina Beard's testimony when questioned by the defense, she "Did not remember," or "Did not know," 298 times.

20

Deliberations Conclude

Mr. DeGuerin and the other attorney's decided I did not need to testify because they were certain I would be found not guilty because it appeared the State did not prove their case. Dick said that, in the event we would need to file an appeal, it would be advantageous for me to not testify. I tearfully agreed with their decision. I was seated at the defense table and was warned by the sheriff to not turn around to face my supporters. One juror was a lone hold out, not convinced of my guilt, which made for a lengthy debate. After four long days of deliberations, I could not control my emotions, I was sobbing and emotionally exhausted. I was terrified and relieved at the same time, wanting this nightmare to be over. The pressure was immense. When I heard the words "guilty" I shut down. I was shocked that the jury missed all that we disproved. I could not reconcile being punished for a crime I did not commit. I wished for the death penalty. I had no fight left in me.

Celeste

The Reading of the Verdict

Guilty of the offense of Capital Murder.

Guilty of the offense of Injury to the Elderly.

Punishment

Confinement for life with a $10,000 fine.

The Texas Legislature enacted *The Michael Morton Act* in 2013, requiring "Full disclosure of all police reports and witness statements regardless of whether the evidence is material to guilt or punishment."

Based on this law, had my defense team received the police reports and witness statements for Tracey trying to kill Reginald Breaux (the Judge denied the jury access to this information), the suspicious death of Zan Ray's husband, thefts and forgeries by the teens and Donna Goodson, medical examiner's reports and slides, piecemeal evidence given to ADA Mange by the teens, and all files sealed by Judge Kocurek, I would be a free woman today. Can the 2013 *Michael Morton Act* help me now?

21

Incarceration

After the reading of the verdict, I remained standing, on crutches, with my feet firmly cemented to the floor. I was not able to move my legs, though my knee caps were trembling. It was not a voluntary action. Everything became a blur. People were talking, yet all I could hear was noise. I could not discern words except for hearing Jennifer cry out, "NO!" I remember my attorney speaking to me. His lips moved but I could not comprehend what he was saying. I felt like I was underwater with waves of anguish washing over me like a tide rushing in. My blood pressure must have been extremely high because I felt my eardrums pounding to the beat of my heart.

I knew I was innocent of the charges placed against me. I had faith in my defense team and believed the jury would see through the thinly veiled circumstantial evidence presented by the prosecution. I was not prepared to hear "guilty." I was scared to death.

I remember being rushed out of the court room in a

haze of confusion. I could not stop gagging, and even though my stomach was empty, I felt like vomiting. The days that followed were much of the same. As I was being processed, I went through the motions and responded to everything I was being told to do without emotion. I was just there, a void, a lifeless form. I recall being loaded into a prison van with other inmates. I was threatened with assault by a friend of Tracey's and that petrified me. During my life I was always physically and mentally abused, but never fought back. I felt defenseless. I was no match for prison.

Arriving at the prison left me with considerable fear of the unknown. We were locked in a cage, known as "The Dog Pound." We were treated harshly and screamed at by the guards. I was stripped naked and my crutches were taken from me. I was still under doctor's care for my broken leg and could not bear any weight. I was forced to crawl nude to the next area to get my prison issued clothing. An officer even threw my crutches further away from me and laughed as I crawled on my hands and knees to fetch them.

I kept my head down and could feel the prying eyes of other inmates upon me. I pretended not to hear their whispers behind my back. I was given the rules of the system, but had a difficult time registering the information. I was overwhelmed and afraid. I felt so alone; all my life, one of my greatest fears was being alone, and now I was utterly alone. Whenever I see a newbie on the block, I relive my first day all over again.

It did not take long to realize prison is a complete black market environment. Postage stamps and Ramen noodles are the currency.

I was taken to a windowless cell in Segregation where it was unbearably hot. I slept on the cool cement floor for relief. The leg cast made me feel so hot; it had not been changed in weeks and it was rank. My leg itched with intensity. I ended up wearing a cast for nearly three years. I was always housed in the furthest units from where I was to report daily; it was difficult getting around on crutches in a timely manner. What I detested most was the noise, women yelled and screamed 24/7. I yearned for peace and quiet.

I never lived with complete strangers. There were so many women housed together. Some were violent, repeat offenders. This left me in such a state of distress that I never made eye contact with anyone for fear they would cause me harm. Some women are such vile brutes and show no signs of remorse for their actions. They look forward to each new day just for the pleasure of tormenting a weaker foe. I saw a gang of women hold down a woman as the leader of the pack stuffed used feminine products down her throat. I was so repulsed that I threw up. I gag whenever I recall that incident. I am surrounded by bad actors and avoid them at all costs.

Bunking with these women left me sleepless.

Because I suffer from PTSD, I could not turn off the reel of my life that would continually play in my mind, leaving me sleep deprived and desperate for rest. I wanted to be in my own bed buried beneath my down comforter, far away from this nightmare.

Bathing with a room full of women left me without dignity. I longed for my own private, luxurious shower with my favorite shampoos and soaps. I would love to have a large, fluffy towel again.

The prison attire left me aching for my closets full of designer clothing and accessories. Realizing I could no longer get dressed up for special occasions gave me a deeper appreciation for the wonderful times and places Steven and I went together.

Not being able to go to the bathroom privately made me want to not eat or drink so I would not need to void. You take plush, two ply toilet tissue for granted until course, one ply tissue is all that is available. I have to buy my toilet tissue from the commissary and ration every square.

Meal time is nothing to look forward to. Eating is only a means of survival and not enjoyable. I know why it is called the Mess Hall. It is because the slop on the plate is a mess. I would like to return to the days where I ate dinner with my husband, even after it sat in the warming drawer for hours and was dried out.

I miss Steven, my estranged daughters, my mom, and the camaraderie of my friends. I miss our jovial conversations. I miss not being able to confide in someone. Most everyone in prison has a secret agenda for making conversation, leaving me reluctant to trust anyone.

I missed my once vibrant and energetic voice. For the longest time I rarely spoke, and when I did, I talked only when necessary. My voice was robotic and monotone, flat and without emotion. I longed for my musical voice to return and to have laughter like the great days in the past. Steven loved my voice and my laugh. He said he loved my smile most.

I miss my pets very much. I loved them and they loved me, unconditionally. Even my friend's pets loved me and would clamor all over me when I went to visit. Pets are a good judge of character. I would have fared well if dogs and cats were on my jury. There are a few stray cats in the prison and I always cuddle them when they make their way to my unit. Recently, kittens were born and they are so precious and adorable. Just seeing them rekindled the love I had for my pets of yesteryear.

The transition from living in the free world to adjusting to prison life was difficult. I am at the mercy of the guards and strict schedules. In the beginning of my incarceration, I was not on time and in place for the head count. I was punished with 30 days of cell restriction and had a temporary restraint placed on the few privileges to which I was entitled. This gave me plenty of time to think and to understand the rules and regulations. I quickly learned to be compliant.

While I was battling to gain a sense of composure in my life, Dick DeGuerin sent a letter to Judge Kocurek asking for a free transcript of my trial. A Hearing of Indigency took place on July 18, 2003, before Honorable Charles Campbell. I lost and had to pay $41,700 for copies of my trial transcripts. After this hearing, I was forced to sign papers distributing the Marital Trust, so my appeals process could begin. The breaking of the Trust distributed money to Steven's three children and the twins, and to the attorneys for services rendered. Bank of America and David Kuperman wanted me to break the Trust agreement because an error was found to result in Steven's Trust owing the IRS over $3 million. My legal team found the error and Bank of America did not want it reported. They did this to keep me quiet. More proof of unethical behavior; this is tax fraud. The stark reality was hitting me hard, I was penniless and in prison. How could I live under the weight of this lie?

I remained in a dark place for a long time. I attended the mandatory group counseling sessions and rarely participated. I sat and listened to other women, leaving my issues buried deep inside. The more I resisted therapy, the harder it was for me to come to grips with the reality that I was in prison serving a life sentence for a crime I did not commit. I was angry at the world and came to understand I was experiencing the five stages of grief and loss: denial and isolation; anger; bargaining; depression; and acceptance. The only way I was going to overcome the situation was to find a coping mechanism that was right for me. I decided it was time to stop feeling sorry for myself and enrolled in classes. I poured myself into my studies. When one course was completed, I began another. I was diligent with the work and excelled at every curriculum, placing in the top tier of every class. I began to feel better about myself and my outlook slowly began to improve. Getting into an educational rhythm saved me from despair. I am proud of my accomplishments and grateful for the opportunity to participate in such diverse programs.

Someday, God willing, my case will be overturned. Someone will help me. I will be a free woman and my substantial skill set will enable me to become a productive citizen.

To me, it had always seemed hypocritical that people suddenly turned to Christ after being in prison. My experience has taught me that sometimes this is the only way God can get your attention. I have discovered God and I know he loves me. He knows I love him. Because of Joyce Meyer's book,

Beauty for Ashes, I have been able to forgive my father and brother. I still have memories, but know that if I want God's forgiveness, then I must forgive.

I am currently enrolled in the prestigious Seminary program where a select few are chosen to participate. I am enjoying the program and look forward to the classes every day.

Courses I have completed during my incarceration:

Degrees:

Central Texas College:
    Associate of Arts degree in General Studies
    Associate of Science degree in Business
Texas A&M University:
    Bachelor of Science degree in Business
        Administration with an emphasis in Management
Agape Bible College:
    Seminary program for both a Master's and Doctorate
        degree in Biblical Studies (presently enrolled)

Celeste

Certifications:

Adams State University:

    Paralegal

    Legal Investigation

    Alternative Dispute Resolution

    Victim Advocacy

National Library of Congress:

    Literary Braille Transcriber

    Nemeth Mathematics Transcriber

    Literary Proofreader

    Music Transcriber

    Unified English Braille (UEB) Transcriber

The National Braille Association:

    Textbook Formatting (1997 Guidelines)

    Textbook Formatting Recertification (2011
    Guidelines)

Windham School District *On the Job Training* (OJT):

    Braille Typist

    Graphic Designer

    Braille Textbook Formatting Apprenticeship

    General Clerk

    Accounting Clerk

Celeste

Windham School:

    Cognitive Intervention

    Parenting/Family Wellness

 U.S. Department of Labor:

    (OSHA) Safety Training – Lifetime Accreditation

American Community Corrections Institute:

    Anger Management Cognitive Life Skills Course

    Cognitive Awareness

Prisoner Assistance Scholastic Service:

    Victim Awareness

    Anger Management

    Domestic Violence & Violence Against Women

        Parenting

    Nonviolent Communication

    Conflict Resolution

    Living With Purpose

    Reentry Into Society

Intensive Volunteer Treatment Programs:

    Celebrate Recovery

    Breaking Free

    Bridges to Life

    Faith-based dorm (15-month program)

Celeste

Cookbook Author:

From the Big House to Your House 2010

High Fence Foodie 2015

Ramentastic 2019

The prison cookbook, *From The Big House to Your House,* was spearheaded by me to get the recipes typed and edited. Other inmates joined me and formed a group sending recipes and drawings back and forth to my mother. After collecting about 200 recipes, Hans Sherrer, at *Justice Denied,* compiled the final book. All proceeds from sales of *From The Big House to Your House* series are being donated to The Justice Institute.

Through dogged perseverance, Mr. Sherrer wrote *Unreasonable Conviction* and was able to help facilitate the exoneration of Kirstin Blaise Lobato, after she spent over 17 years in prison for a murder she did not commit. Knowing these cookbooks offered some financial assistance towards her release brings meaning to my unjust incarceration.

According to the National Registry of Exonerations, published on April 9, 2019, exonerations in the United States last year cleared 151 innocent people of convictions for crimes they did not commit. This group served 1,639 years in prison, a record, averaging 10.9 years per exoneree.

22

Timeline of Medical Abuse

I had kept a journal documenting all the medical abuse I have sustained since my incarceration. Beginning with the abuse I endured at the hands of Craig when I was a young woman, and throughout the rest of my life, I required medical care. I was not getting the proper treatment in prison and I was not given the medicines prescribed by the specialists at the University of Texas Medical Branch (UTMB) in Galveston, Texas. I especially needed the drugs that would help control my PTSD and depression. My ailments fell on deaf ears. I was told I was being dramatic when I complained about my conditions and was sent on my way without being examined by the doctor. One day I was rustled awake by the guards in the middle of the night and told to gather my things. That is how they do things in prison. I was taken to a new unit. During this move, my medical journal disappeared. All my notes vanished. I lost 14 years of information. I started a new journal and suspect that will suddenly vanish someday too. At least they didn't think to take my calendar – I note everything of importance on my calendar.

Celeste

My "Lifting Restriction" and "Ground Floor Only Restrictions" were taken away. I was denied a wedge for serious acid reflux. I have documented vertigo for 10+ years and used to take Meclizine several times a day and now take it only twice a day. I was transferred to the Lane Murray Unit because of falling as a direct result of medical issues. The falling was brought to Huntsville's attention by a forged letter, purported to be signed by my husband. The letter was sent to Classifications in Huntsville. Lane Murray is the women's handicap accessible unit. Climbing stairs would put others and me in danger. I had the "Ground Floor Only Restriction" since April 2003. I have osteoporosis. It is a safety risk and the "Ground Floor Only" should be reinstated immediately. One-third of my stomach was inside of my esophagus due to a hiatal hernia. Every time the Heimlich maneuver was used, it pushed more of my stomach into the esophagus. One time a rib was broken and had become displaced because of the Heimlich procedure. I have had regular incidents of choking and suffer continual pain on my right side. All these incidents are documented:

07/27/17: I had fundoplication surgery where my stomach was removed and sewn around the esophagus. I stayed in the hospital bed for 12 days. The surgery was a complete success, as seen on the Upper GI.

471

08/9/17: I arrived back to the unit and saw P.A. Bennett. He ordered medications but did not issue a "5-pound Lifting Restriction" as ordered by the Cardio/Thoracic surgeon, Dr. Okereke.

08/17/17: After arriving back to my unit from another hospital trip, I was forced to heavy lift my heavy property and pull a heavy cart because I did NOT have a lifting restriction on record. I immediately felt intense pain and reported it.

08/18/17: Mr. Wright, N.P. gave me a "5-pound Lifting Restriction" that expired on 10/2/17. While I was still experiencing intense pain on my right side, I was also having difficulty swallowing.

08/21/17: I filed a Step-1 grievance against P.A. Bennett for refusing to follow the advice of the specialist and by failing to give me the "5-pound Lifting Restriction."

09/20/17: I filed a Step-2 against P.A. Bennett for injury. I am still suffering pain on my right side and am choking with difficulty swallowing. I am choking again and need the Heimlich often. The wrap slipped and I need surgery to repair it.

09/29/17: I saw the G.I. Doctor for a post-surgery follow-up. When I explained what happened and how I felt, I was referred to the Cardio/Thoracic surgeon. The

GERD is now no longer responding to Prilosec and Zantac, which are each taken twice a day. The G.I. Doctor recommended a wedge, which the LVN Nurse McKandless said, "You won't get that on this unit." I suffer from Barrett's esophagus, and it is exacerbated because of the acid. I wake up gagging with acid burning up to my throat and into my mouth; the wedge would relieve this. I have no pillows to use as a makeshift wedge. I use a rolled up jacket, but it quickly flattens, rendering it useless.

11/1/17: I saw the Vascular Surgeon and explained what happened after I strained myself. I said the pain and choking mirrored how I felt before the stomach surgery. He called the Cardio/Thoracic surgeon, Dr. Okereke, and I was held over to have an Upper GI on 11-3-17 and to see Dr. Okereke on 11-6-17.

11/3/17: The Upper G.I. Barium Swallow showed a new hernia coming out of the surgery site. The Upper GI Barium Swallow test that I had post-surgery, on 7-28-17, showed no leaks, no hernia, and no injury.

11/6/17: I saw Dr. Okereke, and he scheduled a CT scan before he decided the next course of action. The pain remains, and food is getting stuck in the esophagus, leaving me to continually choke.

Celeste

11/8/17: The Property Officer forced me to heavy lift again, and I immediately felt intense pain on my right side, by my navel, and on both sides of my abdomen. I experience intense pain 20 minutes after eating. Due to the pain, I did not eat for five days because after I would eat, I would double over in pain. It now affects my bowel movement.

11/21/17: I filed a Step-1 Grievance against Property Officer Anderson for being a direct cause of injury to my stomach.

11/19/17: I had a CT scan of the esophagus and abdomen. My mom received a letter from Complaints Coordinator, Ms. Buro, dated 12/13/2017. It states "The unit medical can change doctor's orders because they are just SUGGESTIONS of care."

12/18/17: Dr. Okereke informed me that I refused an expedited appointment to see the GI doctor. The GI doctor had to refer me to Dr. Okereke because he is unable to help. I had to wait four weeks for that appointment and continued to suffer, without relief. I did not sign paperwork refusing any appointment have made forty-four trips to Galveston to repair this situation.

*The Supreme Court has ruled that a medical official who only has general knowledge about a particular field of medicine many NOT substitute their judgment for that of a specialist.

8-16-2020: I filed a 42 U.S.C. 1983 Civil Lawsuit in the United States District Court for the Western District of Texas, in Waco, Texas. Case # 6:19-cv-00475.

Not having the prescribed lifting restriction, ground floor only restriction, and the wedge has been a detriment to my health and well-being. The denials for necessary medical orders are a cruel and unusual punishment, which violates my Constitutional Rights.

Every person has the right to be able to eat, swallow, and have reasonable medical help. I just hope I do not die before I am set free.

I now have a permanent lifting restriction and ground floor only restriction. I am still in desperate need of a wedge pillow.

It has been almost three years waiting for the repair surgery and my nutrients cannot be properly digested, leaving me deficient in vitamins B-12 and D. I am required to go to the pill line daily to receive a dose of vitamin D. Every other week I receive a B-12 shot. Also, I am now hypothyroid and take daily medication for this. And I am now a Type 2 diabetic and take Metformin twice daily.

For five months I was so dizzy and lethargic that I could not get out of bed. I complained every few days to medical. Finally, they ordered blood tests and determined deficiencies did exist. To this day, my legs feel like lead weights. Walking short distances causes me to feel like I have run a marathon – I am out of breath and my chest hurts. The only medical relief I get is non-aspirin along with four different blood pressure medications. I recently saw a different PA who is concerned about my heart and ordered additional blood work and tests. Due to the COVID -19 pandemic, it will be a while before I see the specialist.

During the pandemic, Marie Gottschalk reported in, *In These Times*-The Texas Department of Criminal Justice has refused to abide by key CDC health and safety guidelines to stem the spread of COVID-19 in prisons. The state said, with no documented proof, that "hand sanitizer poses a major security risk." To date 72 prisoners and 8 officers died from Covid-19 and 7500 cases are under investigation.

Celeste

Trial Dateline of Events

03/28/2002: Arrested in the Dallas area.

06/14/2002: Writ of Habeas Corpus for reasonable bail. The Grand jury requested a bail to be set at $20 million; court set it at $8 million on June 17, 2002.

10/10/2002: Pretrial began.

03/20/2003: The Judge sentenced Appellant to a mandatory life sentence on count one 47 R.R. 70-71; 4 CR. 726-28. The jury returned a life sentence on count three the same day. 47 R.R. 67-68; 4CR.724.

07/18/2003: Hearing of Indigency. I lost and I paid $41,700 for trial transcripts.

09/10/2004: Solicitation of Murder hearing. Paid $250,000 to go to trial for this only to plead out at full cost.

03/23/2006: Third Court of Appeals affirmed the conviction and sentence. Johnson v. State, 208 S.W. 3d 478 (Tex. App. –Austin 2006, set. ref'd).

07/26/2006: The Court of Criminal Appeals refused Applicant's petition for discretionary review.

Celeste

In re: Johnson, 2006 Tex. Crim. App. LEXIS 1351 Tex. Crim. Appl. 2006).

02/01/2008: In the District Court 390th Judicial District Travis County, Texas came on to be considered the application for Writ of Habeas Corpus in cause (9020236-A). The relief was denied and transmitted the record to Court of Criminal Appeals. (Wanda White)

03/12/2008: Court denied, without written order, the application for Writ Habeas Corpus on the findings of the trial court without a hearing.

03/17/2008: Petition for Writ of Habeas Corpus to United States District Court for the Western District of Texas Austin Division.

03/18/2008: Time-barred because it was four days late, after paying $250,000 and received no refund.

09/11/2008: Brief in support of Appellant.

11/06/2008: Notice of Appeal.

01/26/2009: Certificate of Appealability to appeal the District Court's dismissal to the United States Court of Appeals for the Fifth Circuit.

06/01/2009: Motion for a COA is denied.

Celeste

On a Final Note

On June 24, 2016 I had surgery on my right foot and ankle; screws were placed in my foot and my ankle was fused. I left the hospital on crutches and could not bear weight on my foot.

On July 14, 2016, the bones were not healing in my foot or ankle and my cast was replaced with an Aircast boot and pump. I left the hospital on crutches still, not allowed to bear weight on my right foot.

August, September, and October continued to show no healing and I remained on crutches, the non-weight bearing order still in effect. I was not allowed, nor able to work. To pass my time constructively, I paid Central Texas College and enrolled in a math class.

On October 25, 2016, I was abruptly woken at midnight and told to pack my property because I was being reassigned to Lane Murray. I was confused because I had been housed at Mt. View over 13 years. I had been on crutches for nearly three of those years. The Lieutenant told me that he knew it was a medical transfer, yet he had not seen that particular code before. Lane Murray is handicap accessible, not a medical unit.

I arrived at the back gate of Lane Murray and was not

able to carry my one bag of property, being on crutches and unable to bear weight. At Mt. View they made a "crutch bag" for me to use like a backpack. I was not allowed to take this bag with me when I was ordered to switch units.

Officer Turner started cursing at me to carry my bag. She said, "You have a walking boot, so fucking walk." I tried to pick up my belongings and fell. My knee was gashed open and bleeding through my pants. This is the same leg that I had previously broken in three places and had foot surgery on.

Then, Officer Turner screamed, "Don't move! Don't move!" I was placed in a wheelchair and taken to medical and cleaned up by P.A. Bennett.

I was housed in the furthest dorm from all services. It was over the length of a football field away from the pill line, medical, or the Mess Hall. Reaching any destination was difficult and time consuming.

On the third day there, I was allowed to use the phone and let my mother know I was moved off the medical unit at Mt. View to the handicap accessible unit that does not have 24-hour medical. My restrictions stipulate that I must be on a 24-hour medical unit because of my choking condition and stomach issues. Lane Murray's medical closes at 5:00 pm., making this arrangement unsuitable for me.

My mother was told that my husband requested the transfer. He was unaware of this and called Huntsville and spoke to Melissa Bennett. She read him this letter: "Please move my wife to Lane Murray, she is falling because of her crutches." This letter, postmarked September 20, 2016, came from North Dallas. He lives in Austin, as they knew from my files. My husband said this letter was a forgery. Someone from the free world sent that letter and caused this situation. It was a colossal breach of my security.

Health Services decided, since I was on crutches, they were going to leave me at Lane Murray. I was there for a week and fell in front of the shower. Another woman slipped and fell the same as I had; she broke her kneecap in half. I received a displaced fracture in the same foot in which I had surgery. The non-skid surface on the floor was worn off in the shower area, making slipping and falling inevitable.

Lane Murray is a hard-core prison. The dorms are metal and each side houses 102 women, many are violent offenders. There is no air conditioning and water is hard to come by in the summer, where temperatures exceed 120 °. Inmates are regularly denied access to the respite areas. Heat related deaths are not uncommon.

The Guards curse at the inmates and are very racist toward the white inmates, which I was subjected to on many occasions. The medical staff is rude and uncaring. I wrote 32 grievances against the unit during my 19 month stay. I also advocated for other inmates for their mistreatment. I had a high success rate for resolving issues in favor of the inmates. This did not endear me to the guards, rank, or the administration.

On November 9, 2017, after I had been off the unit and in the hospital, I found out my daughter Jennifer was shot in the stomach on October 29, 2017 at 6:30 am after an all night long Halloween party at her house. The irony had not escaped me that my daughter was shot just as my husband was. Her tenant, Randall Gaston Jones, still dressed in his Santa costume, was angry at being told to go to bed and went into the party with a loaded handgun. Party-goer, Michael McKloskey, tried to retrieve the gun and was shot. He later died at the hospital. Another woman was also shot and another was hit by shrapnel. My daughter, Jennifer, was shot twice with life threatening injuries and was in the ICU fighting for her life when I found out about the shooting.

Two weeks prior to the shooting, Jennifer posted a picture on her Facebook page of her SUV filled with over a dozen handguns and rifles. The caption read, "Can you ever have too many guns?" Did Randall shoot her with one of her guns?

I was told that Jennifer was unable to pay her medical bills and home repair bills because she did not have medical or homeowners insurance. I surmised that Jennifer's recent divorce must have been the reason she had squandered her inheritance.

Her friends started a Go Fund Me account requesting donations. I wrote to everyone I knew and asked them to consider a donation to help Jennifer. I asked everyone to ignore their ill feelings towards her; she was not accepted well by my friends after the trial. No amount was too small to help her.

I wrote to David Kuperman, now the Trust attorney for Bank of America. I did not want her to receive substandard care because she could not pay her medical bills. I reminded him that Steven would be appalled that Jennifer was on the internet begging for money. I asked that he contact the business office at the hospital and make arrangements to pay her medical expenses using the corpus of the Trust. I sent a copy of the letter to the State Bar of Texas so that David could not say he did not receive it.

I never heard from anyone other than my friends until March 13, 2018 at 8:00 am. when Sgt. Hill read me the following Disciplinary case – Level 1; Code 5.0. "Court Prohibited Contact with a Victim." It stated, "On the date and time listed above, and at LM STG Office (Lane Murray Security Threat Group) Offender Johnson Celeste Beard, TDCJ ID # 01157250, did contact Jennifer Beard, who is the offender's victim for which the offender is serving a sentence, by soliciting assistance to contact the victim by third party by letter and the court has included in the Judgment and Sentence that the offender is not to contact the victim."

All of this was a blatant lie. I later found out that Jennifer requested her assigned Victim Services Coordinator, from her shooting, to email Lane Murray and notify them that there is a court order prohibiting contact with Jennifer, and that she was my victim. The Victim Services Coordinator, Lynn Craig, perjured himself and used his position with the court to dupe Lane Murray to cause problems for me. Another unethical person and situation to add to my case.

His former boss, Ellen Halbert, is now the person my daughters, Kristina and Jennifer, call "mom." Kristina named my first born granddaughter, Ashley Ellen Fritz, after her. Ellen was the twin's Victim Services Coordinator, from Steven's shooting, and ethically should have never crossed that line. Ellen now has a TDCJ prison unit named after her, the Ellen Halbert Unit in Burnet, Texas.

The Disciplinary hearing officer ignored my attorney. Dick sent an email letting them know that Jennifer was never considered a victim and that there was never a "No Contact Order" in effect. My mother spent $50 in overnight mailing fees sending my official court documents of my Judgment and Sentence, proving no such order was given by Judge Kocurek. Lane Murry knew this because they had a copy of my Commitment papers in my file. They chose to ignore this because they were retaliating against me for all my grievances and medical complaints filed with the Texas Board of Nursing and the Texas Medical Board.

Captain Sullivan berated me for 19 minutes, going so far as to call himself, "The Governor of Gatesville." He punished me with removing 350 "Good Days", along with restriction of phone for 90 days, and commissary, rec and cell for 45 days. He had me placed in cellblock as a G4 inmate (considered the worst of the worst), and locked down for 24 hours a day for at least twelve months. A wide, red plastic band was placed on my wrist identifying me as a high-level offender.

I was placed in a holding cell to wait for an escort to cell block. I was in the holding cell for hours before being taken to my cell. I was terrified and stressed out. The tension made me sick to my stomach when I arrived in my cell. I laid on top of that dirty, sheetless, plastic mattress for two days without moving. I am no match for cell-block living.

On day three, I filed grievances against Capt. Sullivan and the substitute counsel, Ms. Dewald. I wrote to my mom and she contacted everyone she could think of. Finally, we decided to contact Judge Kocurek. She stepped in and sent a letter along with a court certified copy of my Judgment and Sentence.

Celeste

On day 50, Warden Erwin called me out and asked me if the email she received from the Governor was correct. I confirmed it was correct. She said she would resolve the issue the following morning, due to the fact that it was 5:15 pm that evening and she was on her way out.

At midnight, I was abruptly woken up, again, and was told to pack up to be moved to Crain-Riverside. I was jumping up and down with joy and the inmates on the block were clapping and cheering for me.

Early the next morning I was taken to cell-block at Crain-Riverside. It was even worse than the Lane Murray cell-block. I could not understand why the big red band was not removed. On day six, the band was finally removed and I was sent into general population and back to some sense of normalcy.

Jennifer has had ten surgeries to date. Her core muscles were so weakened that she struggles to walk and is unable to work. Kristina supports her twin sister; without her help Jennifer would be homeless. Her shooter, Randall Jones, received 40 years for murder and aggravated assault with a deadly weapon. He is eligible for parole in 2037, a full five years before my eligibility. The reporter wrote that Jennifer was unhappy with his sentence.

It is surreal to me that I am serving a life sentence based on the testimonies of seven incentivized witnesses who all lied in exchange for immunity from prosecuting them for their crimes.

When I was housed at Mt.View in the Faith-dorm in 2015, I began writing Chaplain Threat at Crain-Riverside requesting to be placed on the waiting list for the T.U.M.I. Seminary dorm. Even though I did not receive replies, I continued to send my request. Now, three and a half years later, I am housed on the same unit as the Chaplain who oversees the dorm. I sent a request to be called out to speak with him.

My request was granted and I brought him a copy of my resume´ showing all my accomplishments while incarcerated. He said he remembered all the requests I sent him and that he had thrown them out because he was only allowed to enroll inmates already housed on the Crain units. He told me I would go in when the new class started in September of 2018. I could hardly wait to tell my friends and family the wonderful news!

The T.U.M.I. dorm is on the Terrace unit. On August 10, 2018, I was moved to Terrace because I was "Medically Unassigned" and not able to work. I wrote the Chaplain to let him know I was at Terrace and filled with anxiety because all of my travels back and forth to Galveston to see medical specialists. I requested to be moved to the T.U.M.I. dorm because I would go back to the same bed when I returned from the hospital. I was moved to the dorm on August 14, 2018!

I now know that all of this happened because I had to get to Lane Murray to advocate for those women. God wanted me to see and experience the real prison. I had to suffer and go through the G4 reassignment in order to be sent to Riverside where Chaplain Threat's office is located. Riverside is the only Crain unit that houses G4's. I would have never made it into the T.U.M.I. dorm without the injustices I faced. I am now enrolled in Agape Bible College working toward my Master's Degree and then a Doctorate in Bible Studies. God worked it all out for the good, just like he did for Joseph. I tell my friends to call me "Josephina" now! God is so good.

Only through God's grace, life behind bars is meaningful. I attend Catholic Mass on Thursdays, led by Father Harry Dean and Deacon Ronnie Lastovica. I take the Eucharist and experience overwhelming comfort. Steve and Diane, volunteers from Our Lady of Lourdes Catholic Church, in Gatesville, faithfully come to teach us about the Catholic faith after mass. I share my Catholic faith with others because I want them to see Jesus when they interact with me.

My life is pain filled, just as Jesus' encounter with the Samaritan woman at the well. She, like me, had spent a lifetime searching for love and friendship and had been repeatedly betrayed. She was an outcast going to the well for water when no one else would be there to mock, ridicule, and judge her. Jesus loved and embraced her, as he loves and embraces me, and he gave her eternal waters. Jesus is within me, he is offering the same healing waters. He holds me close to his heart and will sustain me all the remaining days of my life.

Jesus is my Redeemer. Jesus is my Savior. Jesus loves me for all eternity. Jesus will never let me go.

I firmly believe that everything I have gone through is in preparation for what God has planned for the rest of my life.

I stand at the well, hand-in-hand, with the Lord.

Contact Celeste

Celeste Johnson #1157205
Lane Murray Unit
1916 N. Hwy 36 Bypass
Gatesville, TX 76596

celestebj11@gmail.com

www.jpay.com

*If you send an email or Jpay email, you must include your postal address for Celeste to respond. If you send postal mail, TDCJ only allows white, or white-lined paper and envelopes, no card stock, stickers, return-address labels, or postcards.